Heart's
Delight

A PALISADES CONTEMPORARY ROMANCE

Heart's *Delight*

Karen Ball
Barbara Jean Hicks
Diane Noble

PALISADES

HEART'S DELIGHT
published by Palisades
a division of Multnomah Publishers, Inc.

A Valentine Surprise © 1998 by Karen Ball
Cupid's Chase 1998 © by Barbara Jean Hicks
Birds of a Feather © 1998 by Diane Noble

International Standard Book Number: 1-57673-220-7

Cover illustration by Paul Bachem
Design by Brenda McGee

Scripture quotations marked (NLT) are taken from the *Holy Bible*, New Living Translation, © 1996. Used by permission of Tyndale House Publishers, Inc., Wheaton, Illinois 60189. All rights reserved.

Also quoted:

The Holy Bible, New International Version (NIV), © 1973, 1984 by International Bible Society, used by permission of Zondervan Publishing House.

The Holy Bible; King James Version (KJV)

Printed in the United States of America

For information:
MULTNOMAH PUBLISHERS, INC.
POST OFFICE BOX 1720
SISTERS, OREGON 97759

Library of Congress Cataloging-in-Publication Data:
Heart's Delight/by Karen Ball, Barbara Jean Hicks, Diane Noble
   p.cm.   ISBN 1-57673-220-7 (paper) 1. Love—Fiction. I. Ball, Karen M.
Valentine surprise. II. Hicks, Barbara Jean. Cupid's Chase. III. Noble, Diane.
1945-Birds of a feather.
PS648.L6H4 1998   97-44604
813'.08508–dc21   CIP

98 99 00 01 02 03 04 — 10 9 8 7 6 5 4 3 2 1

To Don, my always Valentine

K.B.

To my friend Mary, who thinks I'm pretty funny.
Thanks for the gift of your laughter!

B.J.H.

To Liz Curtis Higgs
Your joy-filled heart, encouragement, prayers,
and friendship bless me beyond words.
You, dear friend, are a treasure!

D.N.

♥

Valentine
Surprise

by Karen Ball

Slowly, steadily, surely, the time approaches when the vision will be fulfilled. If it seems slow, do not despair, for these things will surely come to pass. Just be patient! They will not be overdue a single day!

HABAKKUK 2:3 (NLT)

CHAPTER
One

Roses are red,
Violets are blue,
My gift is a date, especially for you.
Dress casual, be ready by 10:32—
He'll be on your doorstep.
Love, Big Sister Two.

Corie stared at the Valentine in her hand in stunned disbelief. She'd found it a few moments earlier, slid under her door. Smiling cherubs and bright pink and red hearts glared up at her. She couldn't believe Cecelia had bought anything so garish. But it was the so-called poem written in her older sibling's neat hand that held her attention.

"Cecelia," she muttered after reading it again, "this had better be a joke."

She spun toward the phone. Celie was just going to have to call this thing off! No way was she—

Her thoughts were interrupted when her foot encountered a solid object: Doofus, her snoozing basset hound. He promptly pushed himself up, which only made him a slightly taller obstacle for her stumbling feet, and accompanied her headlong tumble with a sonorous howl of displeasure. She added her own howl to his, filling her apartment with an impromptu duet.

"Aaaroooo! Aaaroooo!" Doofus sang out.

"Aaahhhh!" she yelled as she bounced off the edge of the sofa and landed, facedown, on the carpet.

She lay there, wondering if she'd broken anything. A cold

nose came and pressed against her ear, snuffling heavily. Corie grinned. Sometimes Doofus sounded more like a walking sinus infection than a dog.

Slowly, testing her joints, she rolled onto her back. Doofus responded to this sign of life with a glad wag of his thick tail—which made his entire hindquarters wag—and lumbered forward to lay his heavy head on her chest. As one long ear fell over her face, Corie laughed and hugged the animal close. "Fifty-five pounds of pure love, aren't you, fella?"

Doofus wagged his hindquarters harder.

Corie patted the dog's broad head and scooted into a sitting position, leaning against the sofa. Doofus pressed against her leg, gazing up at her with his sweet, droopy brown eyes. His tail thumped the carpet.

She hugged him again. "Who could resist such devotion?" She laughed. "I'll tell you, Doof, men could take a lesson—"

Men. Oh, good heavens. Celie's ridiculous Valentine.

Corie slid onto the couch and reached out to grab the phone. Quickly she punched in the numbers. One ring, two, and then—

"Salutations!" Cecelia's refined voice greeted her, but before Corie could say anything, the voice went on. "This is the Williams' residence." Ugh. The machine. Corie hated those things. She tapped her foot impatiently. "We are unable to speak with you at present, but if you'd be so kind as to leave a message, we'll return your call in as expeditious a manner as possible."

"Cecelia Rose—" she began, but she was cut off again.

"And if this is Cordelia, you might as well hang up. I refuse to talk with you until tomorrow. And, no, I will not call it off. And don't try to appeal to Amelia or Ophelia for aid. We all think you need to do this. Besides, this man is perfect for you. So go get ready, and for heaven's sake, have fun!"

Corie barely heard the beep that followed. She just stared at the phone in her hand as though it had grown a head and a set of horns.

"Have fun?" she sputtered. "Have *fun?*" She slammed the phone back into the cradle, taking a perverse pleasure in the thought that the sound probably recorded and would make her sister's ears ring.

So her older siblings thought she needed to do this, did they? Well, who had appointed them Grand Pooh-Bahs of her life?

They only want you to be happy, a small inner voice chided her.

"I know," Corie said with a sigh as she settled back against the sofa cushions. "And I want the same thing." Her gaze wandered to the framed photographs on her mantel and came to rest on her sisters' wedding pictures.

The Three Sisters, as Corie called them, were triplets and nearly ten years older than she. Perhaps that was part of the reason they seemed worlds apart from her.

Ophelia, Cecelia, and Amelia were fair and blue eyed, tall and willowy, with long, flowing hair and angelic features. What's more, they were off the charts in intellect. Cecelia was a physicist; Ophelia, a law researcher; and Amelia, a senior professor of mathematics and statistical methods at the university. All wonderful, well-paying, judicious professions. Not jobs, mind you, but professions.

Interestingly enough, all three held a particular dislike of anything domestic. Cooking, cleaning, sewing—even decorating their homes—was left to "someone with a flair for such things."

Someone like Corie.

She sighed. If she'd had a choice, she would have opted for being like her sisters. Then maybe she wouldn't feel so lonely all the time. It wasn't much fun being the family oddity. And it wasn't just their personalities that didn't mesh. Corie was different from them in almost every way.

Shorter than the Three Sisters, she was more athletic in build than willowy. Her hair was a deep auburn, which made her stand out from her sisters like a sore thumb. Still, she had to admit it went rather well with her forest green eyes. As for her profession, well, it was something she loved, but it stymied the Three: Corie was a "creativity specialist." And though her sisters didn't understand what she did—or why—they all were proud of the fact that Corie's workshops on "Freeing Your Creativity" were in demand across the country.

If only they could be proud of her because she was doing what she loved and was gifted at, rather than because she was successful.

She longed to share her dreams with her sisters, but she'd learned early on that the Three weren't particularly nurturing of that side of their younger sibling. Oh, they were creative in their own ways—in very linear ways. But when it came to Corie's everything's-possible, just-close-your-eyes-and-you're-there manner of thinking, they just couldn't understand. She remembered once when she was young, going to her sisters and asking, "What if we're really the reflections in the mirror, and only think we're the real thing?" The Three gave her blank looks and shook their heads in that pitying, at-least-she's-a-pretty-child way. They loved her, she knew that. But they were more comfortable with each other.

About the only things they shared were their unusual names and their faith in God, both given to them by parents who had done their best, but found rearing such different children a daunting task. Corie would always be grateful that her mother and father had done all they could to help their daughters develop a sincere relationship with God. And they'd succeeded. The one thing Corie always knew was that she could ask her sisters to pray for her or with her, and, for that moment, they would be connected.

But it seldom happened any other time.

So Corie had focused her energies on finding outlets for her creativity. Painting, writing, photography, sculpture, origami—they all fascinated her. Many of her favorite creations adorned her spacious apartment, giving it a personality that was a delightful mix of beauty and lighthearted humor.

In the past several years, cooking had become one of her favorite pastimes. And though the Three Sisters found Corie peculiar, they were delighted whenever she brought her culinary abilities to their homes.

In fact, when she went to cook dinner a few weeks ago for Ophelia, it was the first time her sister had ever ventured into that particular room of her own house.

"Oh, my," Ophelia had remarked. "It's yellow. How...cheerful."

Corie shook her head at the memory. Her sisters were quite unique. And ridiculously determined to see her "settled."

Her gaze drifted back to the wedding photos, traveling from one to the next. What was that old saying? "Three times a bridesmaid, never a bride." That was the story of her thirty-five years of life. She'd been a bridesmaid for each of her sisters' weddings.

She picked up Cecelia's picture and studied it, noting how her sister's eyes shone with happiness as she gazed up into Daniel's smiling face. It was the same in all three photos. Her sisters were as blessed in love as in the rest of their lives. Each had found the man of her dreams—tall, handsome, and devoted to God and his family, in that order. As for Corie...well, she had Doofus.

Corie glanced at the photo again. Cecelia's wedding had been five years ago, and she and Dan only grew happier with each passing year. They lived a lovely life in a lovely home, complete with their two lovely children.

She set the picture back in its place with a loud thud and turned to Doofus in frustration. "I love my sisters. You know I do."

Doofus gazed up at her, listening intently. His tail gave one hesitant thump on the carpet—a sign he wasn't sure if she was upset or not.

Well, that was only fair. She wasn't sure either.

"They're all so happy that they just can't wait for me to be in the same state of marital bliss." She paced back and forth in front of the fireplace.

Doofus's head swayed back and forth as he followed her movements.

"It's not like I haven't tried! I mean—" She jerked to a halt and planted her hands firmly on her hips, staring at Doofus— "I was practically a candidate for the Queen of Dating, for Pete's sake! Well, wasn't I? Think about it. How many dates did I go on?"

"Rowf!" Doofus replied.

"Exactly!" Corie said, gesturing for emphasis. "About a million! And how many of them were enjoyable?"

"Rowwruf!"

"That's right! Zero. Zilch. Nada. *Zippo.*" The last word surprised her by coming out as a squeak because of her suddenly tight throat. She clenched her teeth. She was *not* going to cry. She dropped back down onto the sofa and pulled up her knees to rest her chin on them. Doofus scooted toward her and laid his chin on the couch beside her. Swallowing hard, she looked down at him.

"I tried, Doofer. I really did. I prayed about it, and I trusted God to bring Mr. Right into my life. But all I ever met were Mr. Wrongs. Or Mr. Not-on-Your-Lifes. There just wasn't anyone out there who…fit." She leaned her head back and blinked rapidly against the tears. "And I just got tired of it all, you know? Of meeting, then getting to know each other, and trying to sort out the image from the reality. I got tired of the games, especially since I'm so rotten at them."

The tears won out. They trickled down her face in hot streams.

A small whimper drew her attention. Doofus was watching her fixedly, looking for all the world as though he were about to bawl right along with her. The thought made her smile despite the depression that threatened to settle over her.

"Declaring a moratorium on dating was the smartest thing I ever did. I know the Three Sisters were horrified, but that last date was so bad! Do you remember?" She leaned down close to Doofus's ear. "Remember…Gary?"

Doofus jerked back with a growl, and Corie laughed. It worked every time. Gary Brower had been the last man with whom her well-intentioned sisters had set her up.

And he'd been the last man she'd gone out with.

"You're both creative types," Cecelia had said. "You have a great deal in common."

"Creative, eh? What does he do?" Corie had been skeptical. The Three Sisters' definition of "creative" and her own were vastly different.

"He's an editor," Ophelia said with confidence.

"And a writer," Amelia added.

This caught Corie's interest, until Cecelia spoke.

"For a computer company," she said. "He works on books of some sort, to guide people as they work with their software or hardware."

"He writes computer manuals," Corie said, her heart sinking.

"Right." Cecelia beamed at her. "Sounds perfect, doesn't he?"

"And you barely even notice those thick glasses," Amelia said.

Ophelia frowned slightly. "Though you'd think he could find frames in some color other than black."

Corie should have stopped it right there. She knew she should have. But she didn't have the heart to pop her sisters' bubble of hope. Instead, she'd suffered through two dates with Gary "Mr. Creative" Brower. Not only had he bored her to tears with detailed descriptions of the importance of algorithms, but he'd taken one look at Doofus and started to sneeze.

"Allergic," he managed from behind a handful of hastily gathered Kleenex. "To dogs. Unsanditary beadsts. Can'd imagine why anyone would hab one id their hombe." He sneezed again, then fixed her with a look of censure. "Do you hab any idea the number of bacteria one finds id a dog's mouth?"

His dislike of Doofus had been mutual. All Corie had to do was mention Gary's name and the usually easygoing animal growled. And snorted. And—she would swear to this in court—sneezed.

All three of them had been relieved when Corie told Gary she didn't think things were working out between them.

The Three Sisters, on the other hand, had been less than pleased. Especially when Corie informed them that she was finished; she wasn't playing the dating game any longer.

"Are you insane?" Cecelia had screeched in a surprisingly emotional display. "You'll never meet Mr. Right hiding yourself away in your apartment!"

"Cecelia, please," Ophelia said. "I'm sure Cordelia isn't at all serious."

"Yes, I am," Corie said firmly.

"Do you truly believe this is what God wants for you?" Amelia asked.

"Do you truly want to spend the rest of your life with no one to talk to but your dog?" Cecelia added.

"He's a better conversationalist than Gary!" she shot back. Seeing her sister's crestfallen expression, she went to put her arm around Cecelia's shoulders. "Hey, you guys, come on. I've given Mr. Right plenty of time to show. Apparently he's not interested. And neither am I. Not anymore. As for what God wants, well, I don't know. But I trust he'll let me know if I'm off base."

Cecelia had stared at her. "You're hopeless."

She'd met this with her usual equanimity: after sticking her tongue out at Cecelia, she kissed each of the Three and went home. That had been a year and a half ago, and Corie had enjoyed every minute since then of the emotional peace and quiet that came from not being caught up in the search for a "soul mate."

As for those long nights when she stared at the ceiling, blinking back the tears and aching for someone to talk with, for someone who could share her heart and hopes, well, that was just the price one paid for giving up childish fantasies.

Corie glanced at the mantel clock. Almost nine-thirty. Her Valentine date would be here in an hour. It looked as though the Three were going to have the last laugh this time. They'd suckered some poor guy into going out with their sister, knowing full well that Corie wouldn't take off and leave the man standing outside her door.

She sat for a few moments, thinking, then an idea began to dawn. No, she couldn't...could she?

The truth will set you free.

Corie felt goose bumps as the familiar Scripture floated through her mind. "Really, Lord? Can it really be that easy?"

As if in answer, verse after verse flooded her heart: *When the*

Spirit of truth comes, he will guide you into all truth.... Hold to the truth in love, becoming more and more in every way like Christ.... Give me an understanding heart....

The answer was so simple. Why hadn't she seen it before? She jumped up from the couch, startling poor Doofus, who had been snoring away beside her.

"Sorry, Doof, old boy," she said, leaning down to plant a kiss on his sloping snout. She cupped his face in her hands. "It just feels good to know what to do, you know?"

Then, with a little jig, she turned and headed for her room to get ready—and to make a few phone calls.

He couldn't believe he'd agreed to this.

He should have known better. Arrangements like this never worked. Especially not with women. If Jay had learned anything in life, it was that he should just stick to his work and his motorcycles. That's where he felt confident, in control.

With women, well, all he ever felt was used.

Too many times he'd gone out with a woman only to find that what she was looking for was someone to "take her away." But he had yet to find a woman who wanted to go where he did, do what he enjoyed, and just spend time getting to know each other.

He'd been foolish enough to believe he'd found her once. He felt his teeth clench as Gwen's image drifted into his mind. He pushed it—and the anger it always brought with it—away. He wouldn't be that foolish again.

Truth be told, he was tired. Here he was, nearly forty years old, and still going out on dates. Kelley, his younger sister, kept reassuring him that an older man was a much desired commodity on the dating scene. Somehow that did little to encourage him. If anything, it just made him more tired.

But there is one woman you'd like to get to know, an inner voice reminded him.

The image of her face drifted into his mind. Yes, he was interested. Was he going to do anything about it? Not likely. Better just to watch from afar and imagine her to be wonderful than to meet her and find out she was just one more disappointment.

That's what he'd told himself, anyway. Until the weekend before last, when Kelley had insisted on accompanying him to the park. She said it was to get some fresh air, but he knew better. She wanted to check out the woman who'd caught her brother's attention.

When the object of Kelley's curiosity showed up on her usual walk, Jay pointed her out. His sister's eyes widened, and she turned to look at him, surprised.

"I know her."

"Yeah, right."

"No, really." She turned back to watch the woman stop to talk with a group of children. "She goes to my church." A smug expression came over her features. "You would have met her by now if you'd only go to church."

"No, thanks," he replied, unwilling to get into the debate yet another time. "I love God with my whole heart. It's his people I can't stand."

"Well, she's one of them. Are you sure you don't want to meet her?"

"Yes."

"Jay!"

"I told you I wasn't interested in—"

She waved his words away. "Protest all you want, but I know you too well. Besides, you've done nothing but talk about this woman for the last three months. Now, all we need is a plan...."

He hadn't heard anything on the subject for a week so he figured that was it. Determined to get on with life, he immersed himself in his work, resigned to the idea of being a bachelor from now to eternity. Sure, God said it wasn't good for a man to be alone, but it wasn't good to keep being disappointed either.

Then a few days ago, Kelley came up with a wild scheme.

20

And, for some crazy reason, he'd agreed.

"Crazy is the word, all right," he muttered to himself as he stood in his sister's flower shop, arms outstretched.

"It's not crazy at all," Kelley said as she shoved the flowers into his arms. "It'll work, Jay. Trust me."

"Yeah, right." He peered at her over the blossoms. "And why should I do that? Oh, wait. Let me guess. Because you're a woman?"

She smiled. "And all our friends call you dense. Why, they don't know you at all, do they, brother dear?"

"Hmmm," he said, heading for the door. "I don't know about dense, but 'sucker' certainly would seem appropriate."

"You *can* do this. You can *do* this. *You* can—"

Ding-dong.

Corie's pep talk came to an abrupt end. She was standing in the living room, staring into her favorite antique mirror. She shot a quick glance at the mantel clock. No fair! It was only 10:10. He was twenty-two minutes early—

Ding-dong.

Her eyes flew back to her reflection in the mirror. She knew she should answer the door, but she couldn't move. She closed her eyes. *Please, God, just have him go away. Please, please, plea—*

Ding-dong.

"Rowf! Aaaroooo!"

Her eyes flew open, and she began to race for the front door. If the basset really got going, the din of his howling could shake the walls. Her neighbors would not be amused.

"Hush, Doofus," she scolded as she scooted him away from the door and pulled it open.

The dog wasn't listening; he was caught up in the heat of the hunt. "Aaaroooo!"

21

The pictures on the walls started to vibrate.

"Doofus! I said knock it off!"

Startled by her raised voice, Doofus sat down and gaped at her, silenced. At the same moment, a deep voice said, "Sorry. No one answered the first few rings so I thought I'd try one more time."

Corie felt her face flame as she turned to apologize, but the words died before they reached her lips. There in front of her was the most beautiful huge bouquet she'd ever seen. There were roses, carnations, daisies, snapdragons, and several other types of flowers she didn't recognize. The fragrance was heavenly.

"Wow," she managed, and a deep chuckle came from behind the blooms.

"I take it that means you like them?"

"Oh!" Startled, she stepped forward and reached out. "Here, I'll take those."

"I—" the deep voice behind the flowers began, but she stopped him.

"I know. You want to get going." Obviously, considering how early he was. "But do me a favor and just hang on for a minute."

He hesitated, and she took the opportunity to pluck the gorgeous bouquet from his hands. "Let me get these in water. It won't take a minute." She headed for the kitchen, calling over her shoulder, "Just wait right there."

Carefully, she laid the flowers on the counter, then buried her face in the fragrant blooms. Inhaling deeply, she smiled, delighted.

Well, at least he knew how to start things off right.

"These are really beautiful," she called as she found a vase and filled it with water.

"I'm glad you like them."

His voice was nice. Deep, resonant, and kind of warm. As if he were smiling.

She arranged the flowers in the vase, then set it on the kitchen table. She grabbed her jacket and headed back to the door, then came to an abrupt standstill.

Her Valentine date was kneeling down in the hallway outside her apartment, petting an ecstatic Doofus. The basset was leaning his heavy body against the man's leg, gazing up at him with an expression he usually reserved for her.

Corie didn't know whether to be pleased or jealous.

He glanced up as she approached, and her steps slowed. He was a very nice-looking man, striking in a rugged sort of way. With his black leather jacket, a motorcycle helmet on the floor beside him, he reminded her a bit of a dark-haired, dark-eyed version of Harrison Ford in his Indiana Jones persona. Especially when he smiled. He had a slow smile that was lopsided and utterly endearing.

Utterly what? her mind scolded as she quickly occupied herself with putting on her denim jacket. *You don't even know the man's name and he's "endearing"? Good heavens. Get a grip, Cordelia!*

She tugged at the bottom of the jacket, squared her shoulders, and stuck her hand out.

"Cordelia Fox," she said firmly. "But please call me Corie. And the beast at your feet is Doofus."

There was that lopsided smile again. "Great dog," he said, giving Doofus one last pat before he stood to take her proffered hand. "It's nice to meet you."

"Thanks. It's nice to meet you, too."

His hand was strong and large, and it all but engulfed hers. At the contact, an almost electrical jolt shot through her, and her eyes lifted to meet his, startled. Something flickered in those brown depths.

So he'd felt it, too.

She lowered her eyes and noted that Doofus had managed to collapse across the man's feet. "Doof," she scolded, "go to your bed."

With a woebegone glance at her, the dog rolled away from his resting place and lumbered over to the dog bed near the fireplace.

A deep chuckle drew her attention back to her date. She really liked the way he laughed and how his eyes crinkled with humor, as though they performed that action on a regular basis.

She hadn't realized she was staring at him until he cleared his throat. "I'm Jay." There was a slight pause, then he went on. "Jay Darling."

Corie felt her jaw go slack and her mouth drop open. Quickly she clamped it shut. "Jay..." she echoed, drawing the name out, doing her best to contain the laughter bubbling just beneath the surface.

He nodded slowly, and she was delighted to see a slight tinge of red touching his cheeks. A man who blushed? She'd never heard of such a thing.

Maybe he was a Martian. Leave it to her sisters to set her up with an alien entity.

"Right. Jay..." he drew it out as she had with a slight smile of resignation—"Darling."

She bit her lip. She would *not* say any of the things running through her head. But oh, she was tempted.

"Darling, it's so good to meet you."

"Oh, Jay, you're such a Darling to do this for my sisters."

"Come on in, Darling. I've been waiting for you."

"Jay, would you be a Darling and fall in love with me?"

Her eyes widened at this last thought. Where had *that* come from? She'd just met the man. For all she knew he could be a psychopath—or worse, a total bore.

Oh, Lord, help! Don't let my emotions go out of control just because there's a man on my doorstep. I'm not that pathetic, am I?

Do not be dismayed, for I am your God. I will strengthen you.

The familiar words calmed her. *Thank you, Mom and Daddy, for making me memorize all those Scriptures,* she thought. *They come back at the most perfect times.* She looked up to meet Jay's gaze. His expression was enigmatic, as if he weren't sure about something. Her calm fled. Was she already falling short of his expectations?

Hold to the truth in love.

Right. The truth.

She drew a steadying breath. "Okay, let's go," she said briskly as she moved past him and pulled the door shut. She started down the hallway, then stopped when she realized he was still standing there, watching her with a bemused smile on his face.

She marched back to him, leaned down to pick up the helmet, plunked it in his hands, then took his arm, tugging until he fell in step with her.

"Are we leaving?" he asked, and the question was filled with barely restrained laughter.

She glanced at him, then halted. Planting her hands on her hips, she faced him, lifting her chin with determination. "I'm sorry, Jay. I'm sure this seems a bit odd—"

"Just a bit," he agreed, grinning.

"It's really very simple. I don't know what you had in mind for today, but we're going to do this my way, or not at all."

His only response was a slight lifting of his brows. Good. A man who knew how to listen.

"So here's the plan. We spend one day together. Just one.

We don't waste our time or money with a series of dates trying to figure out if we have anything in common. The only investment we make is one day, morning till evening, doing things together and being who we really are. No games, no pretense, no putting on a show to catch each other's interest."

She lowered her hands and stepped toward him. "Come on, Jay, admit it. Aren't you sick and tired of all the games we're expected to play when it comes to dating?"

A response flickered in his eyes, and he tilted his head thoughtfully. "As a matter of fact, I am."

"Well, then. What have you got to lose? Remember the verse about the truth setting you free? When's the last time you remember being truthful on a date? I mean, really truthful?"

"Umm, roughly never," he said.

"Exactly! Dates are custom designed for pretense. But it doesn't have to be that way. We can relax, feel free to be honest about how we feel or think, and by the end of the day, it should be clear to us if this is something we want to pursue."

He studied her carefully, and she felt her face grow warm. Did he think she was a total kook? She swallowed uncomfortably. Oh, why had she said anything at all? In fact, why had she even answered the door? She should have known he wouldn't understand.

Lord, this was a mistake! she wailed. *Why did you let me—*

"It makes sense."

"It—it does?" The words came out in a surprised squeak, and he grinned.

"Yes, it does. So how do we decide what we do for the day?"

She glanced at him in delight. "Oh, I've got some things in mind." Things that would make their suitability—or lack thereof—obvious.

He leaned against the wall, shaking his head. "Now, that doesn't exactly seem fair, does it?"

She bit her lip. He was right. "No, I suppose not."

He pushed away from the wall, took her arm, and started walking again. "Of course it doesn't," he said as he held the door open for her and she stepped out into the cool air.

She loved February in San Francisco. Cool, but seldom cold. She drew a deep, appreciative breath.

"So," Jay went on, "how about you pick out the first activity, then I pick one? And we can go on like that for as long as we have time."

She paused, considering. "Okay, that sounds fair." She gave him a hesitant smile. "Are we set?"

"I hope so," he replied, and his smile was so warm she felt it all the way down to her toes.

D o you think they're having fun?"
Ophelia gave Cecelia a stern look and reached for the teapot. The three of them were gathered in Ophelia's kitchen. That was the safest place to hide from Cordelia. She'd never think to look for them there.

Admittedly, if their youngest sibling were going to hunt them down for what they'd done, she'd have turned up by now. The odds, therefore, were very good that she'd decided to give in and go on the date Cecelia had devised for her. It would all work out, Ophelia was certain. But if Cecelia didn't stop worrying, she was going to scream. "Of course they're having fun. He's neither an idiot nor a dud, Cecelia. Please give the man a bit of credit."

"Really, we've done all we can to make this a success," Amelia added. "We just have to leave the details to him. And to Cordelia."

"That's a horrid thing to say!" Cecelia said in alarm. "Cordelia is an utter disaster at dating."

"True," Ophelia agreed patiently. "Undeniably so. But she's still our sister and, as such, possesses a high degree of intellect. She can handle this, I'm sure. Besides, she's a delightful person, fun to be around, truly interesting—"

"For heaven's sake, Ophelia, you sound as though you're giving a eulogy."

"She probably is," Cecelia said sadly. "For this date."

Ophelia firmly set her cup down in its saucer, making a

loud clatter. "All right now, that's quite enough!" As the eldest—by a few minutes—it had always been her duty to comfort and guide her sisters, but, as Corie would say, she had had it.

She stood and paced back in forth in front of the…what was that called? Oh yes, the oven. "We all agreed this was a worthwhile undertaking, didn't we?"

"Yes, Ophelia," the other two answered in chorus.

"And we felt this young man was, really, when it came down to it, a rather good match for Corie, didn't we?"

"Yes, Ophelia," Amelia said.

Cecelia remained silent. Ophelia fixed her with a stern look. "Well? Didn't we?"

Celie sighed heavily. "Oh, I suppose so. At least as good a match as we could find among our acquaintances."

"All right, then. It seems to me we simply need to relax and let things run their natural course."

"I suppose you're right," Cecelia said in subdued tones.

Ophelia inclined her head. Of course she was right. That was not open to debate. With a sigh of relief, she sipped her tea. A moment later she nearly choked on it when Cecelia added, "Even if Cordelia's most natural course with men is one that leads to disaster."

Wow.

It was the only word that came to Jay's mind. He could scarcely take it all in. Nothing had happened the way he'd expected. It was better. Far better. He was almost positive he was dreaming.

No, not even his dreams were this good.

Corie was seated behind him on the bike, her arms draped

loosely around his middle as they made their way through traffic. He could feel her resting the forehead of her helmet against his back as they accelerated, and his breath caught in his throat.

Wow.

There it was again. That word. Well, it was about as appropriate as it got when you were faced with God working a miracle.

As the motorcycle's speed increased, Corie couldn't keep the broad smile from her lips. With each burst of speed, she'd had to hold on to Jay a bit tighter. Just for safety's sake.

What a shame there were speed limits.

She giggled, then tightened her grip even more as the bike made a sudden move to the left.

"Sorry!" Jay called back. "Debris in the road."

"No problem," she hollered. And it wasn't. Not in the least.

If only the Three Sisters could see her now.

Soon—too soon, in fact—the ride was over. Corie slid from the back of the cycle and pulled off her helmet, tucking it under her arm as she turned to survey the building in front of them.

"Ready?" she asked Jay.

His smile was cocky. "Always."

She knew her answering grin was decidedly fiendish, but she couldn't help herself. "We'll see."

She led the way through the glass doors of the library, then down the stairs to the children's section. Gaily colored decorations greeted them as they entered the room.

"Cordelia, over here," a voice called, and she turned to see her friend Amy, who was the children's librarian, waving to her. Amy was one of the calls she'd made that morning. She'd been delighted to take part in Corie's plans. "Just leave your helmets on the desk there and come join us."

In a circle at her feet sat about thirty children of various ages, all watching them with eager anticipation.

Corie didn't dare look at Jay.

"Let me guess. Story time, right?" His voice was low and right next to her ear.

She nodded.

"I don't suppose there's any chance you're the reader?"

She shook her head. "Nope. No chance at all." She glanced up at him. "Amy was thrilled that a man was willing to read to the kids. Unless, of course, you'd rather not. Remember, no pretense."

He studied her for a moment. "Do I get to pick out the book?"

"I suppose so." Intrigued, she watched as he turned and disappeared between the shelves.

What was he up to? she wondered as she went to join Amy and the children.

"You're right on time," her friend said with approval. "That's great. The children are all ready, aren't you, gang?"

"Yeah!" they chorused.

Amy glanced behind Corie. "Where did your friend go?"

"To——" she started to explain, but suddenly Jay was right there, his hand on her shoulder.

"——pick out a book," he finished. "Can't do story time without the best materials." With a quick squeeze of Corie's shoulder, he stepped past her and went to sit in the storyteller's chair.

"Okay, who's ready for a story?" he asked, and the children cheered as he began to read. Corie's eyes widened. He'd chosen one of her favorite books, *I Love You, Stinky Face*. It was the story of a little child at bedtime asking his mother if she would love him even if he were all kinds of terrible things. Corie loved the mother's responses. She always said she'd love him, no matter what, even if he smelled so awful that his nickname was Stinky Face.

Amy and Corie stood watching as Jay read, changing his voice to match each new creature, gesturing wildly when the creature was a slimy, swamp-dwelling monster or a space alien.

The children were mesmerized.

So was Corie.

"Where did you find this guy?" Amy whispered. "And are there any more of him around?"

Corie chuckled. "I didn't find him; the Three Sisters did."

Amy's jaw dropped. "The Three found him? I don't believe it." Her eyes narrowed as she studied Jay. "Maybe he's some kind of robot they made—"

"Amy!" she said in a choked voice, unwilling to admit she'd entertained similar thoughts.

"Or a cyborg. Or a clone. That's it. I'll bet he's some kind of mutated clone your mad-scientist sister created." She gave a dramatic sigh. "I knew he was too good to be true."

Corie's laughter was interrupted by Jay's "The end!" and the jubilant applause of the children.

"Read us another one!" a sweet-faced little girl sitting beside him begged.

Jay reached out to tug her pigtail playfully. "I will another day, I promise."

Amy looked as though she were about to swoon. "Oh, honey, if you don't keep him, *I* will."

"What if he decides not to keep me?"

Amy's smile was wicked. "Even better. Just let me know in any case." She turned back to the children. "Well, wasn't that fun? Let's thank Mr...?" She looked at Jay.

"Darling," he supplied. "Jay Darling."

Amy's expression was priceless. She shot Corie a look as if to say, "Of course! What else?" then turned her focus back to the kids swarming around Jay.

It took him a few minutes to extricate himself, but soon he came to stand beside Corie.

"So, did I pass the test?" he asked.

She looked up at him, surprised. "Test? What test?"

"Ah, ah, ah," he admonished. "No pretense, remember? You wanted to know if I liked children, right? And if they liked me?"

She opened her mouth to deny it, then stopped. He was right. She'd convinced herself she was just having fun, but truthfully, this *had* been a test. "Yes, I guess that's what I was doing."

"So did I pass?"

"With flying colors," she said, and he nodded, satisfied. Taking her arm, he turned her toward the door.

"'Bye, you two," Amy called out. "And Cordelia, don't forget to let me know if that item becomes available, you hear?"

Heat filled her face, and Jay's curious look didn't help. "Item?"

She shot Amy a glare, then grabbed her helmet and headed out the door. "So where did you learn to get along with children so well?" she asked as she started up the stairs. Sidetracking was one of her best skills.

Usually.

Jay stopped at the bottom of the stairs and leaned against the wall, a stance Corie was beginning to recognize. "The truth will set you free," he said gently. "No games, remember?"

With a sigh she sat on the top stair. "You. The item is you. Amy thinks you're wonderful, and she's offered to take you if things don't work out for us."

"Ah," he said, and pushed away from the wall. "Now, don't you feel better?"

She watched him, bemused, as he came to the top stair and held a hand out for her. She took his hand, and he pulled her

33

to her feet. "That's it?" she asked as they left the building.

"Yup. Since I'm not available at the moment—" he paused and looked at her—"am I?"

"No!"

Amusement lit his eyes, and he reached out to take her helmet from her and gently slide it over her head. "Well, then, it's not something we need to think about." He cupped her face briefly, his fingers warm against her skin. "Is it?"

It took a moment for her to find her voice. "No," she said at last, surprised at the rush of gladness she felt. "No, it certainly isn't."

He pulled his helmet on and got on the bike. She slid into place behind him, and he looked at her over his shoulder.

"Now," he said, a devilish look in his eyes, "it's my turn."

CHAPTER
Four

Jay watched Corie with interest as she slid from the motorcycle, took off her helmet, and looked around.

He restrained a smile as he watched surprise touch her features. "The zoo?" she said, looking at him.

He nodded. "The zoo."

Turning quickly so she wouldn't see his mouth quirk with humor at her confusion, he led the way to the ticket booth. He would have been willing to take bets on what she was thinking. He'd heard it often enough from women: "Men hate going to the zoo."

From what he'd seen so far of Corie's bent for honesty, he figured she was wondering if he'd come here because he thought it would please her, rather than because he wanted to do it himself.

He glanced at her. Sure enough, disappointment was painted all over her face. *Well, it never hurts to have your stereotypes shaken from time to time, does it?*

Clothe yourself with tenderhearted mercy and kindness....

He looked away uneasily. There wouldn't be a need for kindness if she'd trust him to be as honest as she was, he defended himself.

Be considerate of the doubts and fears of others.... Do what helps them.

Why on earth had he thought it was a good idea to memorize Scripture? It always came back at the most inconvenient times.

The most important piece of clothing you must wear is love.

It was true. He knew it. But he just wasn't ready to give in. She had things she was testing him on. Well, he had his own tests. Like whether or not she would be willing to see him for who he really was, not for who she assumed him to be. And if she could admit she was wrong.

Kindness makes a man attractive.

"Knock it off!" he muttered, then cast a quick look at Corie. She hadn't heard. She was staring at the zoo entrance, immersed in thought.

The words were out before he could stop them. "You'd better be careful."

"About what?"

"Getting too much exercise without stretching out first."

She frowned in confusion. "Exercise?"

He shrugged and took her arm, guiding her toward the ticket booth. "You know, jumping to conclusions, leaps of logic, that kind of thing."

Pink tinged her cheeks.

Bingo, he thought, expecting to feel a sense of gratification. But all he felt was mean-spirited. Ashamed, he turned to tell her the truth when a voice called out, "Hey, Jay Bird! Long time no see, eh?"

Corie started, and Jay turned with a sigh to the ticket attendant.

"Hi, Chad," he said, pulling out his wallet.

"Hey, I've seen your pass a million times, bud. I don't need to see it again. But as for this lovely lady here—I'm afraid I'll have to ask for hers."

Corie bit her lip and looked away.

Well, he'd accomplished his goal. He'd taught her not to make assumptions.

So why did he feel so rotten?

"I'm covering her, Chad," he said, pulling money from his wallet.

"You got it, Jay."

Corie took the ticket from Jay in silence and followed him through the turnstile. They found the lockers and secured their helmets.

He couldn't stand it any longer. "Corie, I'm sorry."

She paused and looked at him. "No, Jay, I am. You were right, I thought you picked the zoo because you thought I'd like to come here." She looked down at her hands. "That wasn't very fair of me."

He knew it was possible to feel worse than he did right then—he just wasn't sure how. He took her hand. "Yes, well, I wasn't very fair either. I could have told you right up front that I come here all the time. I wanted to teach you a lesson—"

"You did."

He shook his head. "No, I didn't. At least not the one I intended. I wanted you to give me a chance, to see me for who I am and not who you think men are in general. Instead, I just confirmed your stereotype."

A frown creased her brow. "How did you do that?"

"By being the typical, insensitive, arrogant male. I treated you poorly, Corie, and I'm sorry. God told me this was a rotten idea, and I ignored him."

She surprised him by grinning. "That's never a good idea. I know from personal experience. Ignoring God only makes you sorry. And usually makes you look stupid."

He laughed. "Guilty as charged. But I'm not nearly as stupid as I was five minutes ago." He met her gaze. "Forgive me? And can we start over?"

Her smile was a thing of beauty. It lit her face and sparkled in her eyes and made him feel as if he'd just won the lottery.

"Yes on both counts." She looked around, then back at him, and her expression reminded him of a little girl on Christmas morning. "I really love zoos."

"So do I. It's a good thing my work brings me here so much."

She fell into step beside him. "Your work? What do you do?"

"I'm an artist. A painter, mostly, though I've dabbled in other media. But painting is my true passion. My primary subjects are animals and children. So I spend a lot of time in parks, too. Sketching."

Now she was the one who looked as if she'd won the lottery. "An artist? You're an artist?"

"I take it that's good," he said with a chuckle.

"That's more than good. That's wonderful." Eyes sparkling, she told him about her work. He listened, watching the way her emotions played over her features. Excitement as she talked about her workshops. Joy as she shared her passion of helping others bring their creativity to life. Then a sudden sadness as she described her sisters. "They think I'm a bit odd," she explained with a shrug of her slender shoulders.

A loneliness filled her eyes, and he was taken aback at the powerful urge to take her in his arms and draw her close. He wanted to protect her, to bring her smile back...to let her know she wasn't alone at all.

He was there.

Whoa, buddy. Slow down! Just because her family doesn't understand her is no reason to pledge a lifetime of devotion to the woman.

No, it wasn't. Which only made it that much more astounding that that was exactly what he wanted to do. He was not a man easily swayed by emotion. Oh, he was as drawn to women as the next man—Gwen had more than proven that. But he'd also learned from her to keep his emotions under tight rein, which he'd never had trouble doing.

Until now.

"Oh!" Corie's exclamation pulled him out of his thoughts. She was pointing to a crowd nearby. "They must be getting ready to do something special."

"I saw a sign that said they have a special Valentine's Day tour, beginning at the tiger exhibit. We're just in time."

"Great! Let's see if there's any room in front so we can see everything," she said, tugging him along as she hurried toward the group.

They reached the front just as the zoo employee started talking. "Hello, and welcome to our Valentine's Day tour!" she called out. "We're going to take you on an exciting adventure today...."

Joy bubbled in Corie's laugh and shone in her eyes. "This is great!"

"We've put together a special program for you to give you an insider's look at romance in the animal world," the tour guide continued.

Jay smiled at Corie, feeling very proud of himself. "I told you I knew the perfect place to—"

"Or, in more accurate terms, the mating rituals and habits of the big cats."

He looked at the zoo employee, startled. The *what?* A quick glance at Corie's suddenly pink cheeks told him he'd heard right. He took hold of her arm.

"I think we can do better than this on our own," he told her, and she followed him without question.

His prediction turned out to be accurate. They had a wonderful time. Of course, it helped that the animals—from the big cats to the monkeys to the polar bears—were unusually active and entertaining.

Then came lunch. Jay couldn't believe it when Corie

informed him she wanted a hot dog, cotton candy, a jumbo-sized drink, and a doubled-dipped ice cream cone. "No pretense," she remarked gleefully as she licked ice cream from her fingers.

Their conversation ranged from teasing and humorous to quiet and serious. They discussed their families, their hobbies—many of which they shared—and their faith. He'd been surprised to find himself believing her as she told him how much she wanted to reflect Christ in her actions and words. From what he'd seen, she was sincere. Not that she was a saint, but she wasn't just mouthing a bunch of convenient platitudes. She really tried to live out what she believed.

Quite a trusting conclusion on one day's acquaintance, isn't it? a mocking voice asked.

His response surprised him, for it lacked even a particle of the cynicism he usually felt when talking about such things. *Yes,* he answered. *I've seen more of this woman's heart in one day than I've seen of anyone else's in months of being together.*

So if you trust her so much, why haven't you told her about Gwen?

He had no answer for that, save one: he wasn't ready.

The high point came when they ran into a friend of his who was the manager of the big cat exhibit. He took them to the nursery, where they found three young tiger cubs. Jay wasn't sure which of them had more fun holding and playing with the little beasts.

It was late afternoon by the time they left the zoo grounds and walked out to his motorcycle.

"That," Corie said with a happy sigh, "was wonderful."

"Amen," he replied sincerely. "It was the best."

"I hope not," she said with a laugh. "Seeing as it's my turn now."

"Okay, it was the best so far. How's that?"

"Much better."

"Though how you're going to top it is beyond me," he added teasingly.

"That's simple," she said, her smile as cocky as his had been earlier. "I'm going to make you the best dinner you've ever had."

CHAPTER Five

The idea to cook dinner at her place had been spur of the moment, but Corie was glad she'd offered.

She and Jay had gone to the store together, and shopping for groceries had never been so much fun. In fact, nothing had ever been as much fun as it seemed to be with Jay. The most mundane activities turned hilarious; the briefest conversations held insight and discovery.

As they drove to her house, he pointed to a tall building along the way. "That's where I live," he said, and she looked at him in happy surprise. It wasn't more than half a mile from her own building.

He grinned. "I know, conveniently close, eh? I thought so, too. You'll have to come see my place soon. Apartment 1101. End of the hall. I think you'll like it."

"I'm sure I will." Why wouldn't she? She'd liked everything about the man so far. She had to keep reminding herself she'd known him less than a day. It felt as though he'd been in her life for as long as she could remember. And as she unlocked her apartment door, she found herself hoping he'd stay in her life for a long time.

Maybe forever.

He's the one, isn't he, Lord? she prayed, almost afraid to give voice to what she was feeling so strongly. *He's the one I've been waiting for.*

"Aaroooo! Aarooooo!" Doofus greeted her with his usual exuberance. It never mattered how long she was gone; upon her return, he always acted as though he'd been afraid he'd never see her again. His low-slung, solid body would wag itself from one side to the other, and his ear-splitting howl would bounce off the walls.

"Now that's what I call a heartfelt welcome," Jay said with a laugh.

"It's that all right," she agreed, hugging Doofus and clamping her hand over his muzzle in the same motion. "I just wish there was a volume control."

"Why don't you let me try to calm him down while you get started on dinner?" he suggested.

"Hungry, are we?"

"Count on it!"

She thought for a moment, then nodded. Might as well find out how Jay and Doofus would get along. He came to scoop the dog up as though he were a poodle rather than fifty-five very solid pounds.

With a shrug, she hefted the bags of groceries and went to the kitchen. Some twenty minutes later, the salad was ready, garlic bread was warming in the oven, and she was laying shish kebabs on the grill on her balcony. She had all the ingredients for strawberry shortcake, but she planned to ask Jay to help her with that later.

"Hey, would you like something to drink?" she asked as she came into the living room.

Jay was sitting on the couch, leaning back, looking completely at ease. On the cushion beside him was an equally relaxed Doofus. The basset hound was in his favorite position: stretched out on his back, his legs dangling in the air, paws relaxed and drooped. His massive head was draped across Jay's lap. Contented snores rumbled from Doofus's snout as Jay's lean fingers scratched the dog's long ears.

"Oh, my," she said, a giggle escaping her.

There was the lopsided smile again. She liked it more each

time she saw it—and she liked the way it did something to her, making her heart dance and ache at the same time.

"He does seem rather content, don't you think?" Jay said.

"Ecstatic is more like it," she said, moving toward the love seat opposite him. Obviously Jay had passed the Doofus test. The basset was smitten.

"Well, I like him, too." Jay had the nicest dark brown eyes. She wasn't sure whether she liked them or his smile more. She really liked the way they were smiling at her. And the way they could grow attentive when they discussed something serious. If the eyes were a window to the soul, then Jay Darling's soul had to be in a class all its own—a very appealing class.

Maybe the Three Sisters were right about him; maybe he *was* perfect for her. Since this whole day was about being honest, she didn't even try to deny the fact that she truly hoped so.

"You look like you've got something on your mind," he said, snapping her out of her thoughts.

"The truth?" she asked, scarcely believing what she was saying. *Don't do it!* a voice inside her screamed. *It's too risky!*

But she didn't care. She'd been asking Jay for honesty all day long. She wasn't going to start dodging the truth now.

He met and held her gaze. "Yes."

"I was thinking about us, about today. About the way I'm feeling and how it should scare me silly. But it doesn't."

He remained silent, but oddly that encouraged rather than threatened her. She felt as though he were giving her the chance to sort through her thoughts and express them.

"Jay, when we started out today, I hoped we'd at least have a nice time. If we were lucky, we'd get to know each other a bit better than usual in a dating situation. But what's happened is…" she paused, searching for the right word.

"Extraordinary."

"Remarkable," she agreed. "And rare. I mean, I've certainly

never had anything like this happen before, have you?"

"Only in my dreams."

In any other situation, that would have seemed trite. But she knew what he meant. It was true. She'd dreamed of meeting someone—her soul mate—like this. But she'd never believed it would happen.

Forgive me, Lord. You promised me wonderful things, and I didn't let myself believe. But now...

Tears sprang to her eyes, and, for once, she didn't try to stop them.

Jay gently moved Doofus aside and came to sit with her on the love seat. He reached out to take her hand and, with his other hand, touched a gentle finger to her cheek and captured a tear.

"'You have collected all my tears in your bottle,'" he quoted softly. "'You have recorded each one in your book.'"

He paused. "Corie, I don't know where we're going. I don't know what God intends for us together. All I know is that he's done something today, something inside both of us. We agreed no games, no pretense, so I want you to know this: you're not alone in what you're feeling. You move me like I've never been moved before. I want to care for you, to protect you, to be with you. And if I feel that way after one day, I can't even begin to conceive of how it's going to be after a week, or a month."

She sniffed, nodding. It was as though he were expressing her heart. "I know. I feel that way, too. And I don't know whether to be thrilled or terrified."

He smiled tenderly. "How about if we're just patient? Let's take this slowly, carefully, building on the base God has given us today. I know it feels as though we've known each other a long time, but the truth is we haven't. We have a lot to learn about each other. And I, for one, plan to enjoy that process."

She lifted their joined hands to her cheek and closed her

eyes. "Where did you come from?" she whispered, overcome with wonder.

"From the same place you did." His voice was choked with emotion, and he cupped her face with a gentle hand. "From the heart of the Father."

"Wurf!" Doofus barked.

Corie barely heard him, so focused was she on Jay and the feel of his hands against her skin. She could hardly breathe. "Jay, I—"

"Rowrf! Aaaroooo!" Doofus insisted.

"I—"

"Aaarrrrroooooooooo!"

"What?" Corie bellowed, and turned to scold the dog for interrupting such a sweet moment. But the words died on her lips.

"My shish kebabs!" she cried, racing for the balcony, which was cloaked in a cloud of gray smoke.

"They're ruined," she moaned, staring at the blackened spears. They looked like columns of pure charcoal. She looked at Jay, who stood leaning against the sliding door. He had a smile on his face.

"What?" she demanded, putting her hands on her hips.

"I just think God has an interesting way of letting certain things burn out of control to keep other things under control."

She turned to survey the remains of their dinner, then chuckled. "So much for the best dinner you've ever had."

"No sweat," he replied. "Give me five minutes, and everything will be fine."

"Five minutes?" He couldn't salvage those poor shish kebabs in five hours.

"Yup," he said. "That's how long it will take me to call for pizza."

~ ~ ~ ~ ~

It was after ten o'clock when Jay left. They'd decided it was too soon to share a kiss. "Not until we're sure about this," he said, and she agreed, caught between disappointment and gratitude for his wisdom.

She'd followed him to the door, and he held her hands, then lifted one to place a soft kiss at the wrist, where her pulse beat. She'd read in novels about a woman nearly swooning when a man kissed her, but she'd always dismissed it as fiction.

Now she knew differently.

She grabbed the doorway, dazed. When had she stopped breathing? And could someone tell her how to start again? From Jay's bemused look, he hadn't fared much better.

"Wow," he muttered, and she agreed wholeheartedly.

She closed the door behind him, then leaned against it, wondering how something so small as a kiss to the wrist could have such an enormous impact.

"Wow," she mumbled, echoing Jay's reaction. "Wait'll I tell the Three Sisters."

Better yet, why wait? It wasn't too late to call. She jumped on the phone with glee and punched in the numbers. She would owe them for the rest of her life for this.

"Hello?"

"Celie! You're wonderful! And so are Phelia and Melia. You're all wonderful! I mean it."

Stunned silence met her enthusiasm, then her sister asked in a tentative voice, "I take it the date went well?"

"'Well'? Oh, Celie, it was the most amazing day of my life!" She went on to recount the events of the day in detail, barely giving Cecelia a chance to comment with more than a few "Oh's?" and "my goodness's."

She sighed, ecstatic. "I mean it, Celie. I'll never be able to

47

thank you enough for introducing me to Jay. He's the most perfect man—"

"Who?"

"Jay. He's funny, and so sincere in his faith. I mean, I can tell he's got some issues—"

"Corie…"

"—but who doesn't?"

"Corie…"

"What really matters is that we—"

"Cordelia Renae!"

Corie stopped. "What? What's wrong?"

"Who is Jay?"

"What?"

"You said 'Jay.' Who on earth is Jay?"

A small alarm started sounding in Corie's mind. "My date. The man you sent to take me out today."

"Cordelia," her sister said in slow tones, as though speaking to a dense child, "the man I sent was Alex. Alex Winters. From church."

The alarm was now a full-blown siren, blasting so loudly that she could scarcely think straight.

Cecelia went on. "This Jay person may have been your date, but *I* didn't send him. Corie, I have no idea who that man is."

CHAPTER
Six

Despite a virtually sleepless night, Corie was surprised to find that her anger had abated a little by the time she rolled out of bed the next morning.

There had to be an explanation. Jay wouldn't lie to her. She was sure of it. She'd wracked her brain all night, going over and over the things they'd said. But it was so clouded with emotion she couldn't keep it straight.

Had he said he knew her sisters? That he'd been sent as her Valentine date? She couldn't remember.

All she knew was that she had to find out, from Jay himself, what was going on.

You can't go talk to him, the inner voice cautioned. *Not alone. Call one of your sisters—better yet, call all three!—and ask them to go with you.*

No. She'd gotten into this on her own; she'd get out of it the same way. Besides, she wasn't afraid of Jay.

Aren't you? the voice taunted.

Despair flooded her. No, she wasn't afraid of Jay. How could she be? She was in love with him.

Corie watched the numbers on the panel as the elevator rose. Eight, nine, ten...

Don't do this! You don't know what you'll find.

She couldn't argue the point. *No, but I do know what I'll lose if I don't.*

Do you? Or was it all just make-believe? A well-acted fantasy that you were ready to believe?

Thankfully, the doors opened on the top floor, stopping the inner dialogue. She stepped from the elevator and glanced around.

He'd better be there, she thought darkly. *With answers. And they'd better be good.*

She made her way down the hall. 1110. 1108. 1106. Ah, there. At the end of the hallway, just as he'd said. Apartment 1101.

She raised her hand to knock, then paused. The door was already open. Just a crack, but open nonetheless. Had he somehow known she was coming? No, that wasn't possible...was it?

Suddenly hesitant to knock or announce herself, she reached out a finger to push tentatively at the door. It opened wider. She pressed her face to the crack and whispered, "Jay?"

No answer.

He could hardly have heard you, now, could he? her conscience scolded her.

It was easier to ignore that little bit of truth than address it. She stepped back and looked up and down the hall. No sign of Jay. She leaned forward to peek through the crack in the door, and her eyes widened.

Pushing the door open, she went inside. A large, open room greeted her. The sun poured in through tall windows and sky-lights, making the room feel light and airy. The furnishings were simple but not spartan. Elegant, colorful prints and an assortment of sculptures and objets d'art were displayed with artistic abandon. The chairs were low and overstuffed. Overall, the feel of the room was warm and inviting.

But what caught her attention and drew her like a magnet were the easel and paintings at the far end of the room.

Joy filled her heart. He'd told her the truth. He really was a painter. At least he had all the accoutrements of one. Corie went to one of the canvases that was sitting on the floor, leaning against a chair leg. She knelt and studied it…and again her heart sang.

It was beautiful. A child's face smiled up at her, so realistic in its depiction that she almost expected the little one to speak. The strokes were strong and sure, the detail intricate but not overdone. Soft angel's hair framed a face that was the epitome of innocence and wonder. The round cheeks were flushed with excitement, the blue eyes sparkled with laughter. One small hand reached out toward her, as if wanting to make sure she was real. Dandelion fluffs floated in the air all around the child.

It was a magical, captivating portrayal of delight, of childish discovery.

Jay had indeed told her the truth. He *was* an artist. A gifted one.

She looked at the lower right-hand corner of the painting. A name was scrawled across it: Jai.

Well, that was one way to make his name stand out, she thought with a small smile. Give it an odd spelling.

And there, just below the name, was a Scripture reference: James 1:17–18. She would have to look that up when she got home.

She leaned the painting back in place, then stood, eager to see more. She went to the painting on the easel and smiled again. It was exquisite. A sleeping tiger cub lay curled contentedly in the curve of its mother's enormous paws. The blend of helplessness and power held at bay was surprisingly moving. Corie had a sudden image of God holding her in just such a way: surely, protectively, unconcerned for what might come against her, confident that the battle was already won.

Corie explored further, finding one treasure after another.

Finally, she came to several canvases leaning against the far wall, covered by a tarp. She pulled the covering back and knelt with an exclamation of delight.

A basset hound looked out at her, his soulful eyes filled with adoration. "Doofus," she whispered. Indeed, if she hadn't known better, she would have sworn it was her dog. The coloring, the build, the expression all were vintage Doof.

With a laugh, she pulled the painting forward and looked at the canvas behind it.

Shock jolted through her.

It was like looking into a mirror. Her own face looked out from the panel before her. Here, as with the other paintings, the detail was exquisite. So much so that she had the oddest sensation of having been thrown outside of herself to become an observer. Her hair was windblown, and she was framed by trees in the background, resplendent in their autumn foliage. Leaves of rich, muted colors rained down about her, and she had wrapped her arms about herself in an unconscious gesture of savoring the wonder of the moment. She was laughing, her eyes filled with a warm look, as though she were looking at someone she knew.

No—at someone she loved.

She pushed the painting away and jumped to her feet, her heart racing. She was no artist, but she knew something this detailed, this intricate, this...*intimate* took time. More time than she'd known Jay.

A lot more time.

Then she remembered. One day last fall she'd gone to the nearby park for a walk. It had been a perfect autumn day, and she'd had a wonderful time drinking in the beauty all around her. Then, in one magical moment, a gust of wind kicked up, shaking the limbs of the trees all around her, creating a shower of leaves. It was an experience that had stayed imprinted in her memory.

And, apparently, in Jay's.

She frowned. But that had been months ago. A chill washed over her. How long had he been watching her?

She stepped back, and her foot slipped on something. She looked down and saw a manila folder. It must have been resting against the painting of the basset, and she'd knocked it—

The basset hound. Her eyes went back to the painting that had brought her such delight a few minutes ago. It didn't just look like Doofus. It was him. She was sure of it.

She reached down and picked up the folder, but she did so too quickly. Papers fell out and slid to the floor. With a muttered exclamation, she bent to retrieve them—and froze again. They were sketches, some in pencil, some in charcoal, of her and Doofus. Some were of them together, others of them individually, others showed them with the children who always gathered so eagerly around Doofus when she walked him.

God. It was all her terrified mind could manage. *God, help!*

With quick, frightened movements she put the sketches back in the folder, set it against the painting of Doofus, and pulled the tarp back into place. She ran to the door, careful to pull it nearly shut on her way out, then hurried toward the elevator.

She held her breath, waiting anxiously for the doors to open. "Come on, come on," she muttered, heaving a relieved sigh when the car finally reached her floor. Inside, she reached out an unsteady hand to punch the button for the lobby.

The shaking didn't start until she was in her car, the door securely locked. *Lord, what are you doing?* Frantic, she tried to steady her fingers enough to put the key in the ignition.

Trust in the Lord with all your heart.

Swift anger filled her. *I did trust you, and look where it got me. I spent the day with a crazy man!*

Do not depend on your own understanding.

She pulled into traffic with an angry jerk of the steering wheel. *I'll tell you what I understand. The best thing I can do about Jay Darling is to stay as far away from him as possible.*

CHAPTER
Seven

"You what?"

Corie faced her sisters resolutely. "I went to Jay's apartment. I wanted to get some answers."

"And did you?" Ophelia demanded.

"Yes." More than she'd wanted.

"Well, what did the scoundrel have to say for himself?" Amelia asked.

"Not much." She wasn't going to tell them she'd gone into his empty apartment. Why give them yet another opportunity to tell her how crazy she was?

"Was this—this impostor telling the truth about anything?" Ophelia asked.

"Actually, yes," Corie said. "He really is an artist. A painter."

"Hmpfh!" Cecelia snorted. "I'll bet."

"No, really." For some reason, she didn't want the Sisters to think badly of Jay on every count. "What I saw was exceptional." She smiled slightly, a bit surprised to find she was able to do so about anything that had to do with Jay. "Even his signature on the paintings is unique. He spells his name J-a-i rather than J-a-y."

"What did you say?" Amelia asked, giving her a strange look.

"I said he signs his paintings Jai with an *i.*"

"For heaven's sake, Amelia, what possible diff—" Ophelia began, but Amelia cut her off.

"Good heavens, Corie. You mean he's Jai? *The* Jai?"

Corie shrugged. There was a "*The* Jai"?

"Are you telling me you've never heard of Jai?" Amelia demanded. "You're the artistic one in the family, for heaven's sake."

"Amelia, would you be so kind as to dispense with the histrionics and explain yourself?" Clearly, Ophelia was fed up.

"Do you recall when I invited you all to the fund-raiser for the children's hospital that was cosponsored by the university a few months ago?"

"Who could forget? The food was substandard at best," Cecelia replied.

Amelia shot her a quelling look and went on. "Cordelia, you couldn't come because you were out of town. But you two were there. Don't you remember the art exhibit? They were featuring the work of a much acclaimed artist who lives in the area."

Cecelia nodded. "Oh yes. Those! They were wonderful. All depictions of children at play, and they were simply stunning. I could have sworn the figures were going to step right off the canvas."

"Yes, I recall it now," Ophelia said. Then her eyes widened. "The artist was this Jai?"

"Yes!" Amelia said triumphantly. "I remember because he had a Scripture reference beneath his name, and one of the philosophy professors made an inane remark about faith in God being passé." She grimaced. "I wanted to dump my tea on his head."

"The verse," Corie asked, "was it from James?"

"Yes," Amelia said. "Chapter 1, verses 17 and 18, I believe. I looked it up when I got home that night. It was the section about every good thing coming from God, and that we are his children and his choice possessions." She smiled. "Rather appropriate, I thought."

"Corie, what were the subjects of your friend's paintings?" Cecelia asked.

Her *friend?* What happened to "the scoundrel"? "Children. And animals."

Amelia clapped her hands. "He *has* to be the same artist, don't you think? There can't be two with the same name in the San Francisco area."

"I would think that highly unlikely," Ophelia said. "Do you two remember the prices on those paintings?"

"Quite clearly," Cecelia said. "I wanted one so badly I could almost taste it, but Daniel would have shot me if I'd paid twenty-five thousand dollars for a painting."

Corie felt her mouth drop open. "How much?"

"Oh, that was one of the bargains. There were a couple of large paintings of children playing in a field of flowers that went for twice that."

"Am I remembering correctly that the entire proceeds from the sale of his works were going to the children's hospital?" Ophelia asked.

"Yes," Amelia said. "He didn't want any money at all. It was really quite remarkable."

The Three Sisters turned to scrutinize Corie in silence.

"What?" she asked.

"Well, my dear, it's quite improbable—"

"To say the least—"

"That an artist of such skill—"

"—and craftsmanship—"

"—and what would seem to be devotion to God—"

"It's just not likely such a man would be a common masher," Ophelia finished.

Corie lifted her chin. "Then perhaps he's an uncommon one."

"There's no need to be defensive," Ophelia said. "All we're saying is that the man must have a reason for what he did. And you really should give him the opportunity to explain himself."

"I tried that," she insisted.

"Well, then, what did he say?"

Oops. Caught. "Umm, he wasn't home. But I saw something there...." She looked away. "Something that convinced me I shouldn't see him again."

The Three waited expectantly.

"There was a painting."

"Oh. Well. That explains it," Cecelia said dryly.

"It was of me. And there was one of Doofus, too."

A mixture of confusion and concern swiftly replaced the disdain on her sisters' faces.

"I confess, that does seem odd," Ophelia said.

"It felt odd," Corie said. "And invasive, somehow. It means he's been watching me. For a long time."

"But Cordelia, it just doesn't make sense," Amelia said slowly. "He's well known and respected in the art world. And his philanthropy is well documented."

"Perhaps we should go with you to talk to him," Ophelia suggested.

"No!" came Corie's horrified response. "Really. I'll think over what you've said. And I'll pray about it. I promise. If it seems right, I'll talk with him."

Thankfully, this seemed to satisfy them, and the conversation turned to other topics. Corie knew once they let it go, they most likely wouldn't give it another moment's thought.

If only she could do the same.

CHAPTER Eight

J ay stared at Corie's apartment building. He was sitting on a bus-stop bench across the street. When he decided to go for a walk, he'd had no intention of ending up here. All he knew was that he had to get out.

Actually, he'd considered showing up at her apartment several times over the last three weeks, but every time he headed for the door, he stopped. He couldn't explain it, but he had the distinct feeling that he needed to wait.

Tonight, though, he'd reached the limit of his patience. He'd tried calling Corie one more time, and again there was no answer. She didn't even have an answering machine so he could leave a message. No way to tell her how much their day together had meant to him. How much he wanted to see her again .....

But now, after three weeks of silence, he was starting to wonder if Corie wasn't just another Gwen. Lots of talk about faith and honesty, but when it came down to it, that's all it was. Talk.

Judge not.

"Give me a break," he muttered. "If anyone has a right to judge here, *I* do. Seems to me you just keep letting me down in this area, God. You keep letting me care for people who don't deserve it."

He stood and began to pace angrily. "Is this how it works, Lord? *Pow!* and it's over. No good-bye. No explanation. No nothing. Well, you know what I think? I think you blew it. Big time."

I am the Alpha and Omega, the beginning and the end.

The words rang in his mind as clearly as if someone had leaned over and whispered them in his ear. His reaction was swift. "Then you should have seen this coming! You should have known it wasn't going to work and kept me from caring so much!"

Who is this that questions my wisdom?... Where were you when I laid the foundations of the earth? Who defined the boundaries of the sea?... Have you ever commanded the morning to appear and caused the dawn to rise in the east?... You are God's critic, but do you have the answers?

He sat down again wearily. No. He didn't have the answers. Not for anything. He shoved his hands into his pockets and leaned back against the bench. He couldn't deny it. God's words were as true for him as they'd been for Job. But he couldn't deny his anger, either.

What do I do, God? I want to yell, at you, at myself. I want to say I'll never trust a woman again. But I know that's not the answer any more than blaming you is the answer. I just wish someone would tell me what to do.

He shook his head and glanced at Corie's building again. And then he stiffened in disbelief.

Corie was there, leaving her building, laughing and smiling and talking...with a man!

He rose and stepped off the curb, fully intending to march across the street and confront her, when a horn blared loudly. He jumped back just in time to avoid being turned into a grease spot on the street by the six o' clock bus.

He sat back down on the bench with a thud, clenching his teeth so hard his jaw ached.

Okay, God. You win. I'll wait. For a few hours more. But that's it. He settled back against the bench. *Then I'm going to get some answers.*

Lord, if you don't get me out of this in the next ten seconds, I'm going to scream.

"Did you say something, my dear?"

Call me that one more time and you're going to become one with my lasagna, she thought fiercely as she met her date's curious gaze. "Not a thing, Alex," she said as sweetly as she could through clamped teeth. Why, oh, why had she ever let the Three Sisters talk her into this?

"It's been three weeks, Cordelia," Ophelia had said a few days ago.

"Thanks for the reminder," Corie had said in a near snarl. As though she needed one. She was acutely aware of how many weeks…days…minutes…interminable seconds it had been since she'd last seen Jay.

Fortunately, Ophelia ignored her rancorous reply. "If you're not going to contact Jay Darling and resolve things, then it's time you got on with your life."

"And we have exactly what the doctor ordered," Amelia said. "Alex Winters, your Valentine date. He's willing to forgive you for going off with a total stranger and leaving him to stand in your hallway like a ninny."

"Oh, goody," Corie said.

"Cordelia, please," Ophelia scolded. "Alex is a fine man. Besides, he's perfect for you."

Corie didn't trust her sister's bland expression. "Oh?"

"Absolutely. He's a psychologist."

"Definitely what you need," Cecelia said sweetly.

"Besides, you owe the man a date," Amelia said.

She'd resisted, but they'd worn her down. And now here she was in a nice restaurant, staring at Alex Winters and listening as he expounded on the fact that people brought their trials on themselves and how much better off they would be if they would only get over themselves and show the smallest kernel of intelligence. Of course, one sign of this intelligence would be for them to buy his book, *Living Life the Way You Should.*

If he was what the doctor ordered, she'd rather be ill.

Quick shame filled her over the unkind thought. *Sorry, Lord. It's not Alex's fault I find him pompous and irritating.* She grimaced. Oops. She'd done it again. She never should have left her apartment. It was just that simple.

With as much sincerity as possible, Corie feigned a huge yawn. "Oh, gosh, sorry about that," she said with a self-deprecating smile. "But it's getting to be past my bedtime."

Alex glanced at his watch and frowned. "You go to bed by eight-thirty?"

She thought quickly. "Well, it's, uh, very conducive to creativity."

He wasn't buying it.

This is a punishment, isn't it, Lord? For ignoring you when you've urged me to call Jay. Well, I'm not going to call him. Okay? I'm just not going to.

"Uh, besides, I need to check on Doofus. He...hasn't had his dinner," she finished. "And, you know, there's just nothing worse than a hungry basset hound."

"Indeed?"

I'm not doing it, Father. So you can just knock this off!

"Oh, definitely," she said gravely. "He'll start howling and crying. My neighbors wouldn't like that at all. In fact, they'd probably demand I get rid of him." She managed a trembling lower lip at the thought. "And I just couldn't bear that."

She gave him her best imitation of Doofus's woebegone look. It always worked on her.

And, wonder of wonders, it worked on Alex, too.

"Well, by all means," he said with a pitying smile, "let's get you home to feed the little fellow." He signaled for the bill.

Ha! I can handle things my—

"And while he's enjoying his canine repast, we can treat ourselves to a spot of coffee and a nice little chat about this rather odd fixation you have on your dog. How does that sound, my dear?"

Like her worst nightmare.

Okay, Lord, I give. You win. I'll call Jay, I promise. Just, please, can you get rid of Mr. I-can-fix-you before he gets past my apartment door?

Corie was nearly desperate.

She'd been hoping for a traffic accident or a stickup or an alien abduction; *anything* to distract Alex and convince him to go home. But her prayed-for reprieve hadn't materialized, and they were headed down the hallway to her apartment.

God, this is a test, right? You're not really going to make me go through with—

She stopped, frozen in her tracks.

There, leaning casually against the wall beside her apartment door, was Jay, looking as wonderful as she remembered...except for the hardness around his eyes. That was new.

His gaze rested on her for a moment, then traveled to Alex. His lips thinned. Apparently Jay wasn't any more pleased to have Alex walking behind her than she was.

"Hello, Corie," Jay said. The greeting sounded pleasant enough. "I hope I'm not late."

She blinked. "Late?"

She felt Alex stiffen behind her. Good grief, she hoped he wasn't going to try to defend her from Jay. She turned toward him.

He was looking at her, not Jay, and his expression was one of complete affront.

"Really, Cordelia, all you had to do was tell me you had an engagement, and I would have dropped you off at the door."

"I—"

"May I just say how thoroughly unsatisfactory this evening has been?" he continued. "I had hoped your behavior on Valentine's day was an exception, but I can see you are that careless sort of woman who believes she can use men as she wills. Well, my dear, you shall not use me a moment longer."

With that, he spun on his heel and strode down the hallway and out the door.

Corie stood there, her mouth gaping in astonishment.

"Nice guy," Jay said from behind her. "Astute. I think I like him."

She spun to face him. "What are you doing here?"

His brows arched. "Fine, thanks. And how are you?"

She didn't answer. She just went to shove her key in the door. Her annoyance only increased when she saw her hands were shaking. Before she could turn the key, his hand settled over hers gently.

"Corie."

She stilled, overwhelmed by the sudden urge to bury her face in his broad chest and weep.

"We need to talk. That's all I want to do. Talk."

She rested her forehead against the door. *God, I know I promised. But I'm not ready. I can't do this. I can't.*

I am the Lord, the God of all the peoples of the world. Is anything too hard for me?

No. No, it wasn't.

She straightened and looked at Jay.

"Come on in. I'll make us some coffee."

I'm frightened, Father.

Corie was standing in the kitchen, gripping the countertop as though it were a life preserver. The coffee had been ready for five minutes, but she couldn't force herself to go into the living room.

It wasn't that she was afraid of Jay. When she'd seen him, she'd known he was safe. And sane. She couldn't explain it, but one look at him and she'd been filled with the certainty that he was everything he'd said he was.

No, what held her prisoner, caught between hope and terror, was another realization that she couldn't escape, no matter how desperately she wanted to.

I love him.

The words kept ringing in her mind until she thought she'd go crazy. On impulse, she reached for the phone and quickly dialed Ophelia's number.

Be home. Please.

"Hello?"

"Phelia, it's Corie," she whispered into the receiver.

"Corie? Do you have a cold? I can scarcely hear you."

"Phelia, listen, I haven't got much time. I...would you pray for me?"

Her sister's response was immediate. "You know I will. What's happening, Corie?"

"Jay is here."

"Oh, my! Should I call the police?"

"No!" she cried, half laughing, half frantic. "No, Phelia, just listen. It's good that he's here. We need to talk. I care about him. A great deal. And I want to work things out."

"I see. So I take it he's Prince Charming again." There was a smile behind the words.

Corie smiled in response as a sweet warmth filled her. "Yes. Yes, I think he is."

"All right then, dear. I'll pray for you. And I'll ask God to show you clearly if this isn't the man you can give your heart to."

"Thanks. And Phelia?"

"Yes?"

"I love you."

There was surprised pause, then her sister said, "I love you, too, Cordelia."

Feeling the peace that had been lacking a few moments before, she hung up the phone, then reached down to pick up the two mugs. *Okay, Lord, here we go.* They would talk, bring everything out in the open. Maybe that way she could put this whole episode to rest.

Maybe that way her heart could stop aching.

She entered the room and experienced déjà vu. Jay was sitting on the couch, with Doofus snoozing contentedly beside him. She set one of the mugs on the coffee table in front of him, then went to sit on the love seat.

She held her mug between her hands, staring at the steaming contents, realizing she didn't know where to begin.

Hold to the truth.

The truth. What was the truth? That she was desperately unhappy? That she was sorry for her lack of trust but unable to overcome it? That she was terrified?

Yes. All of the above.

"Jay—"

"Look, Corie—"

They both broke off, and Corie felt a hysterical giggle rising. Leave it to them to start speaking at the same time.

Jay tipped his head. "Please. Ladies first."

She grimaced. "I don't feel like much of a lady. What I feel like is an idiot." *What?* Where had that come from? Okay, so it was probably true, but what a beginning.

He blinked. "Excuse me?"

"I'm an idiot. I've been going crazy—"

"I haven't exactly been having a wonderful time," he growled.

Regret filled her. "I know. But, well...Jay, I went to your apartment." Seeing his confused reaction, she rushed on. "The door was open, but you weren't there."

He nodded. "A bad habit of mine. I leave the door open a crack when I go down to the laundry room."

"Well, I went inside. I—I wanted some answers. I mean, you weren't the date the Three Sisters sent, so even though I was sure I could trust you, I didn't. After all, you were an impostor. But I was almost sure you didn't know you were. I mean, you never said the Three had sent you—"

"The what?"

"At least, I don't think you did. So I had to find out. Because I really cared—"

"Corie..."

"And I was looking around and saw your paintings, and it was so exciting because they're wonderful. You really are gifted, you know? And I was so thrilled that you'd told the truth about being an artist—"

"Corie..."

"—that I was ready to forgive you most anything, and I was sure God had brought us together, and then I found the paintings."

Stillness settled over him.

"The paintings?"

She nodded. "The ones of Doofus. And me."

He sat back slowly.

Say something, Jay. Give me an explanation, one that will make the fear go away.

So she had found the paintings. Well, that at least explained a few things. It didn't excuse her behavior, but it did explain it.

He knew the constructive thing would be to explain, to tell her the truth about that day in the park and about all that had resulted from it. But he couldn't make those words come.

He wanted to yell. *"You left me hanging for three weeks because you saw a stupid painting? Did it ever occur to you just to ask me about it? What happened to being honest, Corie? That doesn't count when it's scary? Is that it?"*

He clenched his jaws shut, holding the tirade back.

One thought kept running through his mind, over and over. It was the thought that had hit him squarely between the eyes when he'd seen her walking down the hallway. It was the thought that had coursed through him like fire as he fought against the urge to grab the man with her and turn him into silly putty.

I love her. God help me, I love her.

But he'd be darned if he'd tell *her* that!

The silence grew between them until Corie wanted to jump up and shake him. Just as she was about to give in to that urge, he sighed.

"Who are the Three?"

She started. "What?"

"The Three. You said you thought they'd sent me?"

"They're my older sisters. I told you about them."

"The brainy triplets."

She nodded. "They sent me an…unusual Valentine gift this year. A date. With a man."

"I didn't think it was with a kumquat," he said dryly.

A smile found its way through her uncertainty. "Anyway, he was supposed to show up Valentine's Day morning, at precisely 10:32."

Jay's brows arched. "About the time I came with the flowers. You thought I was your date."

She nodded. "Right."

"Well, that explains it then."

She shook her head. "No, that doesn't explain it. Not your part, anyway. Jay, you were just there to deliver the flowers, weren't you?"

He paused. "Yes and no."

"I don't understand. Why did you agree to spend the day with me? And what's the deal with those paintings?"

There was no humor in his face now. "I suppose you think I'm some kind of nut case."

"No. Oddly enough, I don't. Not anymore."

"But you did. When you saw the paintings."

She nodded.

"I see. So that's why you pulled your little disappearing act? You saw the paintings, decided I was a maniac, and ran."

"You're angry," she observed.

He fixed her with a glare.

"Well, it's not like it was that unreasonable an assumption—"

"Not if you didn't know me at all," he said, his voice hard.

She looked away. "I'm sorry. I was frightened." She squared her shoulders and met his gaze. "Jay, I know now that I should have just come to you, asked you to tell me about the paintings. Well, I can only hope it's not too late to do so. Jay, please tell me about the paintings."

Jay was torn.

He wanted to explain to Corie, wanted her to understand. But something inside him was still angry she hadn't trusted him.

It's not fair, God. I've trusted her, taken her at her word. Why couldn't she do the same for me?

Be considerate of the doubts and fears of others.

He let out an exasperated breath. *Don't you ever get tired of saying the same things over and over?* But he already knew the answer to the question. *I know, I know, you wouldn't have to if I would just get it; right? Right.*

He pulled his drifting thoughts together and studied Corie as she sat quietly, staring at her hands, waiting.

"I told you before that I mostly paint children and animals," he said, and she jumped at the sound of his voice. Apparently she hadn't expected him to answer. The relief he saw in her eyes pierced him.

"Y-yes," she stammered.

"Because of that, I spend a lot of time at the zoo and in parks. It's a good thing I like them so much." He smiled briefly, and an answering smile touched her lips.

"That's probably why your paintings are so emotive," she said warmly. "I can see why you've enjoyed the success you have."

He looked at her, surprised.

"My sisters told me about you." Her smile broadened a bit. "About Jai with an *i*, as they call you. Amelia works at the university where they had a showing of your work a few months ago."

So she knew about his success, and she'd still avoided him.

Well, at least he didn't have to worry about her loving him because he had money.

No, you just have to wonder if she loves you, period.

"Anyway, I go to the park just down the block several times a week. That's where I first saw you."

She watched him intently.

"It was one day last August. I was at the park, sketching the kids at the playground, when I heard the most amazing laughter. It was so light and uninhibited, it was almost musical. I figured the child who belonged to that laughter would be a great subject, but when I turned, it wasn't a child at all. It was you. You were sitting on the ground, your dog jumping on you, children all around you.

"I don't know what it was about you, but something inside me clicked. It was as though I heard a whisper in my heart: 'That's her. That's the one.' For a moment, just for a moment, I believed it. I almost got up and came over to you right then and there."

His gaze drifted back to her face, and he was caught off guard when he saw tears shimmering in her eyes. He felt a powerful need to be near her, to comfort her. He nearly stood and moved to the love seat. He wanted to be closer, to touch her hand, to find some way to help her understand what their day together had meant to him.

But it wasn't time for that. Might never be. So instead he stood and started pacing behind the sofa.

"I told myself I'd had too much pizza and anchovies the night before," he said in an effort to lighten things a bit, though he wasn't sure whether it was for her sake or his own. "But I couldn't forget you." He gave a short laugh. "I didn't have the chance. You seemed to be there almost as often as I was, walking Doofus, stopping to let the children adore him. Then one day last fall, I was sitting there, just enjoying the colors, and I saw you walking, and this waterfall of leaves suddenly surrounded you, and you looked so...enchanted. Enchanting."

Just as she did this very moment. The way she was watching him, the way she was sitting, even the way she held her hands tightly together—everything about her seemed filled with waiting.

"I almost came up to you then. But I couldn't. I was too afraid you'd be like—" He broke off. "Like too many others," he hedged. "Beautiful on the outside but hollow where it matters the most. I couldn't let myself believe you might be someone I could trust."

And you were right, weren't you? She turned out to be just like the others. Just like Gwen. When it mattered most, she didn't trust you.

The thought hit him with a jolt. For a moment he couldn't breathe, and anger rushed in, filling him to overflowing. How could he have been so stupid? How could he have revealed so much of his heart to her? He hid his resentment in indifference.

"So I decided to do what I always do with images I need to purge. I paint. And that's what I did." He smiled. "That's what you found, Corie. My exorcism, so to speak. My exorcism of you."

Corie sat in stunned silence as a tumble of confused thoughts and emotions assailed her. One moment Jay was warm and open, then—seemingly without cause—he was cold. Mocking.

Startled hurt turned to white-hot anger.

"Well, then, if you're free of me, I guess we don't have anything more to say."

72

His eyes darkened like ominous thunderclouds. "I suppose we don't."

She stood quickly and walked to the door, her back stiff. With any luck, he'd be out the door and gone before her heart shattered into a million pieces.

He followed her without speaking. She threw the door open and spun to glare at him, then faltered. In that moment, she'd caught an unguarded expression on his face, an expression full of helpless desperation.

He didn't want this any more than she did. She was sure of it.

"Jay—" She stepped toward him, one hand outstretched.

He jerked away, and when he spoke his tone was cold. "Thanks, Corie, for letting me see the reality. It makes it much easier to give up the fantasy that way."

With a few long strides he was out the door and down the hall.

Bristling with indignation, she turned to Doofus, who sat on the couch, watching her cautiously. "All I can say is good riddance!" she spat. "Thank goodness he's out of our lives."

She meant it, too. She was glad he was gone. Even if he had taken her heart with him.

Jay stood on the sidewalk in a dumbfounded silence.

What the heck was *that?*

He rubbed his aching eyes wearily, then turned to study the brick building for a few seconds. Suddenly he strode forward, stood next to the wall, and then thumped his head against it, yelling with each blow, "Idiot! Idiot! Idiot!"

After the fourth smack he saw stars, and he staggered back. *So,* he thought, rubbing the spot where a lump was already forming, *this is love. One minute you're looking at her, loving her, wanting to be near her, the next you're a raging idiot. No offense, God, but I'm not so sure I care for it.*

He turned and started the walk back to his apartment building.

It was going to take some time to figure out exactly what had happened tonight. And it was going to take even longer to find a way to convince Corie she should ever speak to him again.

"Y ou *what?*"

Corie faced her sisters resolutely. She'd played this scene once before; she could do it again. She would not let them make her feel foolish. *I made the right decision,* she thought defiantly. *Right, Lord?* Nothing but silence answered her, so she rushed on. *Of course I did,* she insisted. And no one was going to tell her differently.

Fools think they need no advice, but the wise listen to others.

Uh-uh. No way. She'd listened to others too many times. And look where it had gotten her. Disappointed. Hurt.

Alone.

Tears stung her eyes, and she blinked them back. She was not going to shed one more precious tear over Jay Darling.

"I told Jay I didn't want to see him again," she answered, making her tone as calm and reasonable as she could.

"Why on earth would you do that?" Ophelia asked. There was no censure in her tone, only complete confusion.

"I thought he was your Prince Charming," Amelia added. She, too, looked utterly baffled.

"He turned out to be more of a toad," Corie said before she could stop herself. She felt the quick heat in her cheeks as the Three fixed her with chiding looks.

"Cordelia, I'm sure there is no need to be unkind," Ophelia said quietly.

A retort flew to her lips, but she clamped them shut. Phelia was right. Berating Jay wasn't going to help anything. Her sisters would only find fault with the way she'd acted, no matter how justified she'd been. Suddenly an old saying flitted through her mind: Better to keep silent and be thought a fool than to open your mouth and remove all doubt.

Well! What did that have to do with anything?

Help me out here, will you, Lord? she begged. *How do I explain this to them so they'll understand and let it go?*

Silence again. Well, that was just fine. She'd handle this on her own.

"He wasn't what I thought he was," Corie said.

"Oh. He wasn't Jai with an *i?*"

"No, he's Jai…uh, Jay. Whatever. He's the artist." The image of his painting of her came to mind. She could still see the exquisite detail, the way he'd seemed to capture her personality, even her soul, on the canvas. He was definitely an artist.

"Did he explain the paintings?"

She sighed. "Yes."

"And what he said made sense?" Amelia asked.

This was not going well. "Yes, but there were things about him I didn't know—"

"Don't tell me he's married!" Amelia said, aghast.

"No." Corie shook her head, exasperated. "Of course not. It's not that at all. He's single, like he said he was—"

"Well, dear, which is it?" Ophelia broke in. "Was he or wasn't he what he said?"

"Yes, he was what he said, but he wasn't what I thought."

Oh, good heavens. Even she could see the absurdity of this. Not surprisingly, the Three pounced.

"For heaven's sake, Cordelia, make some sense."

"What *are* you talking about?"

"That is the most illogical thing I've heard in years."

The chorus rang in her ears, and her reply jumped out, hot and angry. "So what? So what if it's not logical? *I'm* not logical. I never have been. And what's more, I have no desire to be. Not

76

if it means I have to ignore my feelings and intuition. When will you three *get* that?"

Stop this now! her mind told her. But she wasn't listening. She was on a roll.

"I don't think the way you do. I don't feel the way you do. I'm not you, okay? Considering how off-the-scale you three are in IQ, I fail to understand why that's so hard for you to grasp. But you have to let me be who I am, no matter how inferior you all think that is."

She stopped, not so much because she was finished, but because her throat was too choked with tears to continue.

The silence in the room was deafening.

A sob caught in Corie's throat, and she shook her head helplessly. How could she have said such hateful, resentful things? She couldn't even bear to look at her sisters for fear of the anger she'd see on their faces. Or, worse, the hurt.

She turned to leave, and suddenly they were there beside her, their arms around her, their faces pressed against hers.

"Oh, Corie, no. Don't leave. Please."

The plea was filled with grief, and she looked into Ophelia's face, stunned to find tears coursing down her sister's cheeks.

"We can't let you go. Not believing such things," Ophelia said.

"I—" she started, but again the tightness in her throat cut off the words she so wanted to say.

I'm sorry. I didn't mean it. I'm an idiot! Forgive me.

She closed her eyes tightly, but it did no good. The tears overflowed. *God, God, forgive me....*

"Oh, sweet Corie, don't cry," Amelia begged, taking hold of her hand and leading her to the sofa. She sat her down gently, her arm around Corie's shoulders protectively.

"I'm sorry," Corie finally managed to sob out.

"No, my dear," Celie said. "We're sorry. So dreadfully sorry that you thought we…that we made you feel…oh, bother! Ophelia, where are your blasted Kleenex?"

Soon all four of them were doing their best to sop up the tears. Suddenly Ophelia blew her nose gustily, producing one of the finest impromptu elephant imitations Corie had ever heard.

They all froze, looking at each other in astonishment, then dissolved into giggles, collapsing against each other on the large sofa.

Amelia was the first to regain her composure. She reached out to gently touch Corie's arm. "We love you, Corie. I love you."

Corie blinked back tears again. "I know, Melia. I never doubted that."

"But you doubt we like you," Ophelia said quietly.

Corie was silent, not sure what to say. She nodded reluctantly.

"Or that we respect you," Celie added. "Which we do, Corie."

Corie looked at her sister, dumfounded. "You respect me?"

"A great deal," Ophelia said. "Corie, you have so many wonderful qualities, so many gifts that God has clearly given you. All three of us have watched you, the way you are with people, the ability you have to draw others out and bring them joy—"

"And we've envied that in you."

That was too much. Corie's mouth dropped open.

"It's true, Cordelia," Amelia said. "We've often wished we could reach people the way you do. Make them feel comfortable, rather than intimidated. But since it's just not in our makeup—"

"Definitely not in our makeup," Cecelia said with good humor.

"—we've been thankful to have you."

"You're our bridge, Cordelia," Ophelia said. "The one who connects us with others, and even with ourselves at times."

"You're our heart," Amelia said.

"The wind beneath our wings," Cecelia chimed in, then sat back chagrined when the other two rolled their eyes at her.

"What we're saying," Ophelia went on, "is that we've always considered you a gift, Cordelia. God has used you in our lives to help us to feel and to be honest about our feelings."

Corie shook her head, trying to sort through what she was hearing. "I had no idea."

"I suppose you couldn't have," Ophelia said thoughtfully. "None of the three of us does particularly well at expressing our emotions, I'm afraid."

Amelia touched her arm. "But I promise you, if we had known you were feeling as you were—"

"Left out—"

"Lacking—"

Corie swallowed with difficulty. "Lonely," she said quietly.

Cecelia took her hand. "Oh, my dear, we would have done whatever it took to let you know how we felt."

"And that you are, most certainly, not alone," Ophelia said.

"Though heaven knows, there quite likely have been times when you wished you were," Amelia said.

Corie shook her head. "No, I didn't want to be without you." At their knowing looks, she grinned. "Okay, once in a while, maybe. But not often. I just wanted to feel as though I belonged. That I wasn't just an oddity that you endured as best you could."

"Cordelia, you are not an oddity," Ophelia said.

"After all, my dear, *you* can cook," Amelia said.

"And clean house." Ophelia shuddered.

"And do all those puzzling acts of domesticity that most women learn at their mother's knee," Cecelia finished.

Amelia frowned. "Good heavens," she said, looking at Ophelia and Cecelia. "Do you realize that Corie is the most normal of the four of us?"

"Now *that's* the kind of logic I could learn to love!" Corie said, laughing. Her sisters joined in, and as their laughter surrounded her, she savored the love and acceptance she was feeling. This was what she'd longed for, prayed for for so many years. Who would have imagined it was there all the time? If only she'd said something sooner.

The truth shall set you free.

Oh, yes. Thank you, Father.

"Well, I, for one, need some help recovering from that realization," Ophelia said.

"Absolutely." Amelia's tone was filled with mirth. "In fact, I think it will take nothing less than chocolate to get us through our trauma."

"Oh," sighed Cecelia, "if only some gracious, gifted, creative person would take pity on us—"

"—and bake a pan of double-chocolate—"

"—fudge-frosted—"

"—nut-filled brownies."

Corie's laughter erupted again. "All right, all right. I'll take pity on you." She looked at Ophelia. "I assume you have the ingredients for brownies?"

Ophelia's expression was blank.

"Margarine, flour, sugar, eggs…" Corie said hopefully.

"And I would find these ingredients…where?" Ophelia asked.

"In the pantry!" Amelia said triumphantly.

"No, in the kitchen, in that cold thing," Celie said. "What is it? Ah yes, the refrigerator."

"Do I have one of those?" Ophelia asked, eyes wide.

"Never mind," Corie gasped between her giggles. "I'll go to

the store. You three are hopeless."

"Indubitably," Ophelia said.

"Undeniably," Amelia said.

"Most assuredly," Celie finished.

And not one of them had the grace to look even a little bit repentant.

"Cordelia needs our help," Ophelia said as she and the other two triplets stood waving good-bye to their younger sister later that evening.

"I believe you're right," Cecelia said.

"Maybe it's just as well that she's given up on this Jay Darling person," Amelia said, but the words rang false. "No, you're right. We can't leave things as they are."

They went to sit in the living room.

"Absolutely not," Ophelia said. "Cordelia has finally found a man she cares about. We cannot let emotions muck up such a splendid match."

"Do you think he would let us have a discount on his paintings once he's part of the family?" Cecelia asked.

"Cecelia!" the other two said in chorus.

She looked appropriately chastised. "Well, how should we go about this?"

"I think," Ophelia said carefully, "we should deal with it the way Corie would."

Her sisters stared at her, flummoxed.

"You want us to…think like Corie?" Amelia's brow was creased with confusion.

"Is that even possible?" Cecelia asked.

"We've always said we can do anything if we put our minds to it," Ophelia said confidently. "Now, if you were Corie, how would you get two people together?"

"I'd cook a meal," Cecelia said.

Her eldest sister pinned her with a glare. "Get real."

"Ophelia, we have PhDs. I daresay we can put together one meal."

After a moment, Ophelia nodded. "All right. We'll do it."

"I just have one question," Amelia said, and her sisters looked at her expectantly. She bit her lip and peered over her shoulder toward the kitchen. "Who's going to tell us which of those contraptions we're supposed to use?"

CHAPTER Ten

Corie hung up the phone, wondering if she'd somehow become part of a *Twilight Zone* episode.

Her sisters had just invited her to Ophelia's for dinner tomorrow night. And they were cooking.

I wonder, she thought dazedly, *if you use 911 for the fire department?*

Kelley looked up as the bell at the door jingled, alerting her to the arrival of customers.

Three of the most attractive, elegant women she'd ever seen came in. Kelley blinked her eyes, and then looked again.

They were triplets.

Triplets? The shock of realization hit her full force. The Three Sisters. It had to be them. She'd thought Jay was kidding when he'd told her about them.

"Excuse me," one said in a low, cultured voice. "We'd like to buy some flowers."

"Certainly," Kelley replied, wracking her brain for a way to find out if they were truly the Three.

"Ophelia, wait. I think it would be more effective if we order them to arrive while the meal is going on."

Ophelia pondered this, then tilted her head in a nod. "You're right, Amelia."

"And we should make them from him," the third triplet said.

"Cecelia, you're a genius," Amelia said.

Cecelia smiled. "Well, of course."

They came forward and quickly gave Kelley the address, then pointed to a large bouquet identical to the one she'd sent with Jay when he went to meet Corie.

"That will do nicely."

"Fine," she said. "And how do you want the card to read?"

All three smiled smugly, and Cecelia said, "To Corie. With all my love, Jay."

Kelley dropped her pen. "You *are* them! I knew it. You're the Three Sisters."

Ophelia studied her curiously. "And you are?"

She was all but jumping up and down. "I'm Jay's sister, Kelley. Oh, please tell me you're doing what I think you're doing. Please tell me you're trying to get the two idiots back together."

The triplets exchanged glances.

"An interesting way of putting it," Ophelia said, "but entirely accurate."

"Thank goodness. Jay needs someone to help him, and he won't let me even call her."

"You'd like them to get back together, then?" Cecelia asked.

Kelley nodded. "Absolutely. Jay's in love with your sister; he just doesn't know it yet."

"Typical male," Ophelia said.

Cecelia nudged her excitedly. "I told you God was in this with us! Kelley is the perfect solution to how we'll get Jay to your house."

Ophelia looked from her sisters to Kelley.

"Hey," Kelley said, "whatever you need, I'm available."

A broad smile crossed Ophelia's face. "I can see you're going to be an estimable addition to the family." The Three gathered around Kelley, their eyes sparkling. "Now, here's the plan...."

~ ~ ~ ~ ~

"Where is it we're going again?" Jay asked.

"I told you, to a dinner with some potential clients. They may want me to do the flowers for an upcoming wedding."

"And I'm going…why?"

Kelly glared at him. "To be charming."

"Ah, of course."

"There it is: 422 Standish Drive." Kelley pointed to a house on the right.

"Wow," Jay said, pulling into the circular drive and peering at the marble columns framing the front double doors. "This could be quite a wedding. I might even want to come."

Kelley coughed suddenly, as though she'd choked on something.

"You okay?" he asked, and she nodded, motioning him toward the door.

They walked up the wide stone stairs and rang the bell. No answer. They rang the bell again.

"Are you sure they're—" Jay's question was interrupted as the door flew open, and he turned to face what looked like a tall, slim ghost.

"Well, don't just stand there," the apparition snarled. "Come in."

As he walked past, Jay saw that the creature was a woman, covered in what looked like flour.

"Amelia?" Kelley asked uncertainly. "Is that you?"

"Don't be smug," flour woman said. "We've encountered a bit of an obstacle, but I believe we have it under control now. At least…I hope so."

At that moment, the sound of clanging and clunking came from the direction of what Jay assumed was the kitchen.

"Never mind the man behind the curtain," Amelia muttered.

"This way, please." She brushed ineffectively at her soiled apron as she led the way to a large, elegant dining room.

Well, Jay thought, *the servants are a mess, but the decor is strictly* House Beautiful.

"Have a seat," Amelia said. "We should be ready to start soon."

Jay took in the table. Two places were set, complete with fine china, sparkling crystal, and linen napkins.

A howl of frustration came from behind the closed door of the kitchen, followed by the door crashing open.

A woman stood there, gesturing wildly. Smudges of flour and something dark ran across her face, and her hair stuck out in all directions, as though she'd been caught in a wind tunnel. "Amelia! Quickly! Ophelia's stuck in the refidger-whatsit!"

And then she was gone again, back into what Jay was beginning to think of as the black hole.

Amelia's smile was pained. "You'll excuse me? I believe I'm being paged."

They watched her trudge to the door and push it open, as though it took a Herculean effort.

Jay bit his lip to keep from bursting into laughter. Casting a cautious glance at his sister, he saw she was doing the same. She quickly reached for a glass of water and began to sip.

"I sure hope maid service isn't their day job."

Kelley choked, spewing water everywhere. Jay pounded her on the back.

"Sorry," she wheezed when she could speak again. "I had trouble swallowing something."

"Well, at least we get to enjoy beautiful surroundings," he said, pulling the chair out for his sister.

She hesitated. "Um, I think I'll go see if I can help them in the kitchen."

"Are you sure it's safe in there?" he asked with a laugh.

Just then the tones of a melodic doorbell filled the air. Jay glanced at the front door, then back to his sister.

"Were you expecting someone else?"

Kelley's eyes were wide. "Who, me?" She stepped toward the kitchen door. "Not my house. Not my place to expect anything."

The chime sounded again.

"Well, somebody's here," Jay said.

Kelley took another step backward. "You're absolutely right. Tell you what, why don't you answer the door, and I'll just go see what's holding dinner up."

She pushed the door open and slipped through.

With a shake of his head, Jay went to the front door.

"What's with the locked—"

The question hung there, unfinished, as Jay stared at Corie. She stood there, hair windblown, eyes wide with alarm, a half smile frozen on her face. He thought his heart would burst with the feelings she stirred in him.

"I—" she stammered, "you—what are you doing here?"

"I believe I was invited. And you?"

She came inside, her expression wary. "The same. But I'm getting the distinct feeling it was for something far more than dinner."

They stood there until the silence between them grew unbearable.

"I'm going to find out what's going on," Corie said, turning to march away.

Jay's hand shot out as though it had a mind of its own. He caught her arm and held on. "Wait."

She stood there, her back to him.

You're not going to make this easy, are you, God?

"Did I ever tell you I was engaged once?" He knew he hadn't, but he wasn't sure how else to begin.

Apparently it was a good start. She turned slowly to look at him.

"About five years ago. Her name was Gwen. We met at church, and it was as though we knew God had brought us together."

She watched him silently. And yet, despite her closed expression, he sensed her vulnerability.

"So you can imagine my surprise when Gwen called me about a week before the wedding to say God had told her he knew she wouldn't be happy married to a penniless artist and that she should marry Dewie Dortman."

Her lips twitched. "Dewie?"

He nodded. "One of the more affluent members of the church. Gwen wished me all God's blessings, told me she'd be praying for me, and hung up."

Compassion shone in her eyes, and she reached out to lay her hand over his where he still held her arm.

"I'm so sorry she hurt you that way. She was wrong, Jay."

The simple words hit him like a runaway semi truck. He stood there, his eyes fixed on her face, wanting nothing more than to have her in his arms.

"Yes, she was," he agreed. "But I was wrong, too. I knew I was bitter and I didn't care. I just gave in. Pretty soon I couldn't see anything but deceit in every woman I dated. Then, when my work was suddenly in such demand, all I saw were women who wanted to 'go places' with a famous artist. But the places I wanted to go were to the beach, to the park—"

"To the zoo," she finished for him.

"That day at your apartment, you asked me if I was tired of playing games. I told you I was, but I didn't tell you why. Nor did I tell you the reason I was so quick to believe you were just playing a role."

"Gwen," she said, and he nodded.

"I got so tired of it all that I gave up. On women." He grimaced. "Even on church. I decided I could get along fine without anyone but my family and God. I knew I was just running away. But I didn't care. Until now." He met her gaze. "Until you."

She was silent for a moment, and he watched the emotions play across her expressive face. Compassion, frustration, regret...and then sadness.

Icy fear stabbed through him. "Corie—"

She shook her head. "I understand, Jay. I do, but I don't know that it changes anything. You didn't trust me—"

"Any more than you trusted me," he shot at her, then regretted the words immediately.

"That's true, and that's what worries me." Her stricken eyes met his. "What if I can't be what you want me to be? What if I do something else, make another mistake—" She broke off, and he saw tears shimmering in her eyes. "I want to be a part of a team, Jay. I want to be joined with a man I can depend on, who will be willing to depend on me. What if we can't get past ourselves to find each other?"

I don't know what to say or do, God, and I'm losing her. Please, don't let this happen!

A screech from the kitchen jarred them both. "Call 911! Somebody, call 911!"

Corie and Jay froze for a second, then raced toward the kitchen.

Corie stood in her sister's kitchen, too stupefied to do more than gawk.

The Three Sisters were a disaster. Their faces and arms were covered in flour and who knew what else. Their usually immaculate hair was poking out in all directions, and their aprons sported what looked like some kind of swamp goo.

But they were clean compared to the kitchen. The floors, walls, and cabinets were coated with a layer of grime that Corie was almost sure must have come from a science lab somewhere. Bits of food were splattered here and there, and dirty pots and pans and utensils covered every surface.

A hysterical giggle bubbled inside Corie as she surveyed the carnage. All humor fled, though, when she spotted the Three dancing about the stove, flapping their hands frantically at a pan from which black smoke was billowing. A smoke alarm started to blare.

"Whoa!" Jay exclaimed. "Kelley, call 911," he said to a woman Corie had never seen before. Had the Three sent out invitations for this event?

Jay move swiftly, grasping Ophelia's arm. She spun to stare at him, and Corie saw that her sister's flour-dusted face was streaked from her frantic tears.

"Where's your fire extinguisher?" Jay demanded, but Corie knew the question was wasted.

She rushed forward, snatched a towel from the butcher block, then scooped up the pan lid and slammed it into place.

"Good job, sweetheart!" She turned to find Jay right beside, a towel in his hand as well.

He lifted the pan, holding the lid in place. Corie dashed ahead of him to the sink and turned on the water, then he lowered the pan into the stream.

Their eyes met, and they smiled. "Thanks, partner," Jay murmured.

Corie nodded.

Jay looked toward the ceiling where a thick cloud of smoke hung, then at the windows.

"Got 'em," Corie said. She moved to throw the windows open as he turned on the fan over the stove.

"All I wanted to do was cook potatoes," Ophelia wailed.

"Water would have been helpful!" Amelia snapped.

Ophelia turned on her sister, and Corie rushed to get between them—only to find that Jay had beat her to it. "We need to go outside," he was saying in low, soothing tones. Corie watched in wonder as he led a suddenly compliant Ophelia toward the door.

Corie slid her arms around Amelia's and Cecelia's trembling shoulders. "Come on, you two. I think we could all use some air."

Jay watched in a daze as the firemen went in and out of Ophelia's house. They'd shown up in response to Kelley's frantic phone call and were busy making sure all was safe in the battered kitchen.

He would never, as long as he lived, forget the sight of that kitchen and those three women. But what had struck him the most wasn't the disarray, but the love he had seen between Corie and her sisters.

He wanted to know what it was like to love Corie that deeply. Every day. For the rest of his life.

"I beg your pardon, but *must* you wear boots in my home?"

His lips twitched. Apparently Ophelia had recovered from the trauma of trying to cook a meal.

"Umm, 'scuse me?"

Jay turned to find a young man standing next to him, holding a huge bouquet of flowers. Recognition dawned. Kelley's delivery boy. "Brad?"

He nodded. "Hiya, Mr. D. I was supposed to deliver these...." His voice trailed off as he turned to watch the firemen. "To that house. Do you think they still want them?"

"Yes, they do," came the answer from behind Jay.

He turned to smile at Kelley. "I take it these are your doing?"

She took the flowers from Brad, thanked him, then handed them to Jay. "Actually, they're from you."

"From me?"

Kelley nodded. "Yup. Compliments of the Three Sisters." She grinned. "They think of everything."

Jay glanced back at the house and the firemen, then shook his head.

"Now, don't you think you'd be more comfortable—" she motioned with her head—"over there?"

He followed the direction of her gaze, then turned back to her with a grateful smile. "Did you know I love you?"

"Of course," she said smugly.

Corie sat on the curb, staring at her shoes. No doubt about it. She was in the Twilight Zone.

A large bouquet, identical to the one she'd received on Valentine's Day, was suddenly laid beside her.

"These are for you."

She didn't turn to see who was speaking. She didn't need to.

"May I join you?"

She hesitated, then nodded.

Jay lowered himself beside her, not touching her, but filling her senses all the same.

"We made quite a team in there."

The lump in her throat stopped any words she wanted to say. She nodded again.

"Not bad after knowing one another for only a day, don't you think?"

"No," she managed. "Not bad at all."

"Corie. Look at me."

She closed her eyes, suddenly afraid.

"Please."

Slowly, carefully, she opened her eyes and turned to him. It was all there, in his eyes: the promise, the regret, the determination to hold on to what they'd found.

He opened his arms and she moved almost without conscious thought. No hesitation, no debate. She was coming home.

"I'm sorry I hurt you," she said against his shirt. "I should have trusted you, what I knew of you and your character."

"And I should have realized that a single day, no matter how wonderful, wasn't enough for either of us to build a basis for that kind of trust." His arms tightened. "I was an idiot," he whispered against her hair.

"It's only fair," she replied. "I was one first."

"Yes," he agreed, the teasing laughter back in his voice, "you were. But I did it best."

"Okay," she murmured. "You win."

He reached out, lifting her chin gently until their eyes locked. "Do I, Corie? Do I really?"

She didn't have to ask what he meant. "I love you," she said. The words seemed to free her heart, and she was suddenly overwhelmed with a bottomless peace and contentment.

Emotion flickered in his dark eyes. "And I love you. Now. Always."

He lowered his head to kiss first her nose, then her eyes, and finally, satisfyingly, her mouth.

When he lifted his head, she reached up to trace his face with tender fingers. "I take it we're sure about this, then."

The smile she'd come to love so well tipped his mouth. "Oh, absolutely." And he claimed her lips again.

ᨆ ᨆ ᨆ ᨆ ᨆ

Kelley nudged Ophelia. "Well, this wasn't exactly the plan you told me about, but apparently it worked."

Ophelia and her sisters looked to where Jay and Corie were deeply engrossed in each other, then turned back to Kelley.

"Well!" Cecelia exclaimed. "It was all worth it then."

Ophelia shot her a dark look.

"Well done, sisters," Kelley said. "You definitely went way beyond anything I would have done."

"You can't possibly believe we did this on purpose!" Amelia said.

Kelley met their exasperated gazes. "You're kidding, right?"

They didn't smile. Not even a little.

"But…you've all got PhDs."

"Exactly," Ophelia said. "We have far more important things to do than cook." Her trembling lower lip made this confident assertion less than believable.

Kelley slipped her arm around Ophelia. "Now, now, don't you worry. I come from a long line of culinary masters." She cast another glance at Jay and Corie. "Since odds are good that we're going to be family now, what say I teach you a few things about that mean old kitchen?"

"I'm never darkening the door of that horrid place again!" Ophelia said.

"None of us are!" Amelia said.

"I am," Cecelia said, and her sisters turned to look at her. "Well, I am! I'm not going to let that beastly place beat me."

"Well," Ophelia said after a moment, "I suppose you're right."

"You'll protect us?" Amelia asked Kelley.

She nodded. "I promise." She hooked her arms with theirs,

and they started toward the house. "We'll start with something easy." She looked at them carefully, taking in the smoke smudges and dusting of flour still clinging to their skin and clothes.

"So, how do you feel about toast?"

~ ~ ~ ~ ~

I loved Valentine's Day as a kid. My mom was the queen of celebrations, so the house was decorated to perfection. For dinner, we would come to a table decked out in red and white, complete with Valentine's Day gifts. As an adult I've had Valentine's dinners for my friends to celebrate marriage and love. I've followed my mother's lead on decorations and fixing meals that are as much a delight to the eye as to the palate. And there is always a small gift at each person's place just to say, You're loved. My favorite time of the evening, though, is when we stand in a circle, hands clasped, and thank God for his perfect love in our lives. Keeping in mind that love—and the wondrous gift of his Son—makes every day a Valentine's celebration.

Frozen Raspberry Macadamia Dessert

Crust
1 cup (20 wafers) crushed vanilla wafers
1/2 cup finely chopped macadamia nuts or almonds
1/4 cup margarine or butter, melted
Filling
14-ounce can sweetened condensed milk
3 tablespoons lemon juice
3 tablespoons orange juice
10-ounce package frozen raspberries, thawed
1 cup whipping cream, whipped

Crust: Heat oven to 375 degrees. Combine all ingredients; mix well. Press into bottom of 8-inch springform pan. Bake at 375 degrees for 8 to10 minutes. Cool.

Filling: Combine first three ingredients in large bowl; beat until smooth. Add berries; beat at low speed until well blended. Fold in whipped cream. Pour over cooled crust. Freeze until firm. Before serving, let stand at room temperature for 15 minutes. Garnish with a dollop of whipped cream and a chocolate kiss.

Karen Ball is senior editor for women's fiction at Multnomah Publishers. She lives in Illinois with her husband, Don, and their "kids": two Siberian huskies and a beagle-basset mix. Her work includes the novel, *Reunion*, and a novella in *Mistletoe*.

♥

Cupid's
Chase

by Barbara Jean Hicks

CHAPTER
One

"H ey, Kincaid!"

Reid pulled his head out from the cabinet he'd been cleaning as the kitchen doors swung inward. Franco Fortunato strolled in and leaned jauntily against the counter. Franco, to his credit, hadn't used the fact that he was the boss's son to try to get out of the closing shift tonight. Not that Lorenzo Fortunato would have let him.

"Hey yourself," Reid answered cheerfully. "Side stands all done?"

Franco snapped his damp towel in Reid's direction. "Clean as a whistle. I am ready to party! What do we have left to do back here?"

"Almost done." Reid straightened his back and stretched his shoulders. "Your choice: finish the cabinets or marry the condiments?"

Franco shuddered and raised his hands as if to protect himself. "Don't use that word around me!"

"What—marry?" Reid grinned. "Getting some pressure from the girlfriend, Franco?"

"Nah." Franco hesitated, uncertainty blurring his usual brash self-confidence. "She broke up with me last week. *After* she got her Christmas present. Women!"

"Yeah. Women. Tough luck, man."

Franco's cocky expression was already back in place. "I'll get over it. Plenty of other fish in the sea. The deejay setting up in the dining room, for instance. What a knockout!"

Ah, the resiliency of youth, Reid thought, smiling. Except

that he knew from experience a lost love wasn't as easy to get over as Franco pretended, youth or not.

"You got a date for the party tonight?"

"No." Reid didn't elaborate. He could have invited someone to the year-end party the Fortunato brothers were throwing for the restaurant staff, but seeing in the new year with a woman he knew only casually felt too much like making promises he wasn't ready to keep.

He wondered how long it would be before he got beyond casual with a woman again. He hadn't been serious about anyone since high school. Since Rae Ann. No time, for one thing—between waiting tables and directing the music program at the church, his four-year degree had already stretched out to nearly seven. But now that all he had left was student teaching...

It was something to think about. All women weren't like Rae Ann.

He took out the mustard jars and the cruets of oil and vinegar for cleaning and refilling. "Is the New Year's Eve party an annual bash, Franco?"

"Since I was a kid. Uncle Leander and my father go all out for it, too. I'm talkin' serious fun."

"Yeah?" Reid was dubious. Lorenzo he could see throwing a party in appreciation of his employees. But Leander? Leander was such a tightwad his brother probably had to sit on him to get him to put out the money. He still had Nonna Pippa—at seventy-five—working the hostess desk for him.

Was it Leander who got out every day to sweep the sidewalk? Was it a busboy he could have paid minimum wage for the work? No, it was his old mother whose back was bent over the broom. "One day, I retire," Nonna Pippa would say, coming in off the street to sink onto a bench in the waiting area, a sheen of perspiration on her upper lip.

And while Lorenzo knew everyone who worked at Fortunato's by name, Leander rarely showed his face outside his office, which was tucked into a corner of the flagship restaurant near Seattle's Pioneer Square. He'd certainly never said hello to Reid.

Franco rambled on about last year's New Year's Eve party while Reid listened with half an ear. Reid had been working part-time at Fortunato's Ristorante for four months now. The Italian restaurant was a classy place, his best job since he'd started waiting tables as a freshman to help pay his way through school. The managers worked with his class schedule, and the upscale clientele regularly left 20 percent tips on tabs higher than Reid's monthly food budget.

He felt lucky to have landed the job. It was rare to have a position at Fortunato's without a family connection. But by now, he almost did have a family connection: Lorenzo and Leander's mother insisted Reid call her "Nonna" Pippa—Grandma Pippa—just as her eight grandchildren did. She was every bit as delightful as her name sounded rolling off his tongue.

It was Nonna Pippa who'd told him the history of Fortunato's Ristorante. The family business begun by her sons Lorenzo and Leander twenty-seven years ago had expanded to four locations in the Seattle area over a period of twenty-two years. "But this location, she is the first," Nonna Pippa told him. "Like home for this old woman."

Five years ago the Fortunato brothers had franchised the operation, and now there were Fortunato's Ristorantes everywhere. "Even Rome," the family matriarch told him proudly. "Even Genoa!"

The twang of steel guitar sounded from the dining room.

"All right!" Franco shoved the last rack of glasses under the counter. "Let's party!" He gestured toward the dining room. "Check out the redhead running the music, Kincaid. She looks like some fun."

Reid followed him out the door. The main dining room was enormous, wrapped in a sweeping mural of vineyard-covered hills. It had been cleared out, except for chairs lining the wall and one long buffet table laden with food, leaving the hardwood floor open for dancing. The surface of the bar was crowded with chilled bottles of Asti Spumante.

Dozens of green, red, and white balloons floated against the ceiling, their long streamers of curling ribbon hanging like a forest of colorful seaweed over the dance floor. A crowd of people in semiformal attire stood around the marble fountain in the foyer, talking and laughing. A pretty teenager in a short velvet dress—another of Lorenzo's seven children—was draping a sash with the new year emblazoned on it across the marble cupid in the center of the fountain.

Reid glanced across the room to the makeshift stage, where Franco's redhead was plugging a cord into a microphone. He did a double take. Just then she looked up, and a grin broke across her features.

"Reid! Where you been?" she called across the room.

Franco yelped. "You know her? Be still, my heart! Introduce me, Kincaid."

"She's a little old for you, Franco," he answered dryly.

"Not enough to—"

"She's my mother."

"Ohh-kay." Franco suddenly changed direction. "Think I'll see if Marcella needs any help over here...." He headed for the group by the fountain.

Reid hurried across to the makeshift stage. "Mom! What are you doing here?"

"Told you I had a gig for New Year's Eve, darlin'."

"I know, but—why didn't you tell me it was *here?*"

She grinned again, her green eyes sparkling. "Wanted to surprise you," she drawled. Even after twenty years in Seattle, her faint accent revealed her Texas roots.

"Mom, you never cease to surprise me." Reid eyed her outfit, a short black denim skirt and jacket studded with gold stars and worn with a hot pink satin shirt and matching cowboy boots. Wavy red hair, topped by a black, gold-banded cowboy hat, bounced around her shoulders. Her recent trip to the Caribbean had doubled the number of freckles on her nose and cheeks. Franco's mistake had been an honest one; she didn't look nearly old enough to be his mother.

Dolly Kincaid reached over and scraped at a spot of dried pasta sauce on her son's tuxedo shirt. The sleeves were still rolled up, and a black bow tie hung loose around his neck. "You're not wearin' your workin' clothes to the party, I hope."

"Something wrong with my clothes?" At her look of horror, he added, "Mom, I'm kidding! I brought a turtleneck and a blazer. I'm on my way to change. What about you? You sure you're not supposed to be at the Western barbecue pit down the street?" he teased.

She placed her hands on her hips and tossed her hair. "Get with the picture, darlin'! You never heard of spaghetti westerns? Besides, I'm honorin' a special request with this outfit." She lifted one eyebrow in a saucy look he didn't know what to make of.

"Oh? Just who was it hired you for this gig?" he asked curiously.

"Someone who just loves my heart-wrenchin', toe-stompin', deep-thinkin' country music."

"Deep-thinkin'?" Reid rolled his eyes. "Mom, I'm afraid you've gone off the deep *end!* Promise you won't tell anyone you're my mother?"

"You kiddin'? Gonna make sure everybody knows, son!" She gave him an exaggerated wink, then turned her attention to the knobs and levers of her karaoke equipment. "Be ready, darlin'."

But no warning could have been enough to prepare him for the night that lay ahead.

Carina Fortunato turned down the wick on the kerosene lantern swinging over the dining table. The twelve-volt light she'd left on over the sink in the tiny galley cast ghostly shadows across the cabin.

Even in the protected marina with the sails furled tight, on a night like tonight the sloop rolled like Uncle Lorenzo when he walked. The north wind wailed and moaned. The halyards clanged against the mast and echoed through the cabin. Carina hadn't liked the noises when she first moved aboard, but by now they seemed comforting. The wind was out there; she was inside, warm and protected.

The *Portofino* had been Carina's home for more months than she cared to think about. Not that she hadn't enjoyed being a live-aboard, especially in August and September, when the weather in Seattle was as close to perfect as it got this side of heaven. Her father had torn himself away from work to join her for a sail at least half a dozen times. A record.

"Why did you buy the boat when you never use it?" she'd been asking him for years. But she'd been glad he had it when the contractors started to tear apart her house to replace the ancient pipes and wiring and strip the shingles from the roof. There was a reason she'd gotten the little bungalow for such a bargain; she was lucky she hadn't flooded it out or burned it down before she discovered how much work it needed.

"Two months, max," the contractors had assured her. That had been five months ago.

She pulled her warmest coat off the hook in the forward stateroom and slipped it on. Temperatures were expected to dip into the twenties tonight, which was cold for Seattle.

Not a night to be out. But everyone would be; it was New Year's Eve.

She punched in the number for the ristorante on her cellular phone. The line was busy. Maybe Babbo was trying to call, wondering where she was.

The party would be in full swing by now. Uncle Lorenzo and Babbo—her pet name for her father—had closed the dining room an hour early, at nine o'clock, to clear the floor for dancing and to set up the buffet table. The yearly bash was Leander and Lorenzo Fortunato's thank-you to their hardworking staff. Lorenzo cooked and Babbo poured the vino, like in the old days.

Uncle Lorenzo was probably swinging Zia Felicia around the dance floor even now. For a man who liked his pasta as much as Uncle Lorenzo did, he could hoof it with the best of them. Felicia would be wearing sequins, her eyes closed, and for once the permanent crease between her brows would be so slight as to be barely noticeable.

Babbo might be dancing with the widow Giotti. Carina sincerely hoped he was. She'd hinted a month ago that he invite the widow for New Year's Eve. She was a nice woman, alone for almost two years now, someone her father had known through the church for as long as Carina could remember.

"She comes to Fortunato's for dinner twice a week," Carina had told her father. "She eats a lot. She brings her friends. You ought to thank her properly."

"She does eat a lot," was all Leander said.

He hadn't dated at all since his short-lived marriage to April Dawn had ended. What a disaster that had been. It was no wonder he'd steered clear of women since.

But the widow Giotti was nothing like April Dawn. Surely her father knew that. Especially now, after spending a week aboard the same cruise ship over Christmas. They had to have bumped into each other, maybe talked a little, shared some fun. Danced the night away, Carina hoped. It would be so nice for Babbo, having a good woman in his life.

"What's this?" Babbo had frowned when Lorenzo handed him the cruise packet at Thanksgiving.

"Your Christmas present from the family." Nonna Pippa beamed.

"Because you need a vacation," Zia Felicia told him.

"Because *we* need a vacation," Lorenzo said. When Babbo worked too hard, everybody suffered. Uncle Lorenzo wasn't afraid to call a spade a spade.

"But at Christmas?" Leander shook his head. "Christmas is to share with family."

"Family you got coming out your ears," Uncle Lorenzo said. "Every day in this business. Go have a good time without family for a change."

"But a cruise?" Leander protested. "Cruises are for doddering old—"

Carina's pleading look stopped him. "It's a gift, Babbo. Accept it with grace."

He had accepted the gift, much to the family's relief, but three days before Christmas, he called his daughter's office from Miami an hour before the *Ysolda* was scheduled to set sail.

"So did you know all along about the widow Giotti?" he demanded without even saying hello.

"What about the widow?"

"The cruise. The widow. The widow on the cruise."

"Well, of course! She told me about it, Babbo. That's what gave me the idea."

"Which idea?" he asked suspiciously.

"Why, the cruise!" She should have known he'd take a dim view of anything that smacked of matchmaking. And sending her father on a cruise she knew the widow was taking more than smacked.

"Oh, Babbo, what's so bad about wanting to see you have a good time?" she asked. "Can't you just enjoy yourself?"

Was it wrong of me, God? she prayed more than once while he was gone. *To arrange it without asking him?* She didn't like thinking she was meddlesome. And she especially didn't like thinking Babbo might have reason to be angry with her. *You know I only want him to be happy....*

The extent of her relief when he came back home refreshed and energetic told her how anxious she'd been. "I did enjoy myself, very much," he said as he gave her a bone-crunching hug.

She hadn't gotten the details yet. He and the widow had been home only two days.

Hitting the redial button on the phone, she lifted it to her ear again and waited. Two rings, three, four.

Nonna Pippa was probably dancing with her broom, she thought.

She smiled at the picture in her mind. Her grandmother was seventy-five years old and still insisted on sweeping the sidewalk in front of Fortunato's every morning and every afternoon. Weather permitting, which in Seattle meant she took a good number of days off.

Zia Felicia carried on about it, of course; having customers greeted by an old woman nearly as broad as Lorenzo, with a shapeless apron over her shapeless dress and her stockings slipping down around her ankles, didn't project the proper image. And she didn't like the fact that the old woman hung about the dining room during the evenings, "getting in the way of the hostesses," either. But Leander said it made her feel useful and refused to send her upstairs to her apartment all alone. Besides, since the fifth-floor apartment was only a short elevator ride from the ristorante, it would have been difficult to keep her away.

The ringing stopped. Finally!

"Fortunato's Ristorante, Signore Leander here."

She could hardly hear his voice over the noise and music in the background. "Babbo! I didn't think *you'd* answer the phone. How's the party?"

"Such a good time, cara! Where are you?"

"Just leaving the boat. My neighbor was late getting back. I knew he'd want to see his baby." Carina had been cat sitting for a week while the live-aboard across the dock visited his daughter in Los Angeles.

"Such a good girl you are. Always thinking of others. Come soon! We'll save a karaoke song for you."

"Karaoke!" But she was speaking to the dial tone. She held the phone at arm's length, her eyebrows lifted in surprise, then dropped it into her leather shoulder bag. Karaoke?

A blast of cold air greeted her when she climbed through the main hatch a moment later. She tightened her scarf around her head and snuggled deeper into her heavy camel-hair coat. Her high heels tottered precariously as she stepped off the boat and onto the pier.

At the end of the dock she turned the handle on the metal gate and swung it open, eyeing the steep angle of the ramp up to the parking lot. This was not going to be easy. High heels and low tide were as incompatible as Leander and April Dawn.

She gripped the handrail and started up the ramp. *Please, God, let the widow Giotti be at the party,* she prayed. A nice, respectable woman, the widow was. A lady.

Babbo needs a lady, God. You must see that.

Nineteen years he'd been alone after Carina's mother died, but he was too busy building the business and raising a daughter by himself to think about being lonely. Until April Dawn. She'd been hardly older than Carina, but the woman had a way about her that could make a man think he was lonely even when he wasn't.

Carina hadn't liked her from the start, but Babbo was a grown man, so she hadn't voiced her misgivings. What a mistake!

April Dawn had not an ounce of conscience to her. After less than two years of free-spending, high-living marriage, she'd left him. And taken him to the cleaners in the divorce. One thing about April Dawn—she wasn't stupid.

As for Babbo—about most things, he was practical and down to earth.

But when it came to women, he clearly needed help.

Leander Fortunato was pouring drinks behind the bar. He was a handsome man, in a craggy sort of way, Reid conceded. Tall and lean in contrast to his brother's portliness, he looked at the world through sharp, dark eyes under heavy black brows and a thatch of gray hair. A wiry mustache tickled his upper lip under a strong Roman nose. Reid wondered where he'd been to have such a tan in the middle of winter. Somewhere other than Seattle, that was sure.

"Ah, Signore Kincaid!" he said as Reid approached the bar. He held up a bottle. "Vino?"

Reid lifted his brows in surprise. Leander knew who he was after all. "No, thank you. A soda will do."

"How about a *granita? Nocciola*—hazelnut. *Mia favorita.*" Before Reid could answer, he was filling a tall glass with shaved ice. He turned to reach for a bottle of syrup from the row behind the counter, selected one, and poured a generous dollop over the ice. "A splash of syrup…a little latte…fill with soda water," he said aloud as he added each ingredient. "And here she is!" He placed a tall spoon in the glass and handed it to Reid with a flourish.

"Grazie." Reid hesitated. "I didn't realize you knew me, Signore Fortunato."

"Try it," Leander prompted, pointing to the glass, as if Reid's approval were of the utmost importance.

Reid took a spoonful of the creamy iced drink, closing his eyes as he savored the sweet, nutty concoction. Maybe he'd misjudged Leander. He opened his eyes and nodded. "Mmm—good."

Leander clapped his hands together, beaming. "You are the one Mama calls *Zampogna*," he said, stretching his arms along the bar and leaning forward.

Reid grinned. Nonna Pippa had thought his name very odd. "Like the pipe of reeds?" she'd asked, mimicking the playing of panpipes, when he'd first come to work at the ristorante.

And so he'd become Zampogna, the reed pipe. He'd even brought his clarinet and saxophone to work to play for Nonna Pippa to show her how appropriate his new name was.

"She's something else, your mama," Reid told Leander. He eyed the man over the rim of his glass as he took another spoonful. "But I worry that she works so hard."

Leander laughed heartily. "Mama will work till the day she dies—God forbid it should happen soon."

Reid's feelings of goodwill toward Leander quickly evaporated. He turned away from the bar with a sour taste in his mouth that had nothing to do with the granita.

There were Fortunatos everywhere he looked, from Franco, acting as if he hadn't a care in the world, to Nonna Pippa, who had actually abandoned her apron for the occasion. Her dress was as shapeless as the dresses she wore for everyday, but glittery with sequins. He caught her eye and waved.

"Zampogna!" she called, gesturing.

"Go say hello to Mama," Leander urged. Reid was already on his way.

"Signora Pippa," he said formally, lifting her hand for a kiss when he reached her side. "You look smashing. Will you honor me with a dance?"

It didn't take much to talk her into a turn around the dance floor to his mother's lively music. Nonna Pippa loved to dance.

He grinned at his mother over Nonna Pippa's head as he guided her around the floor. Dolly Kincaid was in splendid form tonight. She'd already started to warm up the crowd for karaoke with her upbeat patter and a couple of twangy country songs she'd wailed out between the dance tunes. Everybody loved her.

It was hard not to like Dolly, Reid reflected as he spun Nonna Pippa under his arm. She was great fun, vivacious and good-humored. A little quirky. Compassionate. Tenderhearted in the extreme. Reid worried about people taking advantage of her.

He'd had his share of arguments with his mother, of course—they both had strong opinions, a stubborn streak a mile wide, and the same quick temper. But since his surgeon father had deserted them eight years ago, when Reid was seventeen, to marry someone "younger and more interesting," Reid's role with Dolly had been more like father than son.

Not that she encouraged him. "Reid McAllister Kincaid," she'd told him more than once, "I know you're tryin' to help, but I really can take care of myself."

When he finished his dance with Nonna Pippa, Reid led her to the stage, where Dolly was pulling CDs from her portable library.

"Nonna Pippa, I'd like you to meet my mother, Dolly Kincaid. Mom, I've told you about Signora Pippa."

Dolly reached down to take the old woman's hand between hers. "I'm so pleased to meet you, Signora Fortunato," she said. "You must be very proud of your sons and their families."

The Fortunato family matriarch bowed her head modestly. "The pleasure belongs to me. You got a fine son, too, Signora. And can he dance!" She patted Reid on the cheek. "A good boy. I got my eye on him for Carina Sabine."

"You do?" Dolly and Reid said in unison.

It was the first Reid had heard of it. He'd never met Leander's daughter, though her office was in the same dark corner of the restaurant as her father's. As director of training for the franchise operations, she was often out of town. Apparently when she was home, she worked during the early hours of the day. In his four months working dinner shifts, he'd never run into her.

"She's older than I am, isn't she?" Reid asked.

The old woman looked surprised. "One, two years. What does it matter? You are a man. She is a woman."

Couldn't argue with that logic, Reid thought, grinning. At least not with Nonna Pippa. Somehow he'd got the idea Carina Fortunato—Carina Sabine Fortunato—was much older than twenty-six or -seven. Maybe because she held such a responsible position in the Fortunato family business. But then, she was Leander's daughter. His only child, in contrast to Lorenzo's seven.

"You're quite enough for me, Nonna Pippa," he teased. "What would I want with your granddaughter?"

She snorted. *"Basta*—enough." But she looked pleased. "Carina will come, and you will see. Now you got to meet *mia famiglia.*" She took him by the arm and led him around the room to meet the rest of the clan, beginning with Lorenzo's wife, Felicia—who was as unlike her large, jovial husband as a pumpkin and a pickle—and going on to all seven of their children, eldest to youngest in proper order.

There was Romo, attached at the hip to his young bride, and Franco, in earnest conversation with a different girl every time Reid saw him. Marcella, with her big brown eyes and flirtatious smile, had several young men following behind her like puppy dogs. Salvatore, who at fifteen had nearly the girth of his father, didn't move away from his spot next to the buffet table for more than a few minutes at a time. The ten-year-old twins, Tiara and Aurora, were holy terrors, chasing each other around the room and nearly knocking Nonna Pippa off her feet.

Finally there was six-year-old Santo in his pint-sized tuxedo, who, despite the fact that he was clearly spoiled by everyone, was respectful, polite, and serious beyond his years. He, too, took Nonna Pippa for a clumsy but determined turn around the dance floor.

"Be lookin' in those notebooks for a song to sing," Dolly told the crowd breathlessly after she'd regaled them with what Reid knew was one of her favorite country songs, Pam Tillis's *"Mi Vida Loca."* "My Crazy Life." She called it her theme song.

She'd trilled her tongue like a Spanish cowboy and tripped into a high-pitched "yi, yi, yi, yi, yi!" that had Felicia stamping her high heels like a flamenco dancer. "Brava!" Leander had cried from the bar.

Reid might be biased, but he'd never seen a karaoke hostess as good as his mother at getting people up on stage. She flattered and coaxed and cajoled with the best of them, but mostly she so clearly was having the time of her life that everybody else wanted to be in on it.

"Leander Fortunato," Dolly drawled into the microphone, "you come out from behind that bar sometime tonight, you hear?"

"You got a duet?" he called from across the room. "For me and you?"

"I think I can find somethin'," she answered, her tone coquettish.

Reid frowned. Was his mother flirting with Leander Fortunato? Just how had she landed this gig tonight, anyway?

Feeling a need for air, he escaped the crush of people around the dance floor and made his way to the fountain in the foyer, dropping down onto its marble edge next to Santo, who was scraping a bowl of orange *sorbetto* with his spoon.

"Pretty good?" he asked the boy.

Santo nodded but said nothing. They sat quietly, listening to the sound of water trickling from the fountain as if it were music. The winged statue of Cupid, his bow pulled back and his marble eyes vacant, seemed to be aiming his arrow directly at Reid's heart. Copper and silver coins glinted in the fountain's pool like pieces of private dreams rubbing shoulders with each other.

Fortunato's Ristorante had one of the most dramatic entryways of any building Reid had ever visited. A sweep of curved marble stairs descended from the ornately detailed bronze-and-copper doors at street level to the elegant waiting area, with its marble fountain and velvet-upholstered benches on either side.

A flash of movement outside the high, street-level windows caught Reid's eye. He pointed. "Look, Santo."

To the right of the doors, a Pembroke Welsh corgi and a pair of jeans-clad legs with white athletic shoes attached were splashing through the puddles on the sidewalk. The corgi's short legs took a dozen steps for every one of his person's. It was a wild night for walking the dog.

The legs slowed, and the corgi strained at its leash as a miniature poodle and a pair of stretch pants tucked into stylish boots approached from the opposite direction. Another pair of die-hard Seattleites, undeterred by the wind and rain.

The jeans stopped. The stretch pants stopped. The poodle wagged its tail, and the tailless corgi wagged its entire hind end. They barked joyfully, touched noses, and then, as both pairs of legs moved on, reluctantly left each other behind, peering over their shoulders. "Love at first bark," Reid observed.

Santo looked at him solemnly.

A pair of nicely turned ankles in high heels appeared through the window in the wake of the late-night dog walkers, the length of their owner's stride indicating a pair of extra long legs beneath the coat that swished around them. Legs with a purpose, Reid thought as they disappeared at the end of the last window.

The front door opened, and the legs reappeared suddenly, with an entire woman attached. A very lovely woman. Reid sat up straighter.

"Who is that?" he breathed.

"My cousin, Carina," Santo said.

Reid stood up automatically, spine straight and shoulders back, clasping his hands behind him. Carina Fortunato commanded attention.

Unbuttoning her coat, she stood at the top of the stairs and surveyed the scene as if she owned the place. Which in a manner of speaking, Reid thought, she did. Or would one day.

She descended the stairs. Beneath her camel-hair coat she wore a chocolate brown suit with a fitted jacket and velvet collar and a short straight skirt. A gold heart hung on a rope chain around her neck. She moved like a cat, sinuous and surefooted.

There was a catlike quality to her face as well. Prominent cheekbones and a square jaw narrowed to a small but resolute chin. Her short, dark brown hair, shining with good health, was brushed behind one ear and left to swoop over the opposite cheek from a deep side part. Gold earrings gleamed against her olive skin. Her nose was long and straight, her lips full. Very Italian, he thought. Sophia Loren Italian.

His eyes met hers for a brief moment as she reached the bottom of the stairs and began to slip out of her coat. Her eyes were toffee colored and somnolent.

Suddenly she stopped, her head snapping away from him and her coat dropping unnoticed to the floor. "Babbo!" she gasped.

He automatically stooped to retrieve the coat, turning his

head at the same time to follow her stunned gaze. Dolly had somehow cajoled Leander up on stage. Each of them held a microphone. The introduction to Natalie and Nat King Cole's "Unforgettable" boomed through the speakers.

Dolly was really playing this one up, Reid thought, rolling his eyes at his mother's theatrics. She'd removed her cowboy hat so her red hair fell in waves around her face and down her back. The hat she held across her heart. She looked about twenty years old—no, younger. She looked like a love-struck teenager, gazing up at Leander as if she adored him, stars in her eyes and all.

He frowned as Leander started to sing, gazing down at Reid's mother with a look of adoration mirroring her own. Whoever would have thought Leander had such talent—not just the singing but the acting, too?

"Babbo!" Carina cried again. "What is he doing up there?"

CHAPTER
Three

Reid's hazel eyes and blond good looks were lost on Carina after a brief initial impression. The sight of her father on stage with microphone in hand wiped out everything else. And then when he started to sing...

Babbo didn't sing. At least, she'd never *heard* Babbo sing. Not along with the radio in the car, not in church, where he held the hymnal as far away as he could and frowned at it. She'd never even heard him sing alone in the shower when she was growing up. Where had he acquired such a voice?

And where had he gotten the daring to get up on a stage? Babbo never got up in front of people. "Terminal stage fright," he called it. Even conducting business, Leander wrote the presentations, but Lorenzo delivered them. Life had always been that way. Her father admired Carina profusely for the work she did as a trainer for the franchise stores. "All those eyes on you!" he'd say. "Everybody listening!"

"I just pretend they're in their underwear, Babbo," she'd tease him, just to see his horrified expression.

She glanced at the urban cowgirl sharing the stage with her father. Definitely not the widow Giotti. The deejay, then. The karaoke hostess.

Whose idea had karaoke been? Lorenzo, maybe—Lorenzo leaned toward the flamboyant.

Even "flamboyant" seemed a mild term for her father's singing partner, Carina thought as she took in the glittering gold stars on the woman's skirt and the eye-popping pink of her shirt and boots. Her hair was the color of ripe persimmons, no exaggeration. Big hair, country western hair, poufed out in a halo around her head.

Not the kind of woman Carina was used to seeing in the elegant, upscale atmosphere of Fortunato's Ristorante. How on earth had she gotten Babbo on that stage? He was singing his heart out like a regular Pavarotti.

The duet sounded halfway decent—no, she conceded, it was actually good. She shook her head, still not quite believing it was her father up there singing. And apparently enjoying it.

The voices stopped. The music stopped. Babbo and the redhead were still gazing into each other's eyes. No one was clapping. Carina looked around and realized everyone else was as stunned as she was.

Her father lifted the microphone once more, his eyes searching the room and stopping when they spotted her. "Ah, cara! We've been waiting for you before we make the announcement!" Leander pulled the redhead close and nestled her under his arm, where she seemed to fit perfectly.

Announcement! What was going on?

"Reid, darlin'?" the redhead called out, lifting a hand to shade her eyes as she searched the room. A diamond so gargantuan it could only be a fake winked on one finger.

Carina felt a movement at her side and glanced over to see that the blond man who'd been standing with Santo at the fountain was now at her elbow, raising his arm to acknowledge the woman on stage.

Reid, darlin'?

"Tonight you must all meet Dolly Kincaid," Leander said. *"Mia fiammetta."* His face was flushed, and he was wearing a silly grin. For that matter, so was the woman.

"Mia fia-what?" the man next to Carina muttered fiercely.

"Fiammetta. His 'fluttering flame.'" Carina wondered if she sounded as shell-shocked as she felt. "Who on earth is she?"

"What in the world is she doing with *him?*"

Leander answered both their questions as if he'd heard. "On Christmas Eve, aboard the cruise ship *Ysolda* in the Caribbean, it was my great good fortune to meet this *bella donna*—this beautiful lady," he said. "A gift from God. She has taught me to sing again, my Dolly."

His eyes again found Carina. "God and my family I have to thank for this: Mama, Lorenzo, Felicia, Carina." He blew kisses around the room.

"And now—" He paused dramatically. "And now Dolly Kincaid and I would like to invite you to our wedding!"

A moment of stunned silence, then a "Bravo!" from Lorenzo, and the room erupted.

Leander grabbed Dolly and swept her into a back-bending kiss. When they came up for air, flushed and breathless, Dolly threw her cowboy hat in the air. "Yi, yi, yi, yi, yi!" she cried and caught the hat on its way down.

Without further ado, Carina fainted.

Frankly, Reid was glad for the distraction. He felt Carina sag against him and grabbed her just in time to keep her from crumpling to the floor.

"Valentine's Day," Leander was saying. "Everyone's invited!"

Valentine's Day! Reid pulled Carina back from the edge of the crowd and laid her on one of the benches in the foyer. Getting married in six weeks, after meeting Leander eight days ago? Had his mother gone crazy?

Santo was the only other person in the crowd who'd seen Carina faint. Reid sent him for a glass of water and began to slap Carina's face gently, one cheek and then the other. Her eyes opened just as Santo returned and threw the water into her face.

She sat up abruptly, blinking and sputtering. It was all Reid could do to keep from sputtering himself, as Santo looked on with an owlish expression. Perhaps he should have explained he'd wanted the water for her to *drink*.

"What are you doing?" she gasped.

"Good, your color's coming back." Reid fished for a handkerchief in his pocket and thrust it at her.

"Sorry about the drenching," he said. "Your cousin got a little carried away. Are you all right?"

She closed her eyes, shook the water from her hair, and dabbed at her face with the handkerchief. "No, I'm not all right! I'm wet. What are you doing?" she asked again.

"Reviving you," he answered patiently. "You fainted."

She looked up at him as if she had no idea who he was or what he was talking about. "What do you mean, fainted?"

He ignored her for a moment. "Santo, find Nonna Pippa for me."

The boy nodded solemnly and disappeared into the crowd. Reid sat down next to Carina. "Keeled over. Passed out. Swooned."

"I know what *faint* means," she said irritably, sitting up. "Why would I have fainted?"

He raised his eyebrows. "I must say it seemed like an overreaction," he said. "But I got the impression you were about as thrilled with the engagement announcement as I was."

Carina stopped mopping her brow and buried her face in the handkerchief instead, groaning and mumbling unintelligibly.

"What?"

She dropped the hankie into her lap. Her hair was mussed and her mascara smudged beneath one eye. Somehow it made her more approachable. "I can't believe he'd spring that on me like this!" she wailed.

"I know what you mean," Reid muttered.

"And what could she want but Babbo's money, this—this karaoke hostess?" She grimaced, as if the words left a bad taste in her mouth. "Why does he do this to himself? What's so hard about choosing a lady?"

"Dolly Kincaid happens to *be* a lady," Reid said, his voice frigid. "She also happens to be my mother."

"Your mother!" She looked at him, aghast. "Who are you?"

"My name is Reid Kincaid. I've worked here since September." *Little you or Leander would know—or care,* he added grimly to himself.

"And you're the one who introduced my father to that—to your mother?"

He narrowed his eyes and set his mouth in a grim line. "If he were the last man on earth, I wouldn't wish your workaholic skinflint of a father on my mother."

"I beg your pardon?"

"You heard me. My mother deserves to be happy. Leander Fortunato doesn't have a clue how to treat a woman like her."

"A woman like her," Carina repeated. "A woman like her? *Look* at her! She's nothing but a dance-hall girl. How do you think she got her hooks into my father? And *why,* do you think? I will not let another gold digger ruin his life."

"Gold digger? Excuse me if I find your judgments ironic, considering your father is a hardheaded, coldhearted penny-pincher who doesn't deserve a woman with one-tenth the warmth and love my mother has to offer."

"Now, wait a minute!"

"Look, he's so cheap he makes his own mother do the grunt work around here so he doesn't have to hire someone. Seventy-five years old and sweeping the sidewalks. His own mother!"

Carina opened her mouth, but nothing came out for a moment. "You haven't the faintest idea what you're talking about," she finally said. "Nonna Pippa would wither away and die without her work to do."

Reid wouldn't listen. "And you have no idea what *you're* talking about. My mother doesn't care about money! My father gave her a generous settlement—which she'll lose by marrying your father, by the way—and she's perfectly capable of making her own living, anyway."

"Oh, she's *divorced*." Carina's voice dripped with derision. "I'll just bet she got a generous settlement."

They glared at each other.

"Carina Sabine?"

They both looked up at the sound of Nonna Pippa's anxious voice.

"Santo says you had a fainting spell."

"She's fine," Reid said, his face red with fury. He stood. "If you'll excuse me, *I'm* the one not feeling so good."

Carina let Nonna Pippa fuss over her for a minute or two, but then couldn't take any more of her flurry. "I'm all right, Nonna."

Her grandmother looked at her with her bright black eyes. "You are swooning for Signore Kincaid, si?"

"I would as much swoon for Signore Kincaid as for the man in the moon," Carina answered darkly.

Nonna Pippa's eyes widened. "A fine boy, Signore Kincaid."

"You wouldn't think so if you'd heard what he said about Babbo. *Babbo!*" she wailed, suddenly remembering. "Nonna, how could he? This cowgirl with her impossible orange hair and her yi-yi-yi. Dolly! April Dawn! How *could* he?"

"She is no April Dawn," Nonna Pippa said firmly. "A good woman, this Signora Kincaid."

Carina drew her brows together in a scowl.

Nonna Pippa held up a warning finger. "Only a good mother could have a son so fine."

"What are you talking about, Nonna? Who is this boy who makes you forget about watching out for your own son?"

"I see that my son is happy. As for Zampogna Kincaid, he is my friend."

"Zampogna?"

"The reed pipe. His name in English is Reid, si? A funny name. I call him Zampogna."

This was serious, Carina thought with alarm. Nonna Pippa had a nickname for Reid Kincaid. Somehow he'd wormed his way into her affections. Were they in on this together, the son and his mother, to con the entire family? Were Kincaid's harsh words about Babbo only meant to throw her off?

"He knows how to treat an old woman," Nonna Pippa continued, her gaze returning to Carina. "He would treat a young lady well, also."

Carina's mouth dropped, but only for a moment. She snapped it shut, narrowed her eyes, and raised her chin to the same angle as her grandmother's. "I cannot believe what you're suggesting!"

Nonna Pippa glanced again across the room and shook her head in disgust. "You two are the pair tonight, anyway, with your sour faces. On New Year's Eve! I go to dance now," she called over her shoulder as she stalked away. "I think so should you!"

Carina's eyes flew past her grandmother straight to Reid Kincaid, who was standing alone across the room with his arms crossed, glowering. They *were* a pair, she admitted to herself as she realized she, too, was standing with her arms crossed, wearing an identical frown.

She dropped her arms and tried to smooth her expression, but Dolly and Babbo suddenly moved across her line of vision, her father doing fancy footwork she hadn't even known he knew how to do. Her scowl returned. She realized that she was rapidly twisting the ring on her pinkie finger. Her father had given it to her on her sixteenth birthday—a small gold ring with a cupid's arrow piercing its ruby heart.

If she hadn't been so happy with the gift, she might have seen it even then as a warning sign of Babbo's fatal weakness for romance. To marry a woman like April Dawn! To believe now he was in love with Dolly Kincaid—after knowing her a week!

Uncle Lorenzo was doing deejay duty on the stage. How much were they paying this woman, Carina wondered peevishly, for Uncle Lorenzo to play her music for her while she danced?

Her eyes found Reid again, flickered away, then returned to spend a moment taking inventory. What was it about him that had taken in Nonna Pippa so completely?

His reddish blond hair was straight, thick, and well cut, short on the sides and longer on the top, falling over his forehead in a boyish way, though he couldn't have been much younger than she was. Tall and broad-shouldered, he was quite good-looking, or would have been if his expression hadn't been so forbidding. Was that it, then—his good looks? Nonna Pippa wasn't ordinarily taken in by a pretty face.

Calling her father a workaholic skinflint! So Babbo did work hard. It wasn't a secret. But since when was working hard a thing to be ashamed of? Furthermore, Fortunato's Ristorante wasn't work to Babbo, it was family. It was home—just as it was for Carina.

She twisted her ring in furious agitation. To hear her father called a hardheaded, coldhearted penny-pincher! Just because a man was careful with his money—that made the man a skinflint? No, it did not.

Besides, look at how generous he'd been when he was

married to April Dawn. The one time he *hadn't* been careful with his money, and look where it had gotten him.

Oh, Babbo! she thought in despair. *What are you doing with this—this karaoke queen, this Dolly?*

She raised a hand to push the hair away from her face and realized she was still clutching Reid's hankie, damp now, and smudged with her makeup. Who carried handkerchiefs these days, anyway? She traced a finger over the initials embroidered in one corner. He must have known she'd ruin it, but he hadn't hesitated.

Reid turned his head, his eyes meeting hers across the room in a direct gaze. For a moment they seemed to spark fire, glinting golden in the soft light of the chandelier. Carina wondered irrelevantly if they crinkled at the corners when he smiled.

If he smiled.

He looked away again, his grim expression unchanged. Had he been smiling when he stood at the fountain watching her come in? Carina wondered. She couldn't remember.

So what if he was or he wasn't, she thought, irritated that she would even wonder. What did it matter to her? The only thing that mattered was Babbo. She would have a big job talking sense into her father, but she had to do it. She couldn't bear to see him with a broken heart. Carina didn't like this Reid Kincaid, who insulted Babbo with his unfounded and unflattering opinions, but she could see that, under the circumstances, he might become an ally. He didn't want this wedding between her father and his mother any more than she did.

She made a beeline toward Reid as the song ended, and tapped him on the arm just as Dolly and Leander stopped breathless and beaming in front of them.

The moment was pure chaos. "Cara!" her father cried, grabbing her by the shoulders and kissing her on both cheeks.

"Reid!" Dolly cried at the same time, putting her arm

through her son's and leaning into his shoulder.

"My two favorite women—"

"The man of my dreams—"

"—must get to know her—"

"—you'll love him like I do—"

"—so glad you two are getting to know each other!"

Carina wanted to shout, *We are not getting to know each other!* She realized, however, that Babbo wouldn't even have heard. He and Dolly were in a world of their own.

She managed to murmur a greeting, but offering congratulations was outside her ability to act. Dolly didn't appear to notice her coolness any more than her father had.

"A dance with your old Babbo?" Leander asked her at the same time Reid Kincaid pulled his mother onto the dance floor.

How could she say no?

"Babbo—" she said as he grabbed her hand. "Babbo, we need to talk."

"So talk!"

"You must know what I'm going to say. Babbo, you've known this woman a week. How can you marry her? Have you forgotten April Dawn?"

"Dolly is no April Dawn," Leander said, parroting Nonna Pippa's sentiments. "Wait till you get to know her. You'll see."

"I don't have to know her. She's after your money!" She felt Leander stiffen.

"Nonsense. I will not allow you to talk this way. If you knew Dolly like I know Dolly, it wouldn't enter your head to think such a thing."

"Knew her like—Babbo, you've known her a week!"

"Maybe so—" He held up his hand when she started to interrupt. "Okay, so I met her a week ago, no 'maybe' about it. But—I cannot explain it, cara—but I also have known her all my life. She is part of me." His voice was tender in a way it rarely was these days. He gazed soulfully across the room.

She knew without looking that his eyes were following Dolly and Reid Kincaid around the dance floor.

She shook her head, refusing to accept his decision. "What was so wrong with the widow Giotti?" she asked. "A perfectly respectable woman."

Leander sighed. "Respectable isn't enough, cara. You should know. Haskell T. Robbins III is respectable enough."

Haskell was the attorney she'd said good-bye to six months ago, after a year of dating off and on. "Respectable" was a good description of Haskell, all right. He was solid. A man with prospects. But when she'd found herself happier during their "off" times than their "on," she'd known it was time to let go. Although with Haskell, there had been other issues. Between him and the widow Giotti there was no comparison.

"I just thought you'd meet a woman of means on a cruise, Babbo—"

"I know exactly what you thought," Leander said, his voice flinty. Carina knew that tone of voice. Her father was digging in. Carina used that tone, too. Stubborn as all get-out, both of them.

She ignored his interruption. "A woman of substance. Not some karaoke singer working on the boat!"

Leander frowned. "You got something now against working women?" he asked, his voice harder than Carina had heard it since she was sixteen and he'd told her she absolutely could not go out with Emilio Pazzo, a boy who wore black leather, had a pierced ear, and played drums in a rock band.

Ironic, isn't it? a little voice whispered inside her head.

"But a woman who makes her living this way!" she said, ignoring the voice.

"Helping people to have a good time—a wonderful calling, si? Cara, you don't know how I've needed to have a good time.

I did not know. Did not know how I buried my heart when your mama died, God rest her soul. Did not see how working, working, working, never taking time to sing, to dance, to play, made me less than I could be. Look at her, would you!"

He turned so Carina could see Dolly across the room, dancing with Reid. She looked young enough to be his sister instead of his mother, alight with life and laughter. As they watched, her smile faded, and she shook her head at something Reid was saying. Light rippled along the length of her persimmon-colored hair like a river of fire.

"Ah, that hair," Leander sighed. His voice had lost its hard edge and held something akin to awe.

Carina shook her head again. Hopeless. Positively hopeless. What was she going to do?

Mom, I just don't get it. What's gotten into you?"

"I love him. He loves me," Dolly said simply, as if that explained everything. She twirled under Reid's arm.

He pulled her back toward him. "Leander Fortunato doesn't know the first thing about love."

"And you're the expert on love, now, are you?" she asked, her green eyes flashing. "You seein' someone I don't know about?"

"I'm not seeing anyone," he said irritably. At least she hadn't brought up Rae Ann.

"Ahh," Dolly said. How could she put such a world of meaning into one simple syllable?

"He can't possibly make you happy."

"He does."

Reid rolled his eyes in frustration. He was getting nowhere. "You could have warned me, at least. Do you think it was fair, not telling me before you announced it to the world?"

"You'd have done just what you're doin' now," she said stubbornly. "And I don't mind tellin' you it's none of your business."

"Mom, be practical."

"You're far too practical for your own good, darlin'."

He pretended she hadn't interrupted. "You met him a week ago."

"Best week of my life," she said, her green eyes starry. "So far. Have a feelin' it's only the beginnin'."

"I've worked for Leander Fortunato for four months, Mom. I—"

"Don't know the first thing about him," Dolly interrupted. "Reid, that's enough. I'm a grown woman. I know what I'm doin'."

"He's no different than Dad."

The sudden hurt in her eyes made him immediately sorry. He knew she was remembering how his father had told her he was filing for divorce.

"You're not interesting to me anymore," he'd said, not bothering to wait until Reid had left the room. "You haven't been for years—with your prattle about babies and the PTA and volunteering at the church."

"I stayed home because you wanted me to!" she'd protested.

His look of disdain could have frozen water in a glass. "Whatever."

Interesting, thought Reid, was the fact that the young lab technician Dr. Kincaid had married was now at home, pregnant with their second child, and living Dolly's old life. *Interesting* was the way Dolly had reinvented herself in the last eight years. Reid had thought about pointing out the irony of the situation to his father but doubted it would serve any useful purpose.

"I'm sorry, Mom," he said. "I just meant—well, Leander's obviously married to his work the same way Dad is. From everything I've seen, he's self-absorbed and cheap on top of it. You deserve more than that."

Dolly shook her head. "You don't know him, Reid."

He bit his lip, knowing it wouldn't do any good to say she didn't know him either.

"I want you to be happy for me."

"And I want *you* to be happy, Mom. I just wish—"

133

He stopped at the warning look in her eyes. *I wish you'd think about it,* he finished in his head.

"I'd better get back to work," she said, letting her arm slide off his shoulder as the music ended. "Lorenzo's eyes are looking glazed."

Carina tapped Reid's arm a few minutes later as he stared bleakly at the stage, where his mother was helping Salvatore through an old Beatles tune, joining in when he faltered, fading out as he gained confidence.

"Care to dance?" she asked.

He agreed only because he thought she might want to apologize for the things she'd said about his mother. It crossed his mind that he owed her as much for what he'd said about Leander, but he couldn't bring himself to say he was sorry. Where was the line between truth and courtesy?

"Look," she told him as they swung around the dance floor, "I've been watching you, and you're no happier about this match—this mismatch—than I am. Maybe we can help each other out."

"What did you have in mind?" he asked suspiciously.

"It's crowded here. And public. Will you meet me in my office? Five minutes." It felt more like a command than a request, but he didn't argue as she spun around and strode away, her dark hair bouncing with the energy of her retreat.

Maybe they could call a truce long enough to figure something out, he thought. Maybe they could come up with a plan.

Anything to keep his mother from making this horrible mistake.

He could see the yellow light spilling through the half-open door to Carina's office when he walked down the dim hallway behind the kitchen a few minutes later, balancing two large cups of cappuccino on their saucers. Clearing his throat to let her know he was there, he entered without knocking.

He glanced around the small office in surprise. He didn't know what he'd expected, but certainly not teddy bears. They were everywhere: peeking between the notebooks on the shelves, around the corners of the computer on the desk, even through the leaves of the silk ficus in the corner.

Jumbo, giant, large, small, mini. White, black, cinnamon, beige, brown. Bears in dresses, bears in pants, bears in glasses, bears in hats. Beautiful and plain. Elegant and ordinary. Curly, plush, plaid, flowered, and everything in between.

His mother, too, collected teddy bears. He would never have guessed Carina Fortunato and Dolly Kincaid would have had one thing in common, and he was already being proved wrong.

Carina didn't explain the stuffed animals, and he didn't ask. On a personal level, they had nothing to say to each other. This meeting in her office, while the party in the dining room raced toward midnight, was strictly business.

"Thought you might want something to drink," he told her as he set the cups on her desk.

"Leaded or unleaded?"

"Decaf. I can live without a caffeine rush at this point."

She nodded as she picked up one of the cups. "Thanks. I have a feeling I'm not going to get much sleep tonight as it is."

She lifted the cup to her lips and took a sip, then set it back in its saucer and met his gaze. "All right. Let's get down to business. We agree we've got to break up this ridiculous match between your mother and my father, right?"

He bristled. "Ridiculous because you think my mother's a gold digger?"

"Look, Kincaid, it's nothing personal, okay? I'm sorry if I offended you. I'm just trying to watch out for my father, all right? He met your mother a week ago. A week ago! He's not so smart sometimes about love. Who else has he got but me to watch out for him?"

"Who else has he got? Who else has *he* got?" Reid, still standing, crossed his arms over his chest. "And who do you think my mother has but me? You don't have to tell me they've known each other only a week. Why do you think I'm here, talking to you, instead of having a good time at the party?"

"So we do agree."

"We agree they have no business getting married. That's what we agree on. Period."

Carina's brown eyes flashed. "Period. What else could we possibly agree on?"

She really was irritating, Reid thought. "What I'd like to know is how your father just happened to end up on the same cruise my mother was working on," he said, ignoring her question. "Doesn't it seem a bit more than coincidental?"

She crossed her arms and narrowed her eyes suspiciously. "Frankly, yes. Very convenient—the karaoke hostess meeting the wealthy businessman from her hometown in the romantic Caribbean. Finding out her son works for him."

Reid bristled again. "You make it sound like I had something to do with your father taking that cruise!"

"You're telling me you didn't set this whole thing up, you and your mother?"

He snorted. "I thought I'd made my feelings abundantly clear about this—this mismatch, as you call it. As I recall, it was your family Leander thanked for sending him on the cruise—and I believe he named you specifically."

"I didn't think he'd fall in love with the—" She stopped at Reid's glare. "Okay. I heard the widow Giotti was signed up for the cruise," she said. "A good match for my father, the widow Giotti, but he refuses to take the initiative. I thought the change of scenery, the moonlight in the tropics…maybe he'd see her in a different light. I thought they might see each other on board, spend a little time together. Have a little romance."

Reid groaned. "The widow Giotti! I wait on her two, three times a week. I heard her talking to friends one night a few months ago. She wanted to take a cruise for Christmas, get away from the cold and the rain and the kids. Of course I told her about Mom and the *Ysolda*. I was making conversation!"

Carina looked aghast. "It's all my fault," she said. "Now I *know* I've got to do something. I can't let her—" She looked up at Reid and stopped, as if thinking better of whatever it was she'd intended to say.

At least she was making an effort to be civil, he thought.

"I did this; I can undo it," she said, her chin firm and her mouth set.

Reid pulled up a chair and sat down across from her. "Listen," he said, "I made some…" He stopped, searching for the right words. "Some strong statements about your father. Can we just agree that Dolly and Leander aren't right for each other and leave it at that? Without either of us bad-mouthing anyone?"

"Yes!" She sounded relieved. "We were both a bit—" She stopped.

"Defensive?" Reid supplied.

"I was going to say childish."

Reid lifted a hand to the back of his neck and massaged the muscles before responding. "Yeah. You're probably right."

Their eyes met and held for a moment before Carina looked away. "You're Dolly's only son?" she asked, picking up her coffee cup once again.

"Yes." *Her only child,* he might have added. *Her protector.* "It hasn't been easy for Mom these last few years," he said instead.

"Nor for Babbo—Daddy." She sighed. "He tells me I'm too

much the mother and not enough the daughter with him, but he doesn't see how much he needs me."

Reid looked at her thoughtfully as she sipped her cappuccino. Maybe she wasn't so hard and brittle as he'd thought. Maybe she loved her father as much as he loved his mother, was driven by the same kind of protective urge. Maybe they could help each other after all.

"We don't have much time," he said, dropping his hand and leaning back in the chair. "The wedding's supposed to be in six weeks. You have a plan?"

Carina grimaced. "I've tried to reason with Babbo, but he won't be reasoned with. I figure we'll have to go underground."

Reid nodded. "Mom wouldn't listen to reason, either. What do you think?" He shifted uncomfortably. "Sow the seeds of doubt?"

Carina looked every bit as uncomfortable, Reid thought, as he watched her twist the ring on her finger. "What's left?" she said. "We can't lie, though. That would be wrong."

"Isn't it just as wrong to mislead them?"

"Wouldn't it be wrong to let them fall into a disastrous marriage? Here's the way I see it: Our parents have fallen in love, or think they have. They're not in a rational state of mind. In a word, they're handicapped."

"Incapacitated," Reid agreed.

"Exactly. They can't be held responsible."

"So we've got to make their decisions for them."

"Exactly," Carina repeated. She clunked her cup back down on its saucer.

The jangle of china scraping china made Reid's nerves jump. Or was it the voice of his conscience that scraped across his nerves like fingernails on a chalkboard?

"Our motives are pure," she argued, as if she could hear his doubts. "We love our parents. We want the best for them."

Reid nodded, pushing his uncertainty into a dark corner of his mind. "If we don't watch out for them, who's going to?"

CHAPTER
Five

Reid Kincaid had a short fuse like her own, Carina thought, but he hadn't been so hard to deal with when they focused on their common ground. And as long as she made a point not to insult his mother.

She had given him a few minutes' head start before she locked the door to her office and made her way through the kitchen and back to the party. It was just a precaution. There was no sense in raising anyone's interest, disappearing and reappearing together. People saw things; people talked.

She could almost forgive his insults to Babbo; clearly he was in a protective mode where his mother was concerned. Much the way she was with her father. He was only trying to save Dolly from making the same mistake she wanted to keep Babbo from making. From the sound of it, he loved Dolly as fiercely as she loved Babbo.

Of course his love would make him nearsighted about Dolly's faults, if not completely blind to them. Not such a bad thing in a son, she thought. She'd just have to keep her own eyes open.

Maybe Nonna Pippa was right about "Zampogna." Maybe he was a "fine boy." He probably would know how to treat a young lady, as her grandmother had suggested. Perhaps under different circumstances…

She glanced around the dining room as she pushed through the kitchen doors. While she and Reid had been cloistered in her office, someone had handed out party hats and whistles. "Ten, nine, eight, seven…"

The countdown to the New Year! Dolly and Babbo were both on stage with microphones in hand. "Six, five, four, three…"

She spotted Reid with Nonna Pippa near the buffet table.

"Two, one. Happy New Year!"

The noise in the dining room nearly drowned out the popping of fireworks outside as the entire city welcomed in the new year. Nonna Pippa reached up to kiss Reid on the cheek. He gave her a hug, grinning widely, then caught sight of Carina, watching him from across the room. His smile faded, but he raised his hand in a smart salute. *We'll get through this,* his eyes seemed to say.

She nodded and looked away. Dolly and Babbo were entangled in another back-bending kiss on stage. When they straightened, Dolly hit a button on the CD player and lifted the microphone. She began to sing "Auld Lang Syne."

Leander joined in, linking his arm through Dolly's and beckoning Santo and the twins up on stage to join them. By the end of the verse, everyone in the room stood in a circle with arms linked, swaying back and forth and singing lustily, or at least stumbling through the words they knew. Carina stood between her cousin Marcella and Zia Felicia, who was flushed and smiling. For the first time this evening, she felt hope that everything would work out as it was meant to.

Babbo would come to his senses once he got back to work. The widow Giotti would seem more sensible and sane to him than this flamboyant cowgirl who had turned his head for the moment with her exuberance and her persimmon-colored hair.

She'd thought it best not to discuss with Reid the details of her plans to sabotage their parents' romance, seeing as she'd decided to prove to Babbo that Dolly was interested only in his money. Reid couldn't be objective; he'd be insulted at the idea. Why push his buttons?

He hadn't shared the specifics of his plans, either, and she hadn't asked. They'd simply agreed to keep an eye on their respective parents, to help each other sow the seeds of doubt, and to keep each other posted on their progress. Carina even gave him the number for her cellular phone, a closely guarded secret, so he could reach her on the boat.

The party began to break up not long after midnight. Dolly went to work tearing down her audio equipment, and Carina offered to help.

Dolly had caught her long hair in a band at the top of her head to keep it out of her way while she worked. Even after several hours on stage, she looked fresh and energetic, her lightly freckled skin flushed like a girl's and her sea green eyes clear and bright. Still, if she was Reid's mother, she couldn't be all that young. Certainly not as young as April Dawn.

She banished the thought as soon as it appeared. If she kept comparing Dolly and that woman, she wouldn't be able to keep a civil tongue.

"How long have you had your business?" she asked as she helped Dolly lift a large speaker from its stand. It seemed as good a question as any to start a conversation.

"Four years now," Dolly answered. "Part-time, of course. I've never been able to make a livin' at it."

Carina was startled to hear her admit she didn't make enough money to support herself. If she was after Babbo's fortune, she wasn't bothering to be subtle about it.

"Thanks, Carina. It helps to have another pair of hands," she said as they set a second speaker on its side. Her expression was sunny. "Especially hands as capable as I hear yours are. I'm lookin' forward to gettin' to know you. Your father's told me a lot, of course."

"Has he?" Carina tried to keep her tone neutral. "I wish I could say the same. Your engagement is such a surprise."

Dolly wasn't fooled. "You're hurt." She sighed. "My son is, too. I hope you'll both forgive us." She tossed a cord into a large plastic tub and began to coil another. "We wanted to tell you privately, but things have been so hectic since we got home. And we couldn't pass up the opportunity to announce it at the party."

Of course not, Carina thought darkly. Going public as soon as possible made it harder for a man to change his mind. After the engagement was official, pride entered into the picture. She'd have to stay on her toes to keep up with this one.

"What do you think of the restaurant?" she asked.

"The nicest I've seen. I could get used to this elegance easy!"

Carina quickly bent over a storage box, where she was packing songbooks, to hide her furious expression. *I'll just bet you could,* she wanted to say.

Biting her tongue, she said instead, "It is nice, isn't it? I hope we can afford to renew the lease when it expires next month." She sighed heavily. "It takes so much money to run a restaurant."

"Is Leander having money problems?"

Carina tried to interpret Dolly's tone. Curious? Cautious? Alarmed? "Oh, Dolly, I shouldn't have said anything. My father will be so angry with me! You won't tell him, will you?"

Dolly was silent for a moment. "No, of course not. But I wish he'd told me...."

Good, Carina thought. She had Dolly worried. Now all she had to do was let nature take its course. Dolly could use whatever excuse she wanted to break the engagement with Babbo, but Carina would know the truth. And tell him.

You'd hurt Babbo that way? a voice inside her asked.

Better now than after they're married, another part of her answered. Still, heaviness weighed on her heart just thinking about it.

He was clearly smitten with Dolly Kincaid. This wasn't going to be easy.

Reid tried to think of a way to approach Leander indirectly and finally decided he didn't have it in him. He was going to have to face him man to man.

Taking a calming breath and letting it out slowly, he walked across the room to the buffet table where his boss—the boss who'd never even spoken to him before tonight—was cleaning up.

"Need some help?"

Leander looked up, his expression surprised and pleased. "Zampogna!" He studied Reid for a moment. "You wish to work, or is it the excuse to talk?"

Reid was glad he'd decided not to resort to subterfuge. Leander was too astute. "Both," he said.

"All this to the kitchen," Leander said with a sweep of his arm. He began to gather up spatulas and serving spoons from empty dishes. "What is it you wish to say?"

Reid followed him around the table, stacking bowls and platters. "I wonder, Signore Fortunato—"

"Please—call me Leander. I do not expect you to think of me as your father, but I would like to think we might be friends."

Reid shifted uncomfortably. "Speaking of my father—I wonder how much my mother's told you about him."

Leander picked up an empty serving tray and placed it on a stack at the end of the table. "Why?"

"Because he hurt her. And I worry that you're like him."

Leander whipped his head around and stared at Reid, his dark eyes spitting fire. "What are you saying? I would never do to Dolly what your father did! Abandon her for another woman. You think so, you don't know the least little bit about Leander Fortunato!"

Reid felt his jaw clench involuntarily. "My father is a doctor," he said. "Years before he left my mother for another woman, he left her for his work. His work is his life, Signore. The way Fortunato's Ristorante is yours." He met Leander's fierce gaze directly. "My mother deserves more."

The older man's mouth had hardened into a ferocious frown beneath his bristly mustache. Reid stood his ground, his chin set, daring the other man to look away.

For a full minute they stared at each other in silence, neither flinching. "I will think about what you say," Leander finally said. Then his face broke into a sudden grin. "You are a good son for Dolly Kincaid," he added approvingly. "She has told me, and now I see." He lifted the stack of trays. "The tables and chairs are in the banquet room. Put back together the main dining room while I finish cleaning. You have had your say. I will think about it."

It was noon before Carina dragged herself out of bed on New Year's Day. It had been nearly two when she made it back home, still brooding about the night's events. Then she'd lain awake forever as the boat rocked and rolled in the storm. Even with her head under a pillow, she couldn't shut out the sounds of rain beating against the deck and the wind howling through the harbor, snapping the halyards against the masts in an eerie echo. When she finally did drift off, her sleep was fitful, interrupted again and again by dreams that left her heart thumping like a jungle drum.

Sunlight was pouring in through the hatch over the stateroom as she pulled on a pair of sweats, a heavy wool sweater, and a pair of rubber thongs. Sometime during the night the storm had passed. Yawning, she picked up the nylon duffel bag she referred to as her "portable beauty shop," draped a towel over her shoulders, and climbed out of the cabin. One big breath of the rain-washed air made her feel immediately more alive.

Her neighbor's black-and-white cat, Sneakers, was sitting on the dock washing himself. She bent to scratch between his ears and felt a sudden unexpected twinge of loneliness as he dropped on his back, his green eyes squinting, and waved a front leg at her.

"Need your tummy scratched, cat? You'll have to come over to visit sometime when Lou doesn't require your company. I miss you already."

She'd liked having Sneakers on the boat the two weeks Lou had been gone. During the day the big cat curled up in his second-favorite spot, the stainless steel sink in the forward head; after dinner he curled up in his favorite spot, Carina's lap, purring raggedly like a lawnmower in tall grass. At night he insisted she let him out. She didn't even want to know what he did in the hours before dawn, when he came around scratching at the hatch.

She gave his tummy one last scratch and headed for the women's restroom at the top of the pier. The boat had a shower, but the coin-operated shower in the marina facility was roomier and didn't drain her water tanks. The light was better for applying makeup, too. Her father hadn't outfitted the boat with a woman's beauty routine in mind.

Did Dolly sail? she wondered. Did her father even know?

The thought of her father with Dolly Kincaid hurried her steps. Today was Babbo's last day of vacation. She had to keep them away from each other.

It's too late, she told herself in a panic as she scrambled for

146

change in her bag. Babbo and Dolly would certainly have made plans to spend the day together. Why hadn't she thought last night about a plan for today? Time—she needed time. Babbo needed time. Time to get perspective, time to rethink this mad rush into marriage.

She dropped a quarter into the pay phone outside the restrooms, punched his number, and waited anxiously. They were probably somewhere together even now, confusing the issue with kisses.

When her father picked up the phone on the second ring, her words tumbled over each other in a rush of relief.

"Hey, Babbo, hope you don't have plans for tonight. I thought I'd fix dinner on the boat, that Mediterranean black beans-and-rice casserole you like, and I've got a new video, the latest Whitbread—I thought we could watch it together, what do you think?"

"I think you gotta slow down before you lift off into orbit! And a happy New Year to you, cara."

"You too, Babbo. Well?" she asked impatiently.

"You talking your special recipe black beans and rice? With the raisins and the sweet red pepper? You make it hard for me. But it's back to work for Dolly and me tomorrow, so I promised already to take her out tonight."

Carina's heart sank. "Back to work for both of you?" she asked. "I thought Dolly only worked part-time. At night, I would have guessed, with karaoke."

"With the karaoke, yes. It is a second job. Dolly is a teacher," he said proudly. "Music lessons for the little ones. Every day she goes from this school to that school to another."

"Really!" Carina didn't know what else to say at the unexpected information.

"You know," Leander said, "I'm thinking this morning about

how you say the widow Giotti is a respectable woman, as if Dolly is not. But what could be more respectable than a school teacher, si?"

Carina couldn't argue with that.

"And the funniest thing I gotta tell you. I'm talking to Dolly this morning on the telephone. She says she was hearing I have problems with the restaurant and did I need some help. 'I got a little saved up,' she says to me. 'You take it if it means saving the restaurant from going under.' 'Going under!' I tell her. 'If going anywhere, Fortunato's Ristorante is going *over*—in a big way! We got no need for your savings. But thank you very much. I love you for the offer.' What a woman, my Dolly!"

Carina was stunned. Offered her savings! "Why, Babbo—" She paused, then hurried on, "Why did she think you were in trouble, Babbo?"

"She thought she heard, is all. I don't know who would say such a crazy thing, when the franchises still are selling like hot-cakes. But never mind that. Don't you see? She wanted to give me her savings, cara! So, what do you think now of your worries about she's after my money?" He sounded nothing short of triumphant.

Carina's brain felt scrambled. Offered him *money!* This wasn't looking good at all.

"Babbo," she said slowly, "why don't you bring Dolly here for dinner tonight? To the boat?" If she couldn't prevent their being together, at least she could keep an eye on them.

"You invite my Dolly along with me? Cara, you make your old *babbo* happy. You and Dolly will be friends, I know you will."

She was definitely going to need moral support. "I'll call her son and see if he wants to come," she said. "If he's not working."

"Good!" Babbo sounded almost too eager.

Reid was scheduled to work but called back after their initial conversation to tell her he'd found someone to cover his shift. "I think we should both be there," he said. "More distraction."

"Kincaid?"

"Yeah?"

"Did you ever think you'd be chaperoning your mother's dates?"

He laughed, his first laugh since Carina had met him. A nice laugh, deep and rumbling. Something inside her resonated to the sound, and she found herself smiling.

CHAPTER
Six

"K incaid!"

Reid looked across the double row of permit-only parking spots at Shilshole Marina and lifted an arm in greeting. Carina Fortunato leaned against the railing at the top of the Pier K ramp, one hand shading her eyes from the late afternoon sun.

She was full of surprises, Reid thought as he zigzagged through the parked cars toward her. He'd never have figured her for a live-aboard. Last night she'd seemed so at home in the elegant atmosphere of Fortunato's Ristorante that he'd pictured her living that way, in a villa overlooking the sound, if not somewhere on a cliff above the Mediterranean. Last night in her velvet-trimmed suit and brushed-gold jewelry, she'd looked sleek and expensive and completely unapproachable, until he'd seen her with her makeup smudged and her hair mussed.

This afternoon Carina looked more like the proverbial girl-next-door. She'd pulled a bright orange windbreaker over a yellow-striped knit shirt. Her baggy jeans were rolled up at the ankles, and her deck shoes, worn without socks, had seen their share of salt spray. As Reid stepped over the curb, a puff of air blew her dark hair away from her face. Her skin glowed golden in the lowering sun. He felt warm just looking at her.

She touched his sleeve. "Thanks for coming, Kincaid."

"Yeah. I figure we're in this together." He followed her down the ramp, standing aside as she unlocked the metal gate to the pier and pushed it open.

The *Portofino* was docked a hundred feet farther on. Reid let out a low whistle as they approached. "Wow! She's a beauty! I'd guess a Liberty?"

Carina nodded, looking pleased. "Liberty 458. You know sailboats."

"My old roommate's family had a little Coronado 15," he said. "Fun, but nothing like this. What is she—about forty-four feet?"

"Forty-six. She's the only boat Babbo could find that had enough clearance in the cabin for all six feet five inches of him." Carina climbed the stairs and jumped across to the deck with catlike grace.

"What's it like, living aboard?" he asked.

Carina slid back the hatch and opened the doors to the cabin. "Sometimes it's cozy, and sometimes it feels like I'm trapped in a sardine can. To tell the truth, I'll be happy when the remodeling's done on my house and I can move back home."

"You have a house?" he asked, surprised. It wasn't unheard of, he supposed, for a working woman of twenty-seven, but after seven years of struggling to pay for school on his own, he could barely imagine what it would be like to own a house.

Carina looked up as she descended the stairs. "Right now, 'fixer-upper' is more accurate. When I bought her, I was naive enough to think all she needed was a little elbow grease and paint. Big mistake!" Sighing, she added, "I knew she'd have to be reroofed at some point, but I didn't know how soon. Or that all the wiring and plumbing would have to be updated. But hey, at least she's mine."

He followed her down the stairs into the cabin. "You seem awfully sure she's a girl."

"Of course! Houses and boats are always girls," she said

confidently as she took his jacket and hung it next to the stairs.

"Once upon a time, hurricanes were always female, too," he said with a grin.

The *Portofino* was beautiful inside. The louvered cabinets, built-in drawers, and closets were all polished teak, and the sole—the cabin floor—was inlaid with strips of lighter-colored holly. The two forward staterooms seemed dark and cramped, but the captain's stateroom in the stern, with an overhead hatch and row of rectangular portholes along the back of the bunk, was light and airy, cozy without feeling crowded.

Reid liked the efficiency of the main cabin as well as the aesthetics. Supplies were tucked into every available nook and cranny, including beneath and behind the cushions on the benches and underneath the stairs. The galley was barely big enough to turn around in but housed an under-the-counter refrigerator and freezer, a gas oven and stovetop, a microwave, and a double sink, as well as cabinets for food and dishes.

"She's a beautiful boat, Carina," Reid said, sliding behind the dining table. He watched as she lifted the glass from the lantern hanging over the dining table and lit the kerosene-soaked wick with a match. A warm glow filled the cabin.

"She is, isn't she?" Carina set a platter of cheese and crackers and a bowl of salmon dip on the table. "I wish Babbo would take more time—" She stopped.

Afraid of confirming his claim that Leander was a workaholic? Reid wondered. So Signore Fortunato didn't spend much time on his boat. How much time would he spend on Dolly Kincaid?

"Help yourself," Carina said, withdrawing to the galley to busy herself with dinner.

They kept their conversation neutral, Carina apparently as reluctant to bring up their parents' impending marriage as he was. What more could be said than had already been said?

They both knew what had to be done.

Reid told Carina about his classes in music education at the university and his hopes to head a high school choral program someday. He'd been directing the choir and the congregational singing at his small church since he'd been a senior in high school, and he'd never wanted to do anything else.

Carina confessed her love for art and literature in college and the struggle she'd gone through before deciding to take the franchise training job with Fortunato's. "I spent my senior year of college studying art history in Florence. I loved it, but I missed Babbo and the restaurant like crazy. It's home to me. It always has been."

She was smart and intense and interesting. She was beautiful.

Reid couldn't keep his eyes off her. He tried. He told himself he was being foolish. She was attractive, yes, but not more so than a lot of other women he'd known. He hadn't had a serious relationship with anyone since Rae Ann, but he'd dated several women, some of them very attractive.

And he'd never found any of them, not even Rae Ann, as compelling as he found Carina. Besides, when Rae Ann left him, she'd been just a girl. Carina was a woman. Smart, successful, confident. There was no comparison.

She looked up and caught him staring. Her toffee-colored eyes were startled. A faint flush appeared along her cheeks as their eyes remained locked for an intensely intimate moment. When she finally broke the gaze, Reid realized he'd been holding his breath.

Neither of them spoke for a moment. Then, as if the moment of connection hadn't happened, she asked him, her voice trembling only slightly, "Want to help with dinner?"

I can do this, he told himself. *I can pretend as well as she can that that look meant nothing.* Besides, he wasn't willing to contemplate what it *might* have meant.

Struggling to change mental gears, he eyed the narrow aisle where she stood and asked, "You think we'll both fit in the galley?"

She laughed, a low, musical sound that made him want to reach across the space between them and take her hand. *Get a grip, man!* he told himself, crossing his arms over his chest. *You are here for one reason, and one reason only.*

"You could toss this Caesar salad right there where you sit," she said, holding up a plastic bag and a large stainless steel bowl. "I want it done before Babbo gets here. He'd be appalled to know I make my salads from a kit."

"From a kit? *I'm* appalled," he teased. "Apparently you didn't inherit your Uncle Lorenzo's cooking skills."

"Who had to? I grew up in the restaurant. The food was always there. Babbo's impressed I can make this one meal we're having tonight. I've never told him it comes out of a box."

"Speaking of Leander…" Reid frowned and looked at his watch. "What time are he and Mom supposed to get here?"

Carina glanced at the chronometer on the wall across the room. "Ten minutes." She leaned over the sink and set the bowl and the bag of salad greens on the table. "Get crackin', Kincaid!"

Reid was sprinkling the Parmesan cheese over the dressed romaine when they heard footsteps on the deck. He could feel the sudden tension in the atmosphere and his own stress level rising. He looked across the sink at Carina. She was twisting her ring and biting her lower lip.

Well, he thought, *it was fun while it lasted.*

Carina tried not to show her surprise as Dolly Kincaid made her way down the steps into the cabin. She looked like a different person from the flashy urban cowgirl of last night's party, though she still exuded the same kind of energy. Her hello was as breathless and eager as an excited puppy barking joyfully at its first cat, not yet knowing what a cat could do.

"Thanks for your invitation to supper, Carina," she said. "I do so want to get to know you."

It was all Carina could do to keep from rolling her eyes. The woman may have lost her cowgirl outfit, but she still had her affected Texas drawl.

Dolly's eyes darted around the boat as Leander helped her out of her navy pea jacket. *Assessing its value?* Carina wondered, her jaw tightening. No way was Dolly getting her hands on the *Portofino*.

"Oh, my—this is lovely!" Dolly exclaimed, turning in a full circle as she took everything in. Dressed in jeans and a bulky, apple green sweater, her orange hair pulled back in a loose chignon at the nape of her neck and her makeup subtly applied, Dolly didn't look anything like the scheming gold digger from the night before. In fact, she looked like a very nice woman.

All the more dangerous, Carina thought grimly. She'd have to keep her wits about her; Dolly was clever.

"Sit down," she said, her tone more abrupt than she'd intended. No one seemed to notice. Except for Reid, perhaps; he met her eyes briefly before deliberately turning his attention to her father.

She found his eyes intriguing; last night in his off-white turtleneck and neutral houndstooth blazer she'd thought them hazel, that color used to describe any pair of eyes not blue or brown or green. She'd changed her mind. Already tonight she'd seen them thistle gray and olive green, and once, in that moment when she'd looked up to find him watching her, a brown so deep they seemed almost bottomless. Chameleon eyes.

Stop it! she told herself. *Concentrate on Dolly and Babbo.*

"You're quiet tonight, cara," her father said as she finished serving the plates and sat down to dinner with her guests. "What are you thinking?"

She looked at her father, and then at Dolly, and then at Reid. *I'm thinking how confusing life gets sometimes,* she thought. *I'm thinking how little control we have over our own hearts, let alone anyone else's.* Aloud she said only, "I'm thinking maybe you would like to ask the blessing on our meal, Babbo." She reached one hand out to him and the other to Dolly and closed her eyes.

"Thank you, God, for the love Carina shows by sharing this meal she made with her own hands," Leander said. He squeezed her fingers. "Let this love she shows be returned a hundredfold. Amen."

"Amen," Dolly repeated softly and squeezed her hand on the other side.

Carina quickly retrieved both her hands and made a show of unfolding her napkin and placing it on her lap. The blessing made her squirm inside. God knew her motives had nothing to do with love.

They do! she argued with herself. *Whatever I'm doing, it's for love of Babbo.* But her heart felt heavy.

The casserole and salad and crusty Italian bread got rave reviews around the table, but Carina hardly tasted the food. She tried to join in the conversation here and there—pleasant, polite, getting-to-know-you talk, nothing too serious, nothing that might cause conflict.

"Seconds, Babbo?" she asked as Leander cleaned his plate of rice and beans. At his nod, she got up and lifted the lid of the pan on the stove.

He cleared his throat. "So you kids gonna congratulate us on our engagement, or what?"

She stopped with the serving spoon in midair and looked at Reid. He choked and coughed, his face going red, and reached for his glass of ice water. For a long moment no one said anything.

Dolly finally broke the silence with a nervous laugh. "Well! Talk about your awkward moment."

Carina placed the spoon back in the pan, and Reid set down his glass. Then they both spoke at once.

"Leander's right—"

"I'm sorry, Dolly—"

"—haven't said—"

"—so rude of me—"

"Congratulations," they finished in unison. But even with their voices joined together, it sounded weak.

Leander, scowling fiercely, opened his mouth as if to speak, but Dolly held up her hand. "No, Leander, we need to talk about it. They have a right to their reactions."

"And so do we!"

Dolly took Leander's hand across the table, gripping his fingers hard enough to make her knuckles turn white. "Reid. Carina." She looked from one to the other. "We know how sudden this seems to you. Our engagement. It *is* sudden. For us, too."

Her thumb began to make small circles on Leander's hand. To calm him or to calm herself? Carina wondered.

Dolly looked at her son. "Haven't you ever had the sense that when somethin' happened in your life, whatever it might've been—well, that it was meant to be?" She shifted her gaze to Carina. "The feelin' that this somethin' had been in the works for eons, but the universe was waitin' for just the right time to let you in on it?"

Reid and Carina exchanged glances. "I'm not sure what you mean," Carina said carefully.

Dolly looked at Leander and smiled. The lines between his brows and on either side of his mouth eased.

She turned again to Reid. "Darlin', after your father left, I really didn't think I'd ever fall in love again. It wasn't just the hurt of his betrayin' me. After I'd worked the hurt through, I realized I'd *lost* myself lovin' your father. A good part of myself, anyway. Tryin' to figure out what it was he wanted, tryin' to please him.

"After he left, I started figurin' out what it was I wanted. What was it that pleased me? I thought about how much I loved music, and how much I loved kids." Her eyes returned to Carina. "The divorce was a hard thing, the hardest thing in my life, but it did somethin' good for me. I didn't see it right away, but now when I look back—well, it was almost like comin' out of retirement. I started the karaoke business, and I made up my mind to finish the teachin' degree I'd started way back before Reid was born."

She smiled again at Leander. "I told God that if he wanted me to have another partner, he'd have to bring him to me because I sure as anything wasn't goin' to go lookin'."

Leander squeezed her hand. "And I was finally saying to God a similar thing."

"I was clear about what I wanted," Dolly added. "'He'll have to be strong enough for a strong woman,' I told God, 'because now that I know who I am, I can't ever go back to bein' less.'"

"For me, it was a longer journey," Leander said. "There was for years a ristorante to keep me busy, and then another and another and another. I did not miss a woman in my life." He looked at Carina. "Except for your mama, God rest her soul. Your mama I missed like a part of my soul in the early years. She spoiled me a good long time for any other woman."

He looked a little sad for a moment, Carina thought. Was it

because his memories of her mother were strong, or because they had faded after so many years?

Still, his voice was cheerful as he went on. "And, too, I had from you and your nonna enough female refinement to make me happy and keep my thinking straight." His eyes twinkled. "Carina to surprise and delight me, her nonna to nag me," he explained to Reid. "And Lorenzo and Felicia to keep having children for me to be uncle and godfather to. A good life I was having."

He sighed dramatically. "Then Carina was off to Florence. A year she was away! Such a year it was for her, and so proud her babbo was! But lonely, too. I saw that she would be having her own life once she came home—and so she should. I saw that I should be having my own life, too." The sadness had crept back into his voice.

Carina wanted to say something, tell him she'd never meant for him to feel abandoned, that she could never have stayed away from Fortunato's for too long. But she couldn't speak around the lump in her throat. Her father was right. He had known when it was time to let go.

At least for her sake.

For his own, she thought, it should have been sooner. Maybe then a woman like April Dawn wouldn't have gotten her hooks into him.

"In business," Leander said to Reid, "a better partner than my brother Lorenzo I could never find. In business, I am a smart man." He tapped his head with two fingers. "In love..." He sighed heavily and held a hand over his heart. "In love I think I am not so smart. With April Dawn I learned—"

"Who?" Reid interrupted.

"My former wife. In name alone," he added hastily. "She did not want to be the wife I wanted. But with her I learned a lesson:

when I am lonely, my heart does a lousy job to find a partner right for me. So I tell God, 'God, next time around I let you choose.'"

He stopped.

Carina felt light-headed. "You're saying God brought you together."

Leander nodded. "For me to meet my Dolly on this cruise I did not even want to take—it was like a miracle."

"And I felt from our first meetin' that Leander was a gift to me from God," Dolly said. "No question."

"But how do you *know?*"

They looked at each other, smiling, and said in unison, "We just do!"

"God spoke the word in both our hearts," Dolly added.

"Now," Leander said, "I have a word of my own, but for Zampogna's ears only." He wiped his mouth with his napkin and folded it neatly. "You will walk with me down the dock?"

"Please do, darlin'," Dolly urged. "I'll help Carina clean up here. When you get back—well, I've been lookin' forward to that Whitbread video."

Carina, who was feeling a bit as if the tide had rushed in and swept the sand from beneath her feet, jumped on the topic as if it were a life raft. "You know about the Whitbread?" Among serious sailors, the grueling 'round-the-world race was a common reference point; if Dolly knew about it, she'd had at least some exposure to sailing.

"Reid and I took sailin' lessons from an Aussie who crewed in the '92 race. He had tales to curl your hair."

"I thought his stories would scare Mom off of sailing." Reid laughed. "Did I have her pegged wrong! All those years, I had no idea how much she loved adventure."

"The real me was under wraps," Dolly said. "No more."

Leander shook his head. "No more," he agreed. Admiration shone from his eyes. "What a woman, my Dolly!"

CHAPTER
Seven

Reid and Leander's stroll along the pier was quiet. Leander made a comment here and there on a boat or two that caught his eye. Reid responded to his observations but didn't initiate conversation. He was too busy wondering what it was Signore Fortunato wanted to say to him away from the two women.

He found out, finally, when Leander stopped at the end of the pier and looked out over the dark sound, his hands hooked behind him.

"I have been thinking about your concern," he said. "That I am the same as your father. Leaving the wife behind for the work."

Reid remained silent.

"You are right when you say Fortunato's Ristorante is my life," Leander continued. "But also you are wrong. *Mia famiglia* is my life. The ristorante is not the building, not the accounting books, not even the fine food my brother makes. The ristorante is my brother himself. Lorenzo. And his wife, and their sons and daughters—my nephews and nieces—and Mama and Carina. They are why Fortunato's Ristorante is my life."

Reid tugged at his earlobe. He hadn't thought of that. "But it's still work, Signore Fortunato," he argued. "Long hours of work away from Mom."

"And Dolly will be long hours away from me in the schools," Leander said. "But now that I see how well things run at Fortunato's without me, I will take the holidays she takes. Sometimes I will go with her on the cruises, and sometimes she will take off the time from singing to sail with me on the *Portofino*."

"You've decided this since last night?"

"We talked this morning about it, your mother and I. This is the key, Zampogna, when you find a woman to love: to talk about what you are thinking, to listen well, and to make the compromise. All the time, to keep doing it." He turned his eyes to Reid. "I want to tell you I have made the pledge to your mother, that she will always come first for me. And now I make it to you." He held up one hand. "So help me God," he said solemnly.

Reid was silent for a moment. "You'll need *somebody's* help if you hurt her," he said fiercely.

Leander's smile showed white in the dark. "You protect your mama like I protect mine," he said approvingly. "Mamas need their sons, but sometimes you gotta let them do what they decide." He laughed. "Like my mama working in the ristorante. 'I let you know when I want to retire,' she tells me when Felicia talks about it not looking good, an old woman working the way she does."

"Nonna Pippa *wants* to work?" Reid asked. Carina had implied as much before, but he hadn't wanted to believe it.

"Fortunato's is *her* life, too, Zampogna. What would she do with her days if not for the work?"

What would she do with her days without the work? Reid had never thought to ask.

By the end of the meal, Carina knew for certain the misgivings and twinges of conscience she'd been experiencing over her behavior—and pushing to the back of her mind—were more than social programming. As surely as God had made it clear to Dolly and Leander that he'd brought them together, he was making it clear to Carina that she'd saddened him.

In fact, she knew without question that God had been trying to get through to her ever since she'd decided to do him the favor of taking charge of Babbo's life. As if she knew best. As if God couldn't work his will without her interference.

Judge not, that you be not judged, he'd been whispering. And something about considering the plank in her own eye before she worried about the speck in someone else's. Something about love, too: *Love worketh no ill to his neighbor,* he'd been reminding her.

No ill to her father. No ill to a friend, as Dolly was surely going to be.

Forgive me my presumption, God, she prayed. *Forgive me my unfounded criticism and my lack of love. And thank you for a chance at happiness for Babbo....*

"Penny for your thoughts," Dolly said gently, her eyes searching Carina's face.

"I'm very glad you came for dinner, Dolly Kincaid." She took a deep breath. "And I'm very glad you and my father have found each other."

With her son and fiancé gone, Dolly might easily have called Carina on the carpet for misleading her about Leander's finances. She'd have had every right to question Carina about her motives. But all she said was, "Thank you. I'm very glad you're willin' to share him with me." Generous, gracious, a lady through and through. It was easy to see why Babbo had fallen in love.

As they cleaned up together, Dolly regaled Carina with colorful tales about teaching, growing up in Texas, and what a good son Reid was when he wasn't trying to control her life.

"I know he doesn't mean to drive me crazy," she confided. "It's just that the divorce brought out all his protective instincts. Maybe he'll lighten up now that I've met your father."

Carina had to duck her head to hide her expression. If Dolly only knew.

When Reid and Leander returned to the boat, they were talking amiably—if not enthusiastic, at least respectful of each other. She wished now she hadn't asked Babbo and Dolly to stay for the sailing video; she and Reid needed to talk. "Things aren't the way we thought," she'd tell him. "I think we need to back off. I think we need to let them make their own decisions."

What if he wouldn't back down? What if he'd already said something to Babbo on their walk to give him second thoughts about the engagement? What if he hadn't bought the story that their parents' relationship was from God?

Have you? she asked herself.

I have, she answered back. The couple's candor had disarmed her. God himself had disarmed her.

Watching the sailboat race on video, Dolly and Leander happily sandwiched between their children behind the table, actually turned out to be fun.

"Whew! Sailing the Inside Passage this summer will seem like nothing after that," Leander said when the video was over.

Carina looked at her father curiously. "You've got sailing plans?" The Inside Passage, known for its breathtaking beauty, was the narrow waterway between the coast of British Columbia and the long string of islands that stretched from Vancouver Island all the way to Alaska.

"Our honeymoon has to wait till I'm out of school," Dolly explained. "Leander's promised to take me all the way up to Desolation Sound on the *Portofino* come July."

"Babbo!" Carina was surprised and pleased. "You've talked about making that trip since you bought the boat! I'm glad to hear you're finally going to do something about it."

"Dolly makes me remember how important it is to play,"

Leander said, pulling her toward him. They gave each other foolish, adoring smiles. Carina looked at Reid, who was sitting back with his arms crossed, watching his mother and her father with a thoughtful expression.

"Your house better be done by then, cara," Leander added. "If not, we gotta boot you off the boat."

"If my house isn't done by then, I'm moving back in with you."

Her father pretended dismay. "I'll be calling that contractor tomorrow morning, first thing," he declared. "And speaking of tomorrow morning, we gotta be getting home soon."

Carina found herself reluctant to see the evening end. Filled with laughter and lively conversation, the sloop felt more like home than it had since she'd moved on board. Forget a cat when she moved back to the house—she needed a roommate. She glanced at Reid, who was slipping into his brown suede jacket. Or...

Carina Sabine! she chastised herself. *What are you thinking?*

The four of them walked together from the boat to the parking lot. Reid lingered behind as Dolly and Leander drove off, waving.

"Your mother is a nice woman," Carina said.

"Your father—he surprises me," Reid said.

Carina scuffed the asphalt with the toe of her shoe. "I know we made a bargain, Reid Kincaid. But sometimes when the circumstances change—"

"Or your understanding of the circumstances," Reid interrupted.

"Or your understanding of the circumstances," she agreed. She looked up, startled. Their eyes met in a look as intense and intimate as the one they'd shared earlier in the evening.

"Are you thinking what I'm thinking?" she finally asked.

"I'm thinking your father is good for my mother."

"And vice versa."

"I'm thinking we were wrong to try to break them up."

She breathed a sigh of relief. "I wasn't feeling so good about it," she said. "That still, small voice kept nagging."

"I know what you mean."

Her breath caught in her throat. "You do?"

"I heard it, too. And tried to ignore it. Mom and Leander took care of that."

She nodded.

"Carina." His eyes under the streetlight were a dark, fathomless brown. She imagined she could see into his soul. Her heartbeat quickened at what she thought she saw there.

Reid reached across the space between them and stroked her cheek, gently, as if her skin were something delicate and fragile, as if she herself were precious beyond measure. "I'm thinking something else," he said quietly.

Her breath caught. His gentle caress had set her limbs to trembling. "I'm thinking the same," she whispered.

Funny the little details she remembered about that moment later on. The warmth of his hand. The fringed shadow of his eyelashes across his cheek. A ship's foghorn sounding through the night in the distance—a sound of longing. The smell of clean skin as he leaned forward and kissed her lightly on the lips, a kiss of wonder and promise.

There was a spring to her step as she strode back down the ramp and let herself in the gate. They had a date, lunch on Saturday. Two nights, a day, and a morning to get through first. No matter; anticipation would keep her company.

Reid glanced at his watch, frowning, and once again searched the faces of the weekend crowd streaming through the main courtyard of Grand Central on the Park, the renovated century-old building at the heart of Pioneer Square. He didn't take it as a good sign that Carina was late for their first official date. He himself had been ten minutes early.

"Reid!"

There she was, pushing through the crowd toward his table. He waved and stood to pull out her chair, his frown of irritation changing to one of concern. Something was wrong; he could see it on her face.

"Carina?"

She dropped her leather handbag on the table and sank into the chair. "Have you talked to your mother?" Her voice was strained.

Reid's heart jumped. "No, not since dinner the other night. Carina, what's happened?"

"The engagement is off—Babbo just told me."

"What?"

"Reid, we can't let them break up. They were meant for each other!" She looked as if she might burst into tears at any moment. "It's my fault. I planted the seeds of doubt in Babbo's mind, and now he says I was right—Dolly only wanted his money and he'd been a fool again like he was with April Dawn."

"Where on earth did he…how…like April Dawn!" Reid was dumbfounded.

Carina had told him the whole story of Babbo and April Dawn in a long phone conversation after his dinner shift last night. He empathized wholeheartedly with Leander. April Dawn had married him for his money; Rae Ann had left Reid for his lack of money. The dynamic was the same. What he and Leander had been taught by those women was that love was nothing more than self-interest.

"Babbo wanted her to sign a prenuptial agreement," Carina said, looking as if she might cry.

Reid looked at her blankly.

"To protect himself," she continued. "In the event of divorce."

"Well, that sounds reasonable. Especially after his experience with April Dawn."

"Reasonable! How can you say that?" Carina's expression was horrified. "To bring up the topic of divorce six weeks before the wedding? No wonder Dolly threw the ring in his face and stormed out."

"She did what? You mean my mother broke off the engagement just because he asked her to sign a prenuptial agreement? What's wrong with her? She knows what happened with his last wife. She should know it's only a precaution. Just a piece of paper."

"If they have to take precautions, why are they getting married?" Carina argued. She sounded less distressed and more indignant now. "Of course you'd take his side. You men all stick together."

"Now wait a minute—"

"How can there be love when there isn't trust?" she interrupted. "It isn't Dolly's fault they've broken up. Babbo's wrong. It's ridiculous, this prenuptial thing!"

"But—" Reid stopped. They weren't going to get anywhere arguing. "It doesn't matter whose fault it is," he said soothingly. "What's important is that they work this out. Compromise. Your father knows that that's the key to making love work. He told me."

"I already tried that tack. He set his chin the way he does and said, 'On some things there can be no compromise.' Stubborn old coot."

"I'll talk to Mom," Reid said. "But I think you'd better lay off Leander."

"Oh you do, do you?"

Reid cringed at her sarcasm.

"You barely know him, yet you think you know better than I do how to deal with my father?"

"On this issue...I just think I understand, is all."

She didn't answer, but her silence was thick with anger.

He sighed. "Carina, let's not fight. I'll talk to Mom tomorrow. She has to know how much Leander loves her."

"How could she know?"

"They both just need some time to cool off. You'll see. The whole thing will blow over in a day or two."

Carina stood and grabbed her bag from the table. "I don't believe it should blow over," she said, her expression stormy. "I'm not in the mood for lunch. I'll see you later."

He watched in dismay as she marched off and disappeared into the crowd. If first dates were any indication of a couple's future, he and Carina were already doomed.

And he'd been so sure....

In a foul mood, he returned to his Wallingford apartment, changed into sweats, and drove to Discovery Park, where he went for a long run through the woods. The steady rhythm of his feet pounding against the path restored his sense of calm, enough that he made it through his dinner shift later that evening without snapping anyone's head off.

His mother was missing from church the next morning, which was unusual. He found her afterward holed up at home, still in her pajamas and robe, and looking miserable.

"I'm not feelin' well," she told him through a crack in the door.

"Mom, I know about your disagreement with Leander. Let me in."

"Disagreement? Don't know where you got your information, son, but disagreement's too mild a term. Leander and I have parted ways." But she let him in, reluctantly, and left him with the Sunday paper while she dressed.

He had no more luck reasoning with her than Carina had had with her father. She wasn't angry, only very sad. "If Leander doesn't trust me enough to know I would never, ever do what that woman April Dawn did to him, then he doesn't know me at all," she said. "He doesn't love me the way I thought he did."

"Maybe he thinks if you won't do what he needs you to do to set his mind at rest, you don't love *him* enough," Reid said, tugging at his earlobe.

His mother seemed not to have heard him. "You were right about Leander from the start, darlin'," she said ruefully. "He thinks more about his money than he does about me. At least I found out before I married him."

Reid's heart sank. "I didn't know Leander then, Mom. I was wrong about him. He could make you happy."

She shook her head and got up from the sofa, but not before he saw her eyes, swimming in unshed tears. "Please, darlin'." Her voice choked. "I can't talk about this anymore."

He watched her walk across the room and into the kitchen, her shoulders slumped. What had he and Carina done?

More to the point—how were they going to fix it?

Eight

When Carina needed to release stress, she cleaned. By early evening on Saturday the *Portofino* was spotless. She'd even washed down all the interior woodwork with Murphy's Oil Soap, a job she'd been putting off for weeks.

After a quick dinner of soup and a sandwich, she spent the evening doing laundry in the marina facility near Pier K. She tried to lose herself in a good mystery while she waited through the cycles, but images of Dolly and Babbo kept appearing on the pages: singing together on New Year's Eve, holding hands at dinner, snuggling while they watched the Whitbread video. Talking about their plans. Telling their children with such joy and sincerity how they knew their meeting was a miracle, a gift from God.

She slipped into the pew next to Leander at church the following morning but heard little of the sermon. Probably as much as Babbo did. Afterward, when she invited him to lunch, he said he had things to do at the office and couldn't take the time. She knew it was just an excuse.

Reid was either out or not answering his phone; she tried to ring him several times throughout the afternoon and finally decided to intercept him at Fortunato's before his dinner shift. Between lunch and dinner, Babbo and Uncle Lorenzo provided a limited menu for the staff at reduced prices, and Reid had said he often took advantage of the perk.

She owed him an apology. And she wanted to explain. If

she could make Reid understand, then maybe there was hope for Babbo.

Reid walked in the door with only two minutes to spare before his shift began. He met her eyes directly. "I don't want to fight, Carina."

"I know. It was wrong to walk out on you the way I did. I'm sorry."

"Are you?"

She brushed an imaginary piece of lint off his sleeve. "I wasn't mad at you. I was mad at me," she said. "I feel as if it's all my fault, the trouble between Babbo and your mother. I don't know if he'd have even thought of drawing up a prenuptial agreement if I hadn't questioned Dolly's character."

"It's no more your fault than mine," Reid said. "I don't know if Dolly would be having such a fit about signing the stupid prenup if I hadn't told her I thought Leander was a cheap-skate." He clocked in on the computer in the serving aisle just as Franco breezed through the swinging doors from the dining room.

The other waiter raised one eyebrow and lifted a corner of his mouth in a cocky grin at the sight of Carina straightening Reid's bow tie. "Marcella's seating your section," he said. "You've got a four-top."

"Thanks, Franco." Reid pulled a tray off the overhead shelf and placed four water glasses on its skid-proof surface. "I've been at Mom's all afternoon, or I'd have been here sooner," he told Carina. "No luck changing her mind."

"Babbo hardly talked to me in church this morning."

"Mom didn't even go." He dug the plastic scoop into the ice bin and filled the glasses with ice cubes, then topped them off with water. "We need to talk, Carina."

"I know." She hesitated. "Want to come over to the boat

after work?" At Reid's look, she quickly added, "Just to talk."

"Just to talk? Alone on the boat with you at night, as bad as we're both feeling?" He shook his head, his expression filled with both longing and regret. "I don't think that would be a good idea."

She saw her cousin out of the corner of one eye, obviously eavesdropping, and turned her back on him. "Then how about breakfast tomorrow morning?"

Reid nodded. "I have my student-teaching orientation tomorrow, but not until ten. Meet you at Charlie's at eight?" he asked, naming the coffee shop in the Port building at the marina.

"All right."

He was out the door, the tray of glasses balanced in one hand.

Carina was already seated at a window booth, sipping coffee and staring out over the marina, when Reid arrived at Charlie's a few minutes after eight on Monday morning.

She smiled at him as he slid in across from her, a smile that warmed him from the inside out. He couldn't believe how elated he'd been last night when she apologized. When she let him know she wanted to work things out.

"Good morning," she said. "I'm glad you're here."

"Morning. You look great, Carina." He reached across the table to touch the sleeve of her ivory angora sweater, unable to resist its soft nap. The way she leaned into his hand slightly made him want to pull her into his arms.

We're here to talk, Kincaid, he reminded himself.

"I need to know why you were so angry Saturday," he said. "About me defending your father."

She avoided his eyes. "Could we order first?"

"Because if I'm not allowed to have my opinion without you

174

getting angry," he continued as if she hadn't said anything, "this isn't going to work."

Carina's eyes met his again, studied his face a moment. "You're allowed," she finally said. "But I can't guarantee I won't get angry."

"What *can* you guarantee?"

"That when I'm wrong, I'll say I'm sorry. That I'll talk to you about it." Once more she smiled, a secret Mona Lisa kind of smile. "That being hot-blooded has an upside as well as a down."

"Coffee?"

Saved by the waitress, Reid thought.

With their breakfast orders taken and the menus removed from the table, Carina launched into her tale.

"It's about Haskell T. Robbins III," she said. "A good man with many fine qualities. We dated for a year, off and on. Six months ago I broke up with him."

"And now you're sorry," Reid said, suddenly deflated. "That's why you think Mom and Leander are making a mistake." This wasn't what he'd wanted to hear.

"You're jumping to conclusions, Reid. It's true that Haskell was a good match in some ways, but in one way he was not. A very important way: he didn't trust me." She sent him a significant look. "Every time I had a business lunch with a man, every time he thought I laughed too hard at another man's joke, every time I smiled at another man, he accused me of flirting and sulked for a week."

"Were you flirting?"

"Reid! No, I was being friendly." She threw her hands up in the air. "I'm Italian. We're friendly people."

He grinned. "Just teasing. You've got a lot of your Nonna Pippa in you when it comes to sociability, you know?"

"You think so?"

"Absolutely." *When it comes to stubbornness, too,* he added silently. She and her father both. Could this be a good thing, the Fortunato stubbornness married to the Kincaid stubbornness? He hoped so. Because even if Leander and his mother never resolved their differences and tied the knot...

"Western omelet and sausage and eggs. Anything else I can get for you?"

He looked up at the waitress gratefully. Saved again! What in the world had he been thinking?

"We're fine," he said.

Carina smiled and nodded at the waitress, then turned her attention back to Reid. "So anyway—where was I?"

"Haskell T. Robbins III," he said. "Sulked for a week. Shall we pray?" Without waiting for an answer he bowed his head and offered a short blessing.

"Haskell," he prompted as he cut into his omelet.

Carina absently sliced her sausage into bite-sized pieces. "He was worst when I went out of town for franchise training, which was often," she said. "He called me three or four times a day, left messages at my hotel desk. The last straw was a San Francisco trip last June—he flew down to check up on me.

"We had it out right there. 'How can you say you love me when you can't trust me?' I asked him. 'I've tried to ease your fears every way I know how. What's the use? How can there be love when there isn't trust? I'm sorry,' I told him, 'but this is no good for me anymore.'"

"After the poor man flew all the way to San Francisco to see you?"

She made a face. "You're teasing again, right?"

"I'm teasing. So what did he say?"

"You can't guess? He asked me if I'd met another man." Carina shook her head. "In my book, trust is foundational for love. How much does Babbo trust your mother—how much does he *love* her—if he won't marry her without a prenuptial agreement?" She shook her head again. "She doesn't deserve the way he's treating her."

Reid was silent for a moment. "I see your point," he finally said. "You're right. Mom needs to know Leander trusts her. But he's been burned before, Carina. I know what it's like to believe someone loves you and then find out they were only interested in your money. Mom knows that's not true for her. Why can't she show him that?"

"Someone was interested in you for your money?" Carina asked instead of answering his question. "I didn't know you *had* money."

"I don't. Probably won't ever have a lot. But Rae Ann thought I would someday." He spread strawberry jam on a triangle of toast.

"Rae Ann?"

"My high school girlfriend." He sighed. "My dad's a doctor, you see. A plastic surgeon. A good one, very successful. Dad and I both assumed I'd follow in his footsteps—Dad because he's always gotten whatever he wanted, and me because I wanted to please him. Rae Ann liked the idea that I was going to be a doctor."

He bit into his toast and chewed slowly, aware that Carina was waiting impatiently for him to continue. "And?" she urged as he wiped his mouth with a napkin.

"Something happened when my dad left and my mom started figuring out she'd been living her life for him instead of for herself. Remember how she talked about that the other night? Well, I realized I was in the same boat she'd been in— wanting more than anything to make him proud of me. So I started thinking about what I wanted to do. What I was good at. What gifts God had given me that I could give back to him. That's when I started leading the singing at church, and then directing the choir.

"My dad had always told me he'd pay my tuition and expenses for the first four years of college, but when I told him I wanted to be a music teacher, he changed his mind. 'You go into teaching, you're on your own,' he told me."

"Oh, Reid!" Carina looked pained.

"Yeah. But it was okay, because I knew I'd made the right choice for myself. I applied for scholarships, and I got my first job waiting tables and started to save money. And I had Rae Ann—I was crazy about her. Or at least about who I *thought* she was. I had our whole life planned, our whole future. We didn't talk about it much—I just assumed.

"Then on the night of high school graduation she told me she'd been counting on being a doctor's wife. 'Teachers don't make any money,' she said. That was that."

"Oh, Reid!" Carina said again.

"I understand what's going on in your father's head, Carina. Look at what April Dawn did to him. If his thinking seems irrational to you—well, it is irrational. Totally fear based. If Mom would just understand that's what it's about…"

Carina sighed. "If only they were as sensible as their children."

He grunted. "Yeah, right. Like we haven't made a mess of everything."

Carina pushed her plate away. "We made a mess, all right. So how do we *un*make it?"

"Maybe we should just sit back and hope for the best."

She shook her head. "Unacceptable. We have a responsibility here, Reid. I know we can come up with something."

"No more half deceptions," he warned.

"No deceptions. This time it's the truth, the whole truth, and nothing but the truth. This time, we bring God in on it."

Reid knocked at the door to Leander's office later that afternoon, his sharp rap against the wood sounding more confident than he felt.

"Who is it?" Leander called from inside, his voice grim.

"Reid Kincaid, Signore Fortunato. May I come in?"

He held his breath as he counted off the moments of silence from inside the room. Not more than ten seconds, but it felt like a lifetime.

"Enter," Leander finally growled.

His expression was forbidding beneath his thick gray hair and black brows. "Well? What is it?" he asked fiercely.

"I want to make a confession."

Leander's glare was suspicious. "What do you think, I'm a priest?"

"No. A man who has been wronged."

Reid spilled out his story, how he'd judged Leander without really knowing him, how he'd belittled him to Dolly, how he'd tried to talk her out of their engagement. How he and Carina had taken it into their hands to do whatever they could to break up the relationship.

"My Carina was part of this?"

"I'm afraid so. She thought she was doing what was best for you the same way I thought I was doing what was best for Mom."

"Why do you tell me this?"

"Because when you and Mom told us at dinner that night on the boat about the way you'd prayed and how you met, we changed our minds. We saw how judgmental and presumptuous we'd been. We saw that God had brought you together there on board the *Ysolda*. We saw that you were meant to be together." He took a deep breath. "We still believe that, Signore Fortunato. God has not changed his mind. Only you have. You and Mom."

"And you do not now think you are being judgmental and presumptuous?"

"I hope not. My mother loves you. She wouldn't be so hurt and miserable if she didn't. I understand, more than you can know, why you have to believe she isn't marrying you for your money. But Carina has helped me understand that my mother has to believe you trust her before she marries you." He stood. "I hope you can find the compromise, Signore. It would be very sad for you to lose each other now."

Leander stood as well. "Please," he said, his scowl easing. "Call me Leander." He thrust out his hand.

Carina was getting the tour of Dolly Kincaid's West Seattle home, which was decorated in rustic country style and held almost as many teddy bears as Carina had in her own collection, artfully displayed on window sills, tabletops, and bookshelves throughout the house.

"I have my entire collection crammed into my office at work while my house is being remodeled," Carina said. "It will be so nice to get them home again. Mid-February, my contractor tells me now."

"Mid-February," Dolly repeated sadly.

Valentine's Day was in mid-February, Carina thought. Dolly and Babbo's wedding day. If it was still going to happen.

She nervously twisted her ring. "I have to tell you how upset I am with Babbo," she said.

"Did he send you?" Dolly asked, hope brightening her features.

"No, he didn't. He would be very unhappy knowing that I'm here. His little *impicciona,* he sometimes calls me. 'Busybody.'" Carina hugged herself and rubbed her hands up and down her arms. When had it turned so cold? "Maybe it isn't Babbo I'm upset with so much as I'm upset with me," she said.

Dolly raised her eyebrows.

"May we sit?" Carina asked.

"Of course. Forgive me."

Carina shook her head. "I should ask for *your* forgiveness."

Drawing her brows together in a puzzled frown, Dolly waited.

"It's my fault, the trouble between you and Babbo," Carina said. "Mine and Reid's."

"Oh, no, it has nothing to do with you and Reid, Carina! Your father and I are both happy to see you spending time together. It's how we got to know each other, talking about you—"

"I don't mean that." Carina took a deep breath. "I mean that Reid and I set about to break you up from the beginning. If we hadn't, maybe this trouble would never have happened between you."

Dolly sat back in her chair and crossed her arms. "Oh?"

Carina, looking at her lap more often than at Dolly, told her story. "I was wrong to mislead you about my father's finances," she finished. "I was sure you'd find a way to—unengage yourself, so to speak."

She looked up to find Dolly's eyes riveted on her. "You quickly proved me wrong," she added sheepishly. "Babbo told me the next morning you'd offered to loan him money. I didn't know what to think."

"You were only trying to protect him," Dolly said.

Carina nodded. "Like Reid was trying to protect you. Only neither of us think you need protection from each other anymore." She took a deep breath. "We think you need protection from yourselves."

Dolly frowned. "Go on."

"Reid says you're as stubborn as my father. And if one of you doesn't do something soon—" She stopped. "I don't want him to lose you, Dolly. He has his faults, but he would be very good to you. He loves you. I hope you'll give him a chance."

With a toss of her head, Dolly turned away and stared out the window. "So my son thinks I'm stubborn, does he?" she said.

Carina's heart sank. That was all she had to say?

Hope stirred again when Dolly turned her face back toward Carina. "He's right," she sighed. "Stubborn and proud. Still, after all these years. Thank you for coming, Carina. I promise I will seek God's heart."

T hat was *so* romantic," Carina sighed as Reid handed her into the car on the afternoon of Valentine's Day. "Babbo and Dolly singing to each other at their wedding! If I hadn't heard them New Year's Eve, I never would have believed it."

"I'm still not sure I do," Reid said. "Who would have thought? Two months ago they'd never even met."

"Six weeks ago we were frantically trying to break them up," Carina reminded him.

"Five weeks ago we were frantically trying to get them back together."

Carina laughed. "It's fitting their disagreement had such an O. Henry ending, don't you think?"

Reid nodded. He wished he could have been a fly on the wall the afternoon his mother swept through the restaurant and into Leander's office, brandishing a long plumed pen and closing the door firmly behind her.

Ten minutes later she and Leander had emerged arm in arm, flushed and triumphant, Leander tossing the torn pieces of the signed prenuptial agreement into the air like so much confetti. "The wedding is on!" he'd cried as the entire staff applauded. Dolly's smile could have lit the far corners of the kitchen.

Taking one hand off the wheel, Reid found Carina's hand and squeezed it. "'The Gift of the Magi' all over again," he agreed. He glanced at her and almost missed the red light at the intersection. She was positively glowing. Was it only the afternoon sun filtering through the windows? The reflection of her apricot-toned dress? Or was it happiness, radiating from the inside out?

"Have I told you how beautiful you look today?" he asked.

"Only twice."

The light turned green. He proceeded through the intersection. "I'm slipping," he said.

She raised her eyebrows. "You also just missed the turn." The wedding ceremony had taken place in the West Seattle church where Reid and his mother were members, but no other place than Fortunato's Ristorante would do for the reception. Lorenzo had been preparing the wedding feast for days.

"A short detour," Reid said. "No one will notice if we're a little late."

"Reid! It's our parents' wedding reception."

"Humor me," he said, lifting her hand to his lips. "I guarantee you won't be sorry."

"Mmm…" she murmured, rubbing her knuckles along his cheek. The touch and the sound of her voice resonated through his body.

The last six weeks had been a wild ride. Inside the dizzying whirlwind of Dolly and Leander's romance, he and Carina had created a tornado all their own.

After their breakfast at Charlie's, they had seen each other every day. They worked together, worshiped together, played together. And talked together, endlessly. Reid couldn't imagine they'd ever run out of conversation, though Carina had told him just last night that in the beginning she'd wondered, briefly, if they'd have anything to talk about once they stopped meddling in their parents' lives.

"Still worried?" he'd asked her.

"Not an ounce."

They argued, but cheerfully, and only about nonessentials.

About the essentials they agreed: commitment to family, to calling, to making mistakes, to learning from them. And especially, after the mess they'd made interfering in their parents' lives, to seeking God's heart in everything.

They had planned adventures and let adventure find them. They'd chased each other down the ski slopes at Snoqualmie and through the woods at Discovery Park. They'd taken the *Portofino* for a turn around Elliot Bay. They'd kidnapped Nonna Pippa for a ferry ride through the islands. They'd baby-sat Santo, Tiara, and Aurora, and afterward made a solemn vow never to have twins.

They'd wandered through the craft booths at Pike's Place Market holding hands, snuggled atop the Space Needle, and kissed in the elevator going down. The elevator attendant's bored expression hadn't even flickered, as if he were used to such foolishness.

Reid knew now exactly how his mother had felt when she'd met Leander—as if the link between them had been there before they'd ever met and all they needed to do to fall in love was to recognize it. Accept it. And hold on tight.

With Carina, he had never felt so exhilarated, so alive, so in love.

Or, suddenly, so nervous.

He let go of her hand to pull into a parking space at Alki Beach. The winter sun, sinking toward the white-capped Olympic Mountains across Puget Sound, had the sky to itself. Not a cloud in sight—a rare Seattle day. A perfect day for a wedding.

Or a proposal.

He reached into the inside pocket of his blazer, his heart beating wildly. "Happy Valentine's Day, Carina."

"Happy Val—"

The sight of the black velvet box in Reid's hand stopped her in midsentence. "Reid Kincaid! Is that what I think it is?"

He opened the box and held his breath. The choice, on his budget, had been either a large zircon or a modest diamond; he'd opted for the diamond. It winked in the late afternoon sun.

"I know it's small," he said anxiously, tugging at his earlobe. "Someday I'll—"

"It's perfect, Reid. I love it."

He pulled it from the box and slipped it on her finger. She was right; it was perfect for her hand.

When he looked up, she was smiling at him, her head cocked to one side. "Well?" she prompted. "Isn't there something you wanted to ask?"

He grinned, his nervousness falling away. Leave it to Carina to get right to the point.

"Carina Sabine, will you marry me?"

"Absolutely! What took you so long?"

Dolly and Leander Fortunato stared at their children in open-mouthed astonishment.

"You're *what?*" Dolly cried.

"No!" Leander stormed. "I will not allow it!"

"You're so young!" protested Dolly.

"You only have known each other for six weeks!"

"Have you thought about it?"

"On our wedding day. That they would tell us this thing on our wedding day!" Leander fumed as if Reid and Carina weren't standing right there.

"It's all our fault," Dolly moaned. "We've been so caught up in weddin' plans, we didn't see what was happenin' before our very eyes."

Leander glowered. "We've got to talk some sense into them."

"Babbo," Carina protested. "Can't you be happy for us?"

"*You* knew in a week," Reid pointed out.

Silence. The newlyweds looked at each other. Dolly started to laugh. Leander threw his hands in the air.

"Who can fight love?" he asked, taking Dolly's hand. His dark eyes glittered with good humor, as if his blustering had been only a joke. "*Mia Fiammetta,* will you dance with me?"

The statue of Cupid hovering over the fountain in the foyer was as blind as ever, Reid noticed when he and Carina whirled by a few minutes later.

But had he always worn that smile?

∧ ∧ ∧ ∧ ∧

Like Carina, I take shortcuts when I cook. But I still like the food I serve to look good and taste great. Here's a simple, elegant, and delicious dessert that's perfect for the end of a Valentine's dinner. In fact, this is Carina's no-cook version of a recipe Lorenzo created for Dolly and Leander's Valentine's Day wedding—*Frutta Felicia.*

Lorenzo's version calls for fresh pears boiled in sugar water with a little vanilla; Carina and I use canned pear halves in light syrup. He has fresh raspberries flown in from South America when they're not in season in Seattle, but frozen unsweetened berries work fine. He makes his own sauces from scratch; we use the juice from the berries and hot fudge sauce from a squeeze bottle, warmed in the microwave. He also makes his own *gelato,* while we settle for a good quality vanilla ice cream.

Drain the pears and the partially-thawed raspberries, reserving the juice from the berries. For each serving, pour two tablespoons of juice in a chilled bowl. (If you're making dessert for more than two, you might need to add a little pear juice to have enough.) Place two pear halves, a scoop of vanilla ice cream, and a handful of raspberries in a pleasing arrangement in the bowl. Drizzle the hot fudge in a crisscross pattern over the fruit and ice cream, and sprinkle finely chopped walnuts on top. If you can find fresh mint leaves, one or two make a beautiful garnish. Easy, elegant, and the combination of flavors is exquisite.

Barbara Jean Hicks is an award-winning author with five novels and two novellas to her credit. She lives in Oregon, where she makes her living solely by her words and wits.

♥

Birds of a
Feather

by Diane Noble

CHAPTER
One

Pearl Flynn stood back, squinting as she scrutinized the nearly completed canvas resting on her easel. She had been painting in her garden since dawn, and now the brilliant autumn sun hung much higher in the sky. Time had slipped away so silently that she'd barely noticed its passage.

In all her sixty-something years, never had such a wonder happened to her. Impatient by nature, she was a list maker and clock-watcher, always ready for the next task at hand, whether it was rounding up the Birds-of-a-Feather gang for a bird-watching expedition or picketing the local gas station because of its company's latest oil spill.

But a year ago, she'd signed up for a painting class at San Francisco City College, and now—she sighed, shaking her head—now? Her life had changed. How she viewed herself had changed.

Because of inherited money from a distant cousin she'd never met, Pearl had never had to work. She'd volunteered her time at Birds of a Feather, Save the California Redwoods, Living Free Wild Animal Clinic, and Friends of the Library. As much as she'd enjoyed all those years of stuffing envelopes or sorting used books, she had never felt the passion that she felt for her painting. For the first time in her life, she realized that when God had handed out gifts, he hadn't forgotten her after all.

Pearl examined the painting, pleased. Her style was an uncomplicated and bright Americana. She smiled. Her painting instructor called it "uniquely Pearl." If she ever were so fortunate to have her own studio and shop, that's exactly what she would call it: Uniquely Pearl.

The snow geese in the background needed a touch more white, so she dipped her brush into the paint on her palette and made the correction. She stood back and squinted again. The light was rapidly changing in her garden, creating a glare against the sheen of the oils on the canvas. It would be better to wait until tomorrow morning to touch up the emerald of the pond in the foreground.

The scene was created from her memory of Annie and Gregory Westbrook's property out by Everlasting. She'd used winter-twilight colors, giving the Queen Anne cottage in the background a warm glow of candlelight spilling from inside, with twinkling white lights around the edge of its steep roof. This painting was one of several she'd done of scenes in and around the historic town.

Reluctantly, Pearl began to put away her paints. She had just moved her easel, canvas, and paint box into the house when a car pulled into the driveway. Good timing. She'd told none of her Birds-of-a-Feather friends about her artwork. Some of the other returning students at the college knew and understood the wonder she was feeling, but she didn't want to share her artwork with those who might not understand.

Besides, she knew the Birds-of-a-Feather members believed that beneath that purple-red hair and ever present plastic visor, there was not a serious thought in her head. Maybe she didn't want to destroy that illusion. It was, after all, what she was comfortable with.

Pearl quickly scrubbed her hands with a fragrant strawberry-scented soap in an attempt to cover up the odor of the oils and turpentine, grabbed a dish towel, and headed to the front door.

When she pulled it open, her mouth dropped in amazement. It was Woodrow Hornberger, whom she had thought

192

was still in South Africa doing work for a nonprofit organization. He smiled and removed his Australian felt hat.

"Why, Woodrow," she said a moment later, when she'd recovered from the surprise. "My goodness, I didn't know you were back."

"Hello, Pearl," he said, and the sound of his voice caused a little skitter in her heartbeat.

"Please, come in." She backed away from the door. As he entered, she glanced about, trying to see her living room through his eyes.

A healthy jungle of houseplants covered every available spot, sprouting up walls from old Chinese pots, cascading down from the fireplace mantel, bookshelves, and window ledges. Worn wicker furniture, placed in the middle of the room because there wasn't space anywhere else, was covered with antique quilts and needlepoint pillows. Books and magazines and crossword puzzles were scattered about on her collection of old steamer trunks that doubled as tables. Sacks of food, gathered by her neighbors, awaited her weekly run to the homeless shelters. The windows faced east, and the whole room was flooded with late morning sunlight, pointing out in stark relief every cat hair on the old Persian carpet or dust mote in the air.

Woodrow didn't seem to notice the room at all. He was watching her, and for the briefest of moments, she thought she saw a hint of something new in his gaze. Tenderness, perhaps? It happened so quickly she was sure it had been her imagination. She looked at him more closely.

He was smiling at her, looking as fresh as a daisy. Not a bit worn from his globe-trotting ways at seventy years of age. Debonair, graceful, and stately, as always. She let out a small sigh. Not her type at all. He was Fred Astaire to her Lucy Ricardo. Water to her oil. They just didn't mix—never had and probably never would. Mostly they just exasperated each other. His tender look must have been her imagination.

"Well, come in, sit down," she said, nodding to a wicker chair overflowing with soft cushions and homemade pillows.

"Thank you," said Woodrow, seating himself. "You're looking well, Pearl."

She patted her hair, wondering how he could think such a thing. But she accepted the compliment anyway, smiling. "What brings you to my neck of the woods, Woodrow?" They might as well get down to business; she knew he wouldn't drop by just for a social call.

"I received a telephone call this morning," he began. She sighed. She'd been right. "Actually," Woodrow continued, "Annie tried to call you first, but there was no answer."

"I unplugged my phone."

He frowned, but he was too polite to ask why, and she volunteered nothing. The hours she spent painting were pure joy. During those hours, she felt as if she'd unzipped her earthly body and stepped out a fresh, young, new creature. As if she were somehow partnering with God in creating something fine and beautiful. As if she were becoming what God had intended from the beginning. Such a feeling—both joy filled and sacred—had never happened to her before. And, by jing, she wasn't about to let any cranky, ringing phone distract her.

"Is everything all right with Annie and the twins?" she asked. "And Greg?"

"Oh, yes," Woodrow said quickly to dispel her fears. "The Westbrooks are all healthy. Annie sends her love."

"I can tell by your voice, Woodrow, that something's wrong. Why did Annie call?"

He settled back in his chair. "I came to you first—just as Annie tried to call you first, Pearl—because I know how much you love Everlasting."

She nodded. "We all do. After those weeks we spent rebuilding Annie and Greg's house, we all fell in love with the place—and the setting." She smiled, thinking of her recent obsession with painting it. Of course she loved Everlasting.

"That's why Annie called." He frowned in thought. "Folks around Everlasting are not sure there's anything wrong, but there are rumors flying that aren't too pleasant."

"Rumors?" she asked. "What kind of rumors?" What could be wrong with the sleepy little gold-rush village, virtually unchanged for a hundred and fifty years? It had been turned into a state historic park several years ago, thanks to the efforts of Annie's great-aunt, Sheridan Anne Hartfield, the woman who'd bequeathed her land to Annie and Greg. The whole community cherished Everlasting's roots.

"No one will substantiate them—and Annie says that Greg's even gone all the way to Sacramento to check on it—"

"Woodrow, would you just tell me about the rumors?"

"Everlasting may be sold to some overseas investors."

"What?" She shook her head incredulously.

"That's the rumor," Woodrow said, a sorrowful note to his voice.

"They can't do that," Pearl sputtered. "Everlasting belongs to the people of California. To the people of, well, of Everlasting."

"It gets worse."

She braced herself. "How could it?"

"It's said that it will be turned into a theme park."

Pearl groaned. "With rides?"

Woodrow nodded.

"Panning for gold with pie tins and fake nuggets?"

"Yes," he said.

She closed her eyes for a minute, picturing asphalt parking lots where a forest of pines now grew, a garish neon entrance with ticket booths and souvenir shops, screaming kids on

Ferris wheels and roller coasters and log rides. They'd probably call it Goldyland, Digginsville, or maybe Bear Flags over Everlasting.

"Oh, no," she moaned. "Oh, no." She opened her eyes, staring hard at Woodrow. "We can't allow this to happen."

A slow smile spread across his face. "That's what Annie was hoping you'd say."

"Shall we get the gang together? Plan our strategy for a bit of undercover work? We do that well." She grinned.

"The sooner the better," said Woodrow. "Annie said that she doesn't have room to put all of us up, but if we'd like to bring campers and tents, we can stay by the pond. Use the house for cooking and bathroom facilities."

"An army encampment," she said happily. "The camp will serve as our war room!" Then she lifted a brow, considering when they'd stayed there last. "Just think, we'll be able to listen to my spotted owls at night."

"You'll never let me live that down, will you, Pearl." He'd been the first to discount her identification of the endangered bird when the group was working on Annie's house. She knew her haphazard identification of birds and mispronunciation of their names irritated him no end. What he didn't know was that she did it just to get his dander up...and to hear the resonance of his voice as he invariably provided the Latin name. "Go ahead, rub it in," he said, his voice surprisingly gentle. "I'm sure none of us will ever hear the last of it."

"Do you want to set up the strategy meeting here?" she asked. "If everyone can make it, tomorrow night works for me. By the weekend we can head to Everlasting. Set up camp."

Woodrow nodded. "Sounds good. You want to make the calls?"

"We both can," Pearl said. "One of us can use the fax phone."

"Don't tell me you've got a fax."

"Birds of a Feather couldn't run without it. We had a donation come in, and the group decided it was a good idea. When there's a good cause, we can flood offices with faxes stating our feelings."

"You'll be getting computerized next."

"Nothing will ever make me give up my Olivetti," she said with pride. The manual typewriter had faithfully served her for twenty-five years. She owed the old machine something, even if only keeping it safe from some cold typewriter graveyard.

Pearl led Woodrow to the sun room, which also served as the Birds-of-a-Feather office. She whisked the dustcover off the fax machine, patting it almost reverently.

"Just poke the 'hook' button. You'll get a dial tone—just like a regular phone." Without waiting for Woodrow to follow her instructions, she reached for the receiver and pressed the button for him. "It's what they call a dedicated line," she added with a sense of importance.

They divided the list of members, Woodrow taking Flora, a city librarian, and Theda, her sister, a beautician. Pearl said she'd call Wyatt, a fireman and part-time search-and-rescue volunteer; Gabe Parker, a best-selling romance writer; and their newest member, Charley Stiles, a burly seventy-something college student Pearl had met at the student center.

Woodrow looked a little surprised when she mentioned Charley. He didn't know a new member had joined Birds of a Feather while he was in South Africa. But Pearl, now standing in the doorway, merely smiled and told Woodrow new blood was good for the group.

She headed to the kitchen and picked up the phone by the table. She reached Wyatt on the first ring. He'd just finished working seventy-two hours straight and could attend the meeting since he would be off for the next four days. Gabe Parker didn't answer his home phone, but she tried his car phone and got him on his way to an interview. He said the timing of the meeting was perfect. He was between deadlines.

Next Pearl dialed Charley's number. She liked the man very much. He was a recent widower, and they often met for tea on the days they were both on campus.

"Charley?"

"Ah, me. It's Pearl!" he said. It pleased her that he knew her voice.

She briefly explained about the meeting and gave him directions to her house. He said he'd be there with bells on, then just as she said good-bye and was about to hang up the receiver, Charley stopped her, clearing his throat a bit nervously.

"Pearl?"

"Yes, Charley?"

"I'm glad you called. Actually, I was going to call you."

"You were?"

"Yes. I was wondering if you would, ah, join me for dinner tonight. There's a great little Italian restaurant over by the college. Someone in one of my classes told me about it. It's a classic kind of place, checkered cloths and Chianti candleholders on the tables, run by a mom and pop from the old country. None of this California cuisine with designer pastas."

"Charley, I would love to go. The place sounds charming," Pearl said, touched that he'd thought of her. How long had it been since someone actually asked her on a date? Forever, it seemed. She smiled into the phone. "I really would. Thanks so much for asking me. Do you want me to meet you there?"

He laughed. "Oh, no, my dear. That may be the way of young whippersnappers, but not me. No, I'll stop by and collect you. What time is good?"

"Seven o'clock would be just about perfect," she said, still smiling.

"Good. I'll see you then."

"Good-bye, Charley. And thank you," Pearl said, feeling her cheeks flush as she replaced the receiver.

She turned toward the doorway. Woodrow was standing there, looking for all the world like a towering thunderhead. "I assume our newest member will be more than happy to attend the meeting."

"Well, yes. Actually, he will be," she said, standing and patting her hair. "The others can come as well. How about Theda and Flora?"

"Affirmative," he said shortly. He checked his watch. "Well, then, I guess that takes care of that. I'll call Annie and let her know we're on top of things."

"Good," said Pearl.

"And I'll see you tomorrow night."

This time Pearl merely nodded. She searched his face. There was no trace of the earlier tenderness there.

The old Woodrow was back, and she wondered why that made her so sad.

T he fall air was crisp the following night when Woodrow pulled his well-worn Land Rover into a parking space in front of Pearl's house. The smell of wood smoke filled the air, and lights beamed a welcome through the windows. A single lamppost, an odd-looking sculptured thing with a verdigris finish, stood by the gate, lighting the yard.

As he strode up the walkway, which was flanked by a wild tangle of plants and flowers, Woodrow counted the other vehicles. Seven, including Pearl's sunflower yellow '67 Camaro, for which she'd traded her old lavender Buick a year ago.

All the members were here, apparently even the newest, Charley Stiles. There was a dark red sports car in the driveway that Woodrow didn't recognize. Had to be Charley's, he thought with a grimace.

Woodrow pulled back the screen door and knocked on the rock-solid oak door. He could hear the easy camaraderie of the others, their conversations punctuated with spurts of laughter.

A moment later, the door opened. A radiant-looking Pearl opened the door, her smile widening when she saw him. "You're here at last," she said. "Come in, Woodrow. We've been waiting for you."

He'd heard that a woman is never more radiant than when she's in love, and as he moved past Pearl, he took in the luster of her eyes, her flushed cheeks, and the glow on her face. With a sinking feeling, he realized his suspicions must be true. And he wondered if it was the new man in her life, the most recent member of Birds of a Feather, Charley Stiles. Whoever it was, Pearl Flynn seemed smitten.

Pearl looped her arm through Woodrow's and led him across the room. "Come, meet Charley," she said.

From a chair near the fireplace, a big-shouldered man stood and turned. "Did I hear my name?" he asked with an easy smile. He stuck out his hand. "Name's Stiles." His shake was firm, vigorous.

"Woodrow Hornberger," said Woodrow, wishing for the first time in his life that he had a name that spoke of prize fighting or major-league baseball. "It's good to meet you."

"Woody, good to meet you!" said Charley. Woodrow groaned inwardly at the hated nickname, wondering if Charley had read his mind.

"I've heard so much about you," Charley continued. "And this group is great. I'm so glad that Pearl invited me to join." He shot a pleased look at Pearl, and she returned his smile. "I'm looking forward to getting to know everyone better."

I bet, thought Woodrow, thinking of the radiant Pearl standing near him. He noticed she smelled of wildflowers and soap, and oddly enough, a bit like turpentine.

"We'd better get started," she said to both men. "Woodrow, I'm sure you've already got this planned down to the gnat's eyelash. Do you want to lead off?"

He was surprised. It wasn't often that Pearl relinquished the gavel to someone else in the group. "Of course," he said quickly, before she changed her mind.

"All right, everyone!" Pearl called out to the rest of the group. "Pull some extra chairs from the kitchen. Grab some coffee and cookies, sit down, and listen up. Woodrow's got some good ideas—as he always does—that we need to listen to. He's also the one who talked with Annie about what's going on in Everlasting. He'll be able to relay the details better than I can."

Woodrow stood to one side of the fireplace, looking down at the intent faces of the members. They took their work very seriously. This was a bit out of the ordinary, but after they'd helped to fix up Annie and Greg's house in Everlasting, the history of the place had settled into their spirits. He knew they'd feel as strongly as he and Pearl did about its preservation.

"Here's the information we have so far, folks," he said, and proceeded to tell them of the rumor about the investors and the theme park. There were groans of disapproval, just as he knew there would be. "I really think those of us who have the time could get to the bottom of this. Nose around in Everlasting. Find out what we can. See what we can do to change their minds."

He paused as some members threw out suggestions; then his tone turned serious as he continued. "We're the perfect ones to act. Greg and Annie are too well known in the community. No one knows us. We could fit right in with the surroundings—"

Pearl suddenly spoke up. "I've got some ideas about that," she said. "Everlasting is always in need of docents—volunteers to lead the tours, dress up in period costumes. Musicians to sit on the street corners. Can anyone here play the fiddle or the harmonica?"

"I used to play the harmonica. Probably could pick it up again," said Wyatt.

Charley raised his hand. "I play both, plus banjo," he said. "Just name the tune. I play a mean 'Oh, Susannah.'" He chuckled. "Anyone for 'Dueling Banjos'?"

Everyone laughed good-naturedly. Woodrow gritted his teeth, wishing he'd learned how to shoe horses somewhere along the line. "Good, Charley," he said evenly. "You'll be in charge of the musician role."

"There's also the theater in town," Pearl reminded them.

202

"Phantom of the Opera is playing right now. I'm sure they could use help in the ticket office or with ushering."

The discussion turned to who could remain in Everlasting full-time and who would have to commute on their days off. It was decided that a camp would be set up at Greg and Annie's. Gabe said he'd bring his camper and his laptop computer and work in the mornings, then help the others in the afternoon. Wyatt planned to stay during his four days off each week, then commute back to San Francisco for work the other three days. He volunteered to bring an extra Airstream if Woodrow would pull it with his Land Rover.

Charley Stiles said that because of his class schedule he could only come on weekends. He looked disappointed, then cheered up considerably when Gabe mentioned that the Thanksgiving and Christmas breaks were right around the corner.

It was soon apparent that only Pearl and Woodrow could be in Everlasting full-time.

"I have a suggestion," he said, asking for their attention once more. "At this point, we don't know if this is just a rumor. Before we gear up for our undercover work, I say that Pearl and I should travel to Everlasting, nose around, and see what we can find out."

"How soon?" Pearl asked, frowning. He was surprised. She usually jumped at the chance to head to the little town.

"Well, I was thinking of tomorrow," he said, watching in dismay as she exchanged a glance with Charley Stiles. He tried not to remember that earlier look of radiance on her face. "But if you, er, have other plans, I can certainly run out alone."

"No, no. I can make arrangements," she said quickly, glancing at Stiles again. "Let's go. We can report back on what we discover. Finalize our plans after that."

There was a general hubbub in the room as tasks were

assigned. Flora said she'd call to see when the next classes were scheduled for docents. Charley said he'd find out about auditions for musicians and playhouse actors.

Finally the meeting broke up, and after a bit more chatting as the Birds members headed out the door, the only three remaining in the living room were Pearl, Charley, and Woodrow. It struck Woodrow that he and Charley were each trying to outwait the other so they could be alone with Pearl.

Alone with Pearl? The idea was a revelation. When had he begun to care? He thought back over the years he'd known Pearl. Even though she exasperated him no end, he had always taken joy in her free-spirited ways. It was during his trip to South Africa that he realized he actually missed her and wished she were with him. When he spotted exotic birds, he thought about her propensity to wear colors resembling their plumage, her annoying inclination to call them variations of their proper names, her childlike delight in their beauty and songs.

While Pearl and Charley chatted, Woodrow gathered the empty cups and carried them into the kitchen. From the corner of his eye, he noticed Pearl showing Charley to the door. But when he returned, instead of being on his merry way, Charley was speaking in low tones to Pearl on the front porch. The door was partly ajar, and Woodrow could see Pearl's animated face in the porch light. As she talked, she gestured with her hands, and he noticed her tapered, artistic fingers, the graceful way she flicked them this way and that to emphasize her point.

I'm turning into a romantic, he thought. But why now? Why, when it was obvious Pearl's affections were elsewhere? He had loved his wife dearly, but never, in all their thirty-two years of marriage, had he considered himself a romantic. Quietly, he found his leather jacket and Australian hat and let himself out through the sunporch and the back door.

By the time he'd rounded the house, Charley Stiles and Pearl were no longer on the porch, though Charley's car was still parked out front. Well, Charley won after all, Woodrow thought. He outwaited my departure, and now he's got Pearl to himself.

As he unlocked the Land Rover and stepped inside, he glanced back toward the house. He could see the two of them sitting before the fire. He started the ignition, then pressed hard on the accelerator. The Land Rover lurched forward with a squeal of rubber. The sound of it made Woodrow chuckle. He hadn't felt this way since adolescence.

And to think of it—over Pearl! Pearl Flynn. Beautiful, red-haired, spirited, funny, wonderful Pearl.

Only now it was too late.

Or was it?

He chuckled again. His suggestion that he and Pearl go alone to Everlasting hadn't been just because their schedules were the only two permitting the trip.

He sped through the city, planning to call Pearl as soon as he got home. He needed to let her know the time they'd leave and how long they might expect to stay. The sound of a ringing phone might be just the ticket for getting Charley Stiles on his way.

Woodrow pulled into his townhouse garage, quickly shut off the engine, and locked the car. He practically sprinted to the front door and into his den, where he picked up the receiver.

He punched in her number from memory. After three rings, Pearl answered the phone.

"Pearl?" he said. "Woodrow here."

"My goodness," she said, with a faint sniffling sound. "It's late. What's up?"

"Pearl, are you all right?" She didn't sound all right. In fact, he suspected that she'd been crying. He'd never known Pearl to cry before.

"Yes, Woodrow. I'm fine," she finally managed after a couple more sniffles. "Really."

"Do you not want to go tomorrow?" For a moment she didn't answer, and his heart dropped to his shoes. "It's all right, really. I understand. I put you in a difficult spot tonight. I'm sorry."

"No, you *don't* understand," she said, a bit of her spirit showing again. "I want to go. It's just that, well, there are other, um, extenuating circumstances that I can't really go into right now." She sighed deeply. "Maybe sometime soon I can tell you," she said lamely. This was not the spunky and direct Pearl he'd always known.

"You can tell me anything," he said. Well, maybe. He really didn't want to hear about her feelings for Mr. Banjo, but he didn't say so. "About tomorrow?"

"I can be ready by dawn," she said, sounding considerably brighter.

"Why don't we have breakfast on the way?"

"Perfect. It's my favorite time of day. I'll pack a picnic breakfast. We can stop along the way." Her childlike exuberance was back, and he took pleasure in the sound of it.

"I'll pick up some gourmet coffee. And squeeze some fresh juice. Is orange okay?"

"What if I said kumquat?" she said, laughing. "You'd have to start right now."

The sweetness in her voice during their phone conversation stayed with him long afterward, as if awakening some strange and wonderful music in his soul.

Through his window, he watched the moon-silvered branches of a pine move in the soft wind. From a distance he heard the lonely call of an owl, an *Otus kennicottii*, judging from the series of single-pitched whistles.

An enormous ivory moon hung low in the sky, reminding him of the radiance he'd seen in Pearl tonight.

And he felt as lonely as the owl sounded.

CHAPTER
Three

Pearl watched Woodrow pour coffee from the thermos into two double paper cups. None of the Birds-of-a-Feather gang used Styrofoam. Pearl made sure each member followed the rules. She also insisted that they snip the plastic six-pack soda pop carriers into little pieces before dropping them into the trash. You had to make sure a raccoon or stray cat wouldn't get his head caught in one at the garbage dump. Or, heaven forbid, if the plastic made its way to the ocean... She shuddered, thinking of the consequences.

She placed a checkered cloth on the tailgate of the Land Rover and laid out the breakfast spread: berry preserves and low-fat honey-wheat muffins; her special egg-substitute, lite-cheese, and bacon-bit casserole; and Woodrow's fresh-squeezed orange juice.

Just as the sun began to crown the Sierra Nevadas, Pearl and Woodrow pulled out their folding aluminum chairs and settled into them, facing a golden valley dotted with live oaks and scrub pines. A covey of California quail scattered from beneath a stand of manzanita, calling out "cha-kee-ta" and beating the air with their wings. In some nearby oaks, scrub jays squawked their greetings as they hopped from branch to branch.

"God's creating another beautiful day for us," Pearl said with a contented sigh. She'd cried last night, thinking about leaving her painting for even one day. But surprisingly, her spirits had lifted, and here she sat with Woodrow Hornberger, a man she once thought unbearably stuffy, enjoying the morning. Enjoying him. Enormously.

Woodrow was intent on watching the sunrise, and Pearl turned to watch with him. The eastern sky was filled with clouds, and as the sun rose, they turned to shades of yellow and orange and pink. Soon the valley was awash with golden light, and the oaks and pines and sycamores were now backlit by the sun. The sun spilled onto the morning dew, spreading millions of miniature jewels across the tall grass and leafy trees.

"'I lift up my eyes to the hills,'" Woodrow quoted softly. "'Where does my help come from? My help comes from the LORD, the Maker of heaven and earth.'"

His voice had a pleasant low rumble to it, and it soothed her as he quoted the psalm. She listened to his words with her heart and joined him in the last four verses:

"'The LORD watches over you—the LORD is your shade at your right hand; the sun will not harm you by day, nor the moon by night. The LORD will keep you from all harm—he will watch over your life; the LORD will watch over your coming and going both now and forevermore.'"

Woodrow turned to Pearl and took her hand. When he offered thanks for their food, it was as natural as speaking to a friend. "Lord," he said, "we praise you for the beauty of your creation. How can we doubt your power when we see such glory! We give you this day, and we ask for wisdom and strength for the task ahead. And bless us today, we pray in Jesus' name."

"Amen," Pearl said with him.

For a moment she kept her head bowed, thinking the words of the psalm: "He will watch over your life." God, the Creator of the earth and all its beauty, was watching over her. Over Woodrow. Their coming and going. She could scarcely take it in. How could anyone—let alone Pearl Flynn—be so precious to him?

She was still contemplating the thought when Woodrow spoke.

"It is beautiful, isn't it?" he said, his gaze on the sunlit valley. "It almost makes me want to take up painting just to try to capture it."

She gazed up at him, her eyes widening in surprise.

He saw her look and laughed. "Now *that's* a silly thought! Can you imagine such a thing?" He laughed again, and Pearl turned away.

She handed him a recycled, no-dye paper plate, and Woodrow helped himself to a scoop of the casserole, a couple of muffins, and some orange juice. Then she served herself, and they sat down together to eat.

"Wonderful!" he said enthusiastically after taking a bite of the egg dish.

Pearl nodded absently, thinking of what he'd said about painting the scene. Her gaze swept across the valley, and she took in every detail, savoring the scent of the air, the light, the color.

But he'd laughed at the thought of painting it. Some people thought of art as frivolous. Perhaps he was one.

"Penny for your thoughts," said Woodrow, almost causing her to jump.

She laughed lightly, shrugged one shoulder, and flicked her fingers toward the sunrise. "You're right. It's a masterpiece," she said simply. "I was taking in the beauty."

He was quiet a moment, seeming lost in thought. "About last night," he said finally. "I noticed that you seemed, well, a bit reluctant to come with me today." He fidgeted with his cup, then stood to scoop up more of the casserole, though he hadn't finished with the serving on his plate.

"Well, yes," she said, taking a sip of coffee. "I had some other obligations."

"So you said." His eyes met hers as he seated himself again.

Pearl saw the curiosity on his face and knew that he was waiting to hear her reasons. She wished she hadn't been so transparent when he'd first mentioned the trip. Her first thought, of course, had been one of dismay. Not only would she miss her early morning painting time in her garden, she would also miss today's ten o'clock class. It was weekly, four hours a session, plus lab in the afternoon. Missing one day was a big chunk of class time.

It had saddened her to skip, but after Charley Stiles said he'd stop by and explain the circumstances to her instructor and pick up any handouts or information she might need, she'd felt better. She sighed as the image of her latest painting came to mind.

Woodrow was still watching her intently. "Is it Charley? Did you not want to leave him today?"

Pearl felt her mouth drop open. "Charley?" she croaked. "Charley?" Then she giggled. Where in the world did Woodrow get such a notion? "Do you mean...our Charley?" By now her face was aflame from holding back an explosion of laughter.

Woodrow nodded. "Yes," he said rather grimly. "*Our* Charley."

"Oh my goodness, Woodrow! How did you ever—"

"Guess?" he finished for her, then went on before she could correct him. "As soon as I saw the two of you together last night, I knew there was a special closeness...." His voice rumbled into a sigh.

Pearl was almost too stunned to speak. She swallowed hard, still fighting to keep the laughter from spilling. Then a slow, amazing realization began to dawn as bright as the sunrise. The man was jealous. Woodrow Hornberger was jealous! Of Charley Stiles. Because of her.

She looked at him with wide eyes, wondering about the quickening of her heart. "Oh, Woodrow," she finally managed. "Surely you didn't think that Charley and I…" Now she blushed in earnest, searching for the right words. "That we are, or shall I say, we've, ah—"

"I'm sorry," said Woodrow, standing abruptly. "I can see that I've embarrassed you. I didn't mean to imply any impropriety—"

"Impropriety?" She stood in surprise, her plate filled with egg casserole and half-eaten muffin spilling to the ground. She didn't know whether to be flattered or offended. "Me?" she finally sputtered, placing her hands on her hips and looking at him incredulously.

"Now I can see I've insulted you, Pearl. Please accept my apology. I promise I won't bring up Charley or your relationship again." He turned to place the ceramic cover on the casserole dish and snap shut the Tupperware container holding the muffins.

"Woodrow!" she exclaimed as he twisted the lid onto the jar of preserves. "Woodrow Hornberger!" He turned, opening the lid to the picnic basket as he watched her. "Now you listen here. There is nothing going on between Charley Stiles and me. Absolutely nothing. At least not in the way you're insinuating."

"But last night—" he began, then seemed to think better of it.

"Last night was about a private matter," she said as gently as possible. But she could see the doubt still lurking on his face. She hadn't convinced him. She sighed again and started over. "You see, we share something very special—"

Woodrow looked stricken, and again, she halted. She was

making matters worse. What she wanted to say was that she and Charley shared a love of learning and growing. Of being college students—at their ages! Charley understood how dear her painting class was to her, just as she understood the importance of his algebra, English, and geology classes.

She could say none of that, at least not yet. Of all the people she wanted to understand this new love of hers, Woodrow was at the top of the list. No, she needed to wait until the time was right.

"Well," he finally said with a shrug, "I suppose we'd better get going. I told Annie and Greg to expect us at about nine o'clock."

Pearl nodded, wishing she could say something to cheer him. "Then let's be on our way."

Precisely an hour later, Woodrow guided the Land Rover onto the long dirt road leading to the Westbrooks'. The sun was higher now, and when they rounded the last curve before starting down to the house, Pearl caught her breath. Fall had turned the shimmering aspens that bordered the property to the color of liquid gold, and the emerald pond sparkled like a jewel as a breeze ruffled its waters.

"It's prettier than ever in the autumn," she said. "More substantial, somehow, as if the color is bringing it a second life."

"Much like people," Woodrow said. He grinned at her, and she noticed that whatever had upset him earlier now appeared to be gone.

She laughed easily, glad for the change. "Just like us, Woodrow. Colorful. Substantial. Ready to celebrate life afresh."

He threw back his head and laughed out loud. "Well, Pearl, I don't think anyone would dispute that you're one of God's most colorful creatures." He glanced down at his khaki pants and black shirt, then to her flowing turquoise-and-fuchsia dress.

"I mean our spirits, Woodrow. Not my hair or penchant for bright clothes. God doesn't want us to sit back and wait to die. He's given us all kinds of choices."

Smiling his agreement, he slowed the Land Rover as they crossed a small bridge by the pond, then steered around another bend and pressed on the brake for a rabbit that scampered across the road.

She turned toward him and touched his arm. "Look at you, Woodrow. You build houses for Habitat for Humanity. You volunteer your time overseas caring for little children who need medical help, food, and clothing. And you work in the office of the Ornithologists Union." She thought a minute. "How many birds are on your life list now? Have you reached five hundred?"

He nodded, his eyes on the road.

"See?" she said. "Talk about colorful! You may wear drab clothes, Woodrow, but you've got one of the most colorful lives I know."

"Drab clothes?" he said, glancing at her. He lifted a teasing brow. "Are you criticizing my clothes?"

She looked him up and down. Again the words *debonair, graceful,* and *stately* came to mind. His clothes fit that image perfectly, from his Australian hat to the leather jacket she'd admired last night. He might turn up his nose at artistic endeavors, but he himself was a work of art. "I wouldn't dare criticize your clothes, Woodrow. They're fine. Just fine."

Woodrow parked the vehicle in the side driveway. Before they opened their car doors, the twins slammed through the front door and raced to meet them.

Mary Beth lifted her arms, and Woodrow swooped her into the air. A peal of giggles followed as she gave him a quick hug then wriggled to get down. Shamus studied Pearl intently for a moment, then a small lopsided smile appeared. Pearl knelt so

214

she could look him in the face. "How about a hug for Auntie Pearl?"

"Auntie Pearlie," he corrected seriously and went happily into her arms. She held the little boy close, then took his hand, and they walked up the stairs together.

The foursome had just reached the front door when Annie appeared, wiping her hands on a tea towel. "Well, look who's here!" she exclaimed, pulling both Woodrow and Pearl into her arms at once, the twins wiggling into the middle of the hug.

Pearl stood back, assessing her friend. "You've got that glow again, Annie. Is there something you want to tell us?"

"Does it show already?" Annie laughed, tucking a stray lock of hair behind one ear. Then she patted her stomach. "Three months along. We're expecting in the spring."

"Twins again, dear?" Woodrow asked politely.

Annie rolled her eyes heavenward. "We weren't expecting them the first time, as you remember." She led them into the comfortable, period-decorated parlor. "Please, sit down. Can I get you anything? Tea? Coffee?"

They both declined, telling her about their picnic. A moment later, Woodrow settled into the love seat, and Pearl sat across from him in a pine rocker. Annie bustled the children back to the kitchen table, where they began playing with homemade play dough.

"You've come at a good time," she said when she returned.

"What do you mean?" Woodrow asked.

"There's a meeting tonight at the theater. The new investors are going to explain their position."

"So it's certain, then," said Pearl. "Everlasting's really going to be sold."

Annie nodded slowly. "They hope to dispel all rumors—or so they say. That's why the open meeting. They want to cover all their bases before the close of escrow."

215

"How about the theme park? Is that still part of their plan?" Woodrow asked.

Annie looked uncertain and shook her head slightly. "They're denying it. They've spread the word that they're going to keep Everlasting just as it is. They say that they're actually saving taxpayers' money by running the historic park as a private enterprise." She paused. "At least that's what was being tossed about until yesterday."

"What happened yesterday?" Pearl asked.

"There was an article in the *Everlasting Gazette* stating that it's a business venture and the whole community will eventually profit."

Woodrow narrowed his eyes in thought. "The only way to do that is to run it as a business. Maybe charge admission—"

"Build roller coasters," Pearl said. "Ferris wheels. The whole kit and caboodle."

Annie nodded slowly. "Exactly what we think," she said. "Can you stay for the meeting?"

"We wouldn't miss it," Woodrow said, then glanced quickly at Pearl as if expecting her to say she had other plans.

She met his look and reassured him with a nod and a smile; then they both turned back to Annie.

"We don't expect them to be up-front about their plans. They've already got quite a cover-up in motion." Just then, the twins raced into the room, and Annie pulled them to her lap. As they settled back, thumbs in mouths, she continued. "Greg suspects there are some state officials involved. Perhaps even organized crime."

Woodrow nodded and glanced at Pearl.

There was concern on Annie's face. "I didn't know about the organized crime connection when I called you. Otherwise, I don't think I would have. You must promise me that you'll only nose around for information—that you won't get involved in any other way."

"But we have a strategy," Pearl said. "We had a meeting just last night, planning it down to the minutest detail." She explained their ideas.

Annie frowned. "We don't know who we're dealing with here. We only know they're in powerful places. There are millions of dollars involved in this transaction. You could be placing yourselves in danger."

"Anything worth doing has risk involved," said Woodrow.

"I agree," said Pearl, looking up at him proudly. He'd worked in war zones feeding starving children, in racially divided communities building houses, in disease-ridden jungles photographing rare birds. He'd met danger head-on. Besides, they were simply going to help save a historic park. How dangerous could that be?

"When I called," Annie continued, "I was thinking more of your helping us find out the whos and whats—not jumping in and doing something about it." She paused. "I don't want anything to happen to you—to any of you."

Pearl dismissed her worry with a light laugh and a flick of her fingertips. "Hey! Not to worry, dear Annie. We're tough old birds!" Then she paused, her tone sobering as she continued. "These scoundrels—whoever they are—won't know what hit them."

CHAPTER
Four

Pearl and Woodrow slipped into the back of the playhouse and took their seats. There were maybe fifty to sixty other people seated in the rows in front of them.

Onstage, the set from *Phantom of the Opera* provided a rather bizarre backdrop, especially with its enormous antique chandelier, which hung precariously above the old wooden table that had been set up for the speakers. Six chairs were lined up on the far side of the table, and a podium was center stage with a microphone to one side. Stage lights illuminated the whole affair.

Pearl turned to Woodrow and muttered, "Rather dramatic, don't you think?"

"Seems appropriate to me. A phantom orchestrating the action from behind the scenes." He gave her a half smile.

"How true." She turned her attention to the six men who were now strolling across the stage. They seated themselves noisily on the metal folding chairs just as the seventh, a jovial-looking, bespectacled, round-faced man carrying a briefcase, hurried to join them. There was light applause from the audience, and smiling, the man nodded his balding head in acknowledgment. He then took his place at the podium.

"That's state senator Roland Thorpe," whispered Woodrow.

"I know," Pearl whispered back. "Champion of the little people."

"That's what he'd like folks to believe," said Woodrow.

"Ladies and gentlemen," said Thorpe after the applause died down, "we're so glad you've joined us to talk about

Everlasting's future, to clarify any questions, and to finally put to rest the rumors that have been circulating."

Thorpe leaned forward, pulled his eyeglasses from his nose, and rested his arms on the podium. His stance suggested intimacy and honesty—a man you could believe and trust.

Pearl couldn't resist rolling her eyes at Woodrow.

"Folks," Thorpe said, "we have an opportunity here that's greater than any I've seen during all my years of public service. Not only is it a wonderful opportunity for this community, but this model will someday be replicated throughout the state, perhaps even the nation."

Woodrow groaned softly. "Not the universe?" he muttered under his breath.

Pearl stifled a snicker.

"For you see, privatization is the wave of the future," Thorpe continued. "Privatization facilitates growth. It grows the economy of the community. It's more economically viable than any state or federal park system now being used. Because, dear folks, privatization cuts through red tape and bureaucracy. The result is a lean-and-mean organization that benefits all. And I believe in my heart of hearts that this is exactly what we all want here in Everlasting—growth in the local economy while maintaining the beauty of the area and keeping intact its glorious history."

There was light clapping, and Thorpe nodded his head, smiling broadly. "You see, there have been rumors and innuendoes that have threatened to derail our project. And that's why we're here tonight—to finally put to rest any more ridiculous scuttlebutt. This project *must* proceed," he said dramatically, hitting the podium with his clenched fist. "And proceed it will!"

Pearl watched the chandelier jiggle as Thorpe struck the podium again.

"Now," he said after a pause, "I want to read to you the legal disclosures pertaining to the purchase of Everlasting by the organization known at the date of this document as Everlasting Enterprises Incorporated, or EEI." He opened his briefcase and pulled out some papers, set them in place on the podium, then put his glasses on his nose, hooking the wire earpieces into place. He began to read in a monotone.

"You know what they've done, don't you?" Pearl whispered to Woodrow. He raised a brow, and she went on. "They've succeeded in keeping us from finding out who the investors are by renaming their investment group. EEI is a front for others." Already her mind was exploring ways to find out who was behind the new name.

Thorpe droned on through the legalese, and by now, half of the audience were yawning. Tapping her foot, Pearl timed the reading of the document. Twenty-seven and a half minutes. Finally, it was time for the other men on stage to take the podium.

The first three were introduced as members of the community who would raise the questions that had been posed to them by Everlasting residents. Several questions were brought up about land usage, environmental impact, and zoning. They finished with each asking a final question: One asked if those employed by the state would retain their jobs. Another brought up the question of a charge for admittance to the park. The last of the three, a younger man who'd been seated at the end of the table, asked if Everlasting would remain historically correct no matter what improvements were made.

A red flag shot to the top of Pearl's mental flagpole. She had already been feeling that the questions were staged, but the word *improvements* was open to interpretation.

Woodrow nudged her and nodded. He'd caught the same word. Pearl reached for her handbag, pulled out a notepad and pencil, and began to scribble questions of her own.

The three remaining men were introduced as representatives of EEI. They all stood to answer those staged questions. There was a quick assurance that all jobs would remain intact and new positions would be opened; the environmental impact would be negligible; and the community would of course remain the quaint, historical village people from all over loved to visit. Then they began to address the questions, answering in such endless, obscure detail that Pearl had forgotten the question by the time the EEI representative finished his lengthy answer. She looked around. Judging by the puzzled expressions, everyone else was just as confused.

Finally, state senator Roland Thorpe stood to thank the participants by name. There was no mention of accepting questions from the floor, and it was apparent that the gathering was about to be dismissed.

Pearl checked her watch. Two and a half hours had passed, and she and Woodrow had discovered nothing they didn't already know. It was time to stir the pot a little.

Just when Thorpe looked as if he were about to adjourn the meeting, Pearl stood and waved her hand. Thorpe looked to the back of the theater where she stood, but it was obvious he was about to ignore her.

There was only one thing to be done.

"Yoo-hoo!" she called out in a loud voice. Everyone craned to see who was speaking. "Senator! Back here—here in the back row. Yoo-hoo! I've got a question!"

He finally acknowledged her with a nod.

She gave the room an amiable and innocent smile. "It's a question that's very important to me. May I ask it?" She could see the men on the podium shuffling their feet and tapping their fingers on the table, anxious to be on their way. She cleared her throat loudly. "May I ask a question?"

The senator took a deep breath. "You must understand, questions were supposed to have been turned in ahead of time—"

She cut him off. "But this is a question no one would have thought of unless they'd been here tonight."

Senator Thorpe picked up his papers from the podium, straightened their edges with a soft thud, and gave her a patronizing smile. "Go ahead. What is it we haven't covered?"

She smiled. "Why aren't there any women on the agenda tonight? I know there's a glass ceiling in the business world, but my goodness, Senator, I would've thought you'd have known better."

There were titters of laughter throughout the room, and beside her, Woodrow groaned softly. But the senator's relief at such a question was palpable.

Thorpe grinned broadly. She'd disarmed him, just as she had planned.

"Can you tell me, Senator, why women weren't chosen as representatives? Or at least as consultants? The impact of EEI's wondrous plans are as important to us as to anyone else."

"They are, Miss, er, Mrs...."

"Ms. Flynn," she said. "And I say that because we females own 49.2 percent of Everlasting's shops, run 78.2 percent of the businesses, and constitute 95.1 percent of the docents. I say that it's unfair for you to have excluded us from the process."

Still smiling, Senator Thorpe raised his hand to regain the attention of the audience. "Yes, yes, I quite agree—"

"And that's not all," Pearl said. "If there are going to be profits in EEI's running of Everlasting, I, for one, want to have the chance to invest. I want to know *how* I can do that. I would like to get in on the ground floor, so to speak, and be part of this marvelous, innovative enterprise."

Again, Senator Thorpe started to speak and Pearl interrupted him. "I have some absolutely wonderful ideas I'd like to present to EEI about—"

This time the senator interrupted Pearl. He was still smiling, but if she was reading his expression correctly, he was beginning to get annoyed. He'd want to bring her tirade to a halt. He'd offer exactly what she wanted.

"Please, Ms. Flynn, let me tell you how glad I am—and I think EEI will be also—to know of your interest in our project." He paused, seeming to measure the sentiment of the audience before continuing. "And you've brought up a valid point. We do need a female perspective. I'm impressed with your homework. I think you would be quite an asset as a representative on behalf of the ladies of Everlasting."

There was applause from around the room.

"I would be honored," Pearl said, glowing a bit from all the attention.

"You *are* part of the community here?" the senator asked.

"Oh, yes, of course," said Pearl. She knew she'd have to move here immediately.

"And what is it you do, Ms. Flynn, if I may ask, that's related to Everlasting?" He seemed to be watching her carefully.

She gave him a wide smile. "Why, I'm glad you asked, Senator. I'm an artist. I paint oils of Everlasting and the vicinity." The words seemed to spill forth unbidden, and she wished she could retract them. She felt her cheeks flush as Woodrow looked up at her. She avoided his gaze.

Again the audience craned to get a better look at her. "Why, yes," said Thorpe, "I do believe you'd be perfect, Ms. Flynn. I'll pass on the word to EEI that you're our new committee representative."

"Thank you, Senator."

"Now, as soon as we're dismissed, I want you to come to the

223

front and meet the other committee members. And Ms. Flynn?"

"Yes, Senator?"

"I would love to see your oils of Everlasting. The next time I'm out this direction, will you promise to show me some of your work?"

"Of course, Senator. You just look me up in town." Now she'd have to set up shop in Everlasting. She hoped there was available space. She swallowed hard. "You just ask for me. Remember, my name's Pearl. Pearl Flynn."

"All right, Ms. Pearl Flynn," he said. "You be expecting me."

Finally the senator dismissed the meeting. Before she could say a word to Woodrow, Pearl was surrounded by audience members. They walked with her to the front of the theater, asking about her ideas, telling her about theirs, asking about her artwork and when they could see it. It seemed she'd become an instant celebrity.

She was met near the stage by the senator, who pumped her hand vigorously. He introduced her to the other committee members. In turn, they shook her hand and offered some bland words of welcome.

After several minutes, she was able to pull herself away from the group and headed back up the aisle, searching for Woodrow.

She finally found him in the foyer, absently browsing through old theater programs that were stacked on a table near the exit.

"Woodrow!" she called, unable to wait any longer to discuss all that had happened. "What did you think?"

When he turned, she was surprised by the cold expression in his eyes. It was as if he didn't know her.

"Woodrow?" she repeated softly, puzzled.

"What do I think?" he said. "You don't know me very well if you have to ask."

She put her hand on his arm, attempting to break through the emotional wall he'd put up between them. But Woodrow turned away from her and walked out of the theater.

CHAPTER
Five

The sun had barely risen when Pearl padded from the guest room to the kitchen in Annie's borrowed robe and slippers.

"Good morning," Annie said with a smile. "How about joining me out on the deck for some coffee?"

"Sounds wonderful," Pearl said sleepily.

Annie poured the steaming liquid into two mugs and handed one to Pearl. They headed through the kitchen door to the redwood deck that Greg had finished building the summer before. Just below it was an autumn vegetable garden, filled with ripe squashes, pumpkins, and herbs. They pulled chairs to the railing where the view was best and settled into them, Pearl letting out a contented sigh.

"Tell me what happened last night," Annie said. "Woodrow seemed awfully grumpy when you two got home. Said we'd talk about it this morning. Then Greg left early for school, and Woodrow left soon afterward to check out something in town. He didn't say what." She took a sip of coffee. "What happened?"

Pearl went over the details of the meeting, how she'd thrown out some statistics, then had been asked to join the committee as a representative.

Annie grinned. "Where did you get those numbers?"

A sheepish smile crept across Pearl's face, and she swallowed hard. "Well, I, ah, made them up from estimates I've seen in the past. I just figured the more precise I sounded, the better. We'll just hope no one double-checks."

Annie laughed. "You're priceless, Pearl!" She took another sip of coffee, then set down the mug. "But what about the paintings? I don't see how you'll be able to get by that prevarication."

"I wasn't lying about that," Pearl said softly, looking out at the forest that ringed the Westbrooks' property.

"You paint?" Annie was watching her carefully. "I mean, really paint?"

Pearl turned back to face her. "Yes, really. I've been taking classes. I've taken to art like a bird to a feeder. And the subject that's drawn me most has been this quaint little village and its surroundings." She sat forward, suddenly glad to tell a friend who would understand. "Even this place, Annie. The canvas I'm working on right now is of your pond, the wild geese, and your house the way it looked that first Christmas."

Annie touched her arm. "Pearl, that's wonderful! I can't wait to see your work."

"Will you help me get a place in Everlasting—something I could rent as a working studio? Right in the heart of downtown."

"Of course. I'll contact Dana. Do you remember her?"

"Oh, yes. Your realtor. How could I forget?" Pearl smiled at the memory. Annie had almost sold this beautiful house, her inheritance, to give Greg the money for a sabbatical to write a book on the mountain man Jedediah Smith. At the same time, Greg had found a rare Smith journal that would be an invaluable resource for his book. He'd put the journal up for sale to buy a house for Annie in San Francisco. Just before Annie was to sign the final papers for the sale of her inheritance, the couple had discovered their cross-purpose gifts of love to each other. "None of us will ever forget Dana," Pearl said, chuckling. "I'm just glad she didn't rush you through escrow. It might have been too late for you and Greg to save this place."

Annie laughed. "Dana is good, and we've stayed in contact. I'll give her a call and see what she can come up with." She paused. "You mean just to rent, right?"

Pearl smiled. "Actually, the more I think about it, the more I'd love for it to be long-term. I've got a little nest egg. Perhaps Dana could check into something that's a lease/option. It would need to be just outside the state-park land. And I would need it quickly—within days, if possible."

Annie nodded. "I'll get right on it. Shall I call you tonight? Or better yet, I'll have Dana call you in San Francisco to let you know what she's found."

"Perfect," said Pearl, looking at the streams of sunlight through the forest. The air smelled of fresh pine mixed with the herbs from Annie's garden. "Who ever would have thought that your great-great-grandmother and grandfather started all of this? Because they picked this very place to live, to build, a hundred and fifty years ago, you and Greg also landed here."

"Actually, if you mean getting my family to Everlasting Diggins, it was my ancestor Sheridan O'Brian's twin brother, Shamus, who turned the family toward this part of the country. He came here during the gold rush to seek his fortune. The story is that he hit quite a big strike, then promptly disappeared." She smiled as she related the story. "Sheridan, who was very Irish and very determined, took it upon herself to search for him."

"I assume she found Shamus?" Pearl asked.

"Aye, but she did!" said Annie. "At least she traced his whereabouts, and he eventually got himself back to Everlasting Diggins to reclaim his mine. Appropriately enough for an Irish lad, he'd named it Rainbow's End."

"For the pot of gold he thought he'd find there," said Pearl.

"The real gold was the community itself. Sheridan married Marcus Jade, the newspaperman who'd helped her search for her brother. Shamus returned from his adventures, and they all settled here to raise their families."

"What happened to Rainbow's End?"

Annie laughed. "The strike didn't amount to much after all. Shamus ended up making his living by opening a mercantile and selling to families who were moving into the area. Greg and I tried to find the mine once, but the area is so overgrown with brush that we gave up." She shrugged. "Maybe someday we'll try again."

Pearl frowned in thought. "I would love to paint it, as part of my Everlasting series. Do you have any old maps or a description of where it's located?"

"There was something tucked into the back of Sheridan Jade's journal. We made photocopies so we wouldn't wear out the original. I'll get you one."

Just then two little voices called out from an upstairs window. "Mommy! Mommy!"

Standing, Annie looked at Pearl. "I do believe our moments of reverie are over. This is when my day begins."

A few minutes later, the children were wriggling in their chairs at the breakfast table, and Pearl was studying the map that Annie had handed her. It was crudely drawn, and she had difficulty making out the names, but she folded it and tucked it into her pocket, then turned her attention to the twins.

"Now," she said, sliding into a seat between them, "who's going to say grace?"

"Me, me, me!" shouted Mary Beth. "It's my turn."

Annie poured their cereal, added a touch of milk, and set the bowls before them. Then she sat opposite Pearl and bowed her head.

"Dear Father," chirped Mary Beth. "Thank you for this food. Thank you for this day. And please make Auntie Pearlie marry Uncle Woodrow. We want them to be our gramma and grampa.

And God bless Mommy and Daddy and our new baby. Amen."

Pearl met Annie's gaze, and they both stifled chuckles as they poured their own bowls of cereal and milk.

On the drive back to San Francisco later that morning, Pearl and Woodrow discussed the move to Everlasting. He said he would call the other members of the group to tell them it was time to carry out their plan.

"I won't be staying with everyone else at the Westbrooks'," she announced when they had almost reached San Francisco.

Woodrow turned to her, surprise showing on his face. "You won't?"

She shook her head. "I'm going to get a studio in town—to set up my paintings." There, she'd finally said it. She held her breath and watched his face, awaiting his reaction.

He let out a long sigh. "You know, Pearl, you didn't have to go to such lengths last night."

"What do you mean?" she asked. "What lengths?"

"Lying to get appointed to the committee. You're stooping to their level by pulling such stunts. And now…you've dug yourself into a hole I don't know how you'll get out of."

"You thought I would do that?"

He ignored her question. "You lied about the statistics. I checked those out this morning."

She didn't trust her voice to answer. How could she defend herself? Woodrow still thought of her as silly, frumpy, nary-a-serious-thought-in-the-head Pearl Flynn. No, actually, his assessment of her was obviously worse than that. Dishonest had now been added to his list. She turned her head to look at the passing scenery. But the tears that stung her eyes made everything wavy and out of focus. She swallowed hard and blinked them back.

Nothing more was said except a curt good-bye when Woodrow dropped Pearl at her house. But as she unlocked her front door and stepped inside, the ringing telephone quickly drew her attention from Woodrow and their uncomfortable ride.

She tossed her handbag onto a wicker chair and hurried to the kitchen.

"Pearl?" said the female voice after Pearl had said hello. "Pearl, this is Dana—out in Everlasting."

"Oh, yes, Dana. I just this minute arrived home."

"Well, Annie told me what you're looking for, and I think I've got the ideal place for you."

"Tell me about it." Pearl settled into a chair at her bright yellow chrome-and-Formica kitchen table.

"It's a lease/option. Located just down the street from the state-park portion of Everlasting but still within the city limits. The lease is less than some of the other centrally located shops, but that's because it's rather small. It's also very rustic—unpainted wood walls, ages old. It's even got an old iron fire door, just like the other buildings in the state park." She told Pearl the lease amount as well as the selling price, should she decide on that option.

Pearl grinned, suddenly feeling better than she had all day. "It sounds perfect. There doesn't happen to be an apartment attached, does there?"

"No, I'm sorry. As I said, it's very small. But when Annie told me what you're up to, I checked with the Candlelight Inn, a bed-and-breakfast up by the old schoolhouse. It's an old Victorian that's been lovingly restored. A beautiful place. The woman who runs it, Bea Blankenship, said because it's off-season, she can give you a good price on a room. Weekly, monthly, whatever you'd like."

"Perfect," said Pearl. "Absolutely, positively perfect. When can I come look at the studio?"

"How about tomorrow?"

"I'll be there," she said without hesitation.

By the time Pearl hung up the phone, she realized that this was something she'd wanted to do for a very long time. Open a studio of her own. Paint right there in front of tourists or anybody else who wandered in. Paint all day and all night if she wanted. Sell her paintings to people who fell in love with Everlasting and wanted to take a bit of it home with them.

The thought of strangers looking at her work didn't bother her one iota. But it was the thought of her friends examining and judging her efforts that caused her mouth to get dry and her heart to skip a beat. Well, she would think about that tomorrow.

For now she had to remember that the studio was the cover she needed to go about her sleuthing while on the EEI committee. But she couldn't help smiling and had to fight the urge to kick up her heels and dance around her living room. How blessed she was at the wonderful age of sixty-something to find something that so delighted her heart!

She quickly dialed Charley's number, glad when he sounded so happy to hear from her. She told him of her new dilemma—she needed to get a dozen or so of her paintings framed in just a few days. Not only was he very happy for her venture, he said he had a friend in the framing business and would call him immediately. By the time Pearl told him good-bye, she was more thankful than ever for his friendship.

As she headed to the sunporch to take inventory of her beloved paintings of Everlasting, she kicked off her shoes and did a little Irish jig—in honor of Sheridan and Marcus Jade and all their descendants, and, of course, the young man who started it all, Shamus O'Brian.

~ ~ ~ ~ ~

That night Pearl got very little sleep, thinking about all that needed to be done to pack and be ready to open her studio by the end of the week. Before dawn, she rose to begin loading her Camaro with canvases, easels, art supplies, and clothing. She had no doubt that the studio and the B & B Dana had found would be perfect. She planned to return once a week to attend her painting class and check on the house.

At half past seven, Charley stopped by to pick up the paintings, telling her they would be ready in three days. He also gave her the notes and handouts from the class she'd missed.

At eight o'clock she crossed the street with a bag of cat food to ask a neighbor if she could bring in the mail and feed the cat. Then at 8:16, Pearl backed out of the driveway and headed the Camaro toward the highway leading to Everlasting.

At 8:22, Woodrow pulled his Land Rover around the corner leading to Pearl's house.

He'd found out about his mistake when he phoned Annie the night before to let her know when Birds of a Feather would arrive in Everlasting. In passing, Annie asked if he'd ever seen Pearl's paintings. When he said no, she proceeded to tell him all that Pearl had said about her newfound love of art and painting.

All night he'd tossed and turned, worried about how to apologize for his terribly rude behavior. The worst part was that he'd accused Pearl of lying—lying about something very dear to her heart. He felt like a heel!

He pressed on the brake and slowed to turn into Pearl's driveway. Even before he got out of his car, he knew he was too late. The Camaro was gone, and the shades were pulled down tight—as if the house would be empty for a very long time.

Three days later, Pearl had signed the lease documents and moved into both the B & B and the small studio.

She'd just finished hanging her quickly designed and hand-painted sign above the door of the studio: Uniquely Pearl. When she stood back to admire her handiwork, she heard the clatter of an engine and turned to see Charley leaning out the window of a decades-old truck she'd never seen before. He smiled and waved as the vehicle rattled to a halt in front of her studio.

"New truck?" she asked as he stepped from the vehicle and slammed the door.

"I borrowed it from a neighbor, just to bring your paintings." He grinned as she walked with him to the back of the pickup. "Can't wait for you to see them. Apparently my friend called in his whole neighborhood to help him finish on time. Very professional job, though. The frames set off your paintings beautifully."

They unpacked the pickup, carrying the paintings one by one into the shop. When they'd finished, Pearl stood back to admire the artistry of the framer. He'd chosen well. The simple wooden frames were perfect for her bright Americana style.

She grinned up at Charley. "Perfect! Absolutely perfect."

"Let's get them hung," he said. "I brought my tools. You just need to say where."

Hands on hips, Pearl surveyed the small shop. "There." She

pointed to one of the largest, a painting of Everlasting's famed City Hotel. Years ago, it had been called the Empress, and that's what she'd named the painting. "Hang *Empress* fairly high on the long wall. Okay, then the smaller one, oh, and that one too, beneath the first." Charley did as she said, then the process was repeated again and again, until finally, two hours later, they had finished.

They stood back, looking at their work. Set against the dark, rough wood walls and illumined by the track lighting Pearl had installed the day before, her paintings literally came to life. The colors seemed deeper and brighter, the balance even better than she'd anticipated. Even her easel, paint table, and high metal stool set up in the side room added to the ambiance of the setting. It was as if this little studio had been designed just for her.

"Uniquely Pearl," Charley said, obviously pleased as punch he'd been able to help.

"Now we sit back and wait for customers."

"One can't sit back and wait," Charley said. "We must get out flyers—all around town. If you'll design them, I'll get them printed and hand them out in all the other businesses around Everlasting."

Pearl nodded, frowning slightly. "I can't lose sight of my real reason for being here. The flyers will also let the other shop-keepers know that I'm their EEI representative. In case EEI checks on my community activities, at least people will know I'm here."

She went behind the counter by the door, propped herself up on a stool, and set about designing the flyer. When she was finished, she handed the paper to Charley.

"Why don't we get together for dinner tonight," he said,

"and we can discuss how they were received?"

"Good idea." She told Charley where she was staying. They agreed on a time, then he departed to get the copies of the flyers made.

Charley had just left when she heard another car stop out front. Hoping for her first customer, she hopped on the stool again, looking businesslike, busy, and friendly—just as she thought all shopkeepers should appear.

But it was Woodrow Hornberger, the last person she expected to darken the doorway of Uniquely Pearl.

For a moment neither spoke. Finally, Woodrow met her gaze. "I came to apologize," he said in his wonderful rumbling voice. "I had no reason to believe that you were lying. I so quickly jumped to the wrong conclusion. Pearl, I'm sorry." He stepped closer and now surprised her by reaching for her hand, which was resting on the countertop.

But Pearl gently removed her hand from his grasp. "Your apology is accepted, Woodrow. How did you find out?"

"Annie told me. I came by to see you a couple of days ago—at home. But you'd already left." He looked around the shop, then stepped closer to a large painting of Everlasting's main street. "This is wonderful," he murmured. He spent several minutes just browsing, looking at each painting carefully, sometimes shaking his head slightly as if in awe. Finally, he turned back to her. "I had no idea, Pearl...." His voice fell off.

Pearl laughed lightly. "I hadn't told anyone. Until, well, the other night at the meeting when I had to come up with something fast. It just didn't feel safe."

"But these are wonderful! You've got real talent, Pearl. You should've been shouting about this from the rooftops." He spotted the nearly completed painting on the easel and strolled into the side room to stand in front of it. Pearl came out from

236

behind the counter and joined him. This was her favorite painting, the one of Annie and Greg's property.

Woodrow turned to look at her. "You said you didn't feel safe, Pearl. Why?"

She looked at him solemnly for a moment before answering. "Think of your own assumptions, Woodrow. I saw the look in your eyes the night of the meeting. You'd placed me in a little box filled with only your expectations—not very high expectations, I might add. You were willing to believe that I'd acted impulsively, that I'd lied to get my way."

Woodrow reached for her hand, and this time she let him hold it as she continued. "All my life I've been labeled silly and thoughtless. I don't know when it started. But rather than dispute others' opinions, I simply played on that image. In a way, I lived up to others' expectations. Funny, silly Pearl. An airhead. Life of the party." She shrugged one shoulder.

"Oh, Pearl…"

But Pearl didn't let him finish. "It took me sixty-some years to realize that I'm not that person. That the depth of my thoughts and the desires of my heart have value. That God created me in his image. And this—" she looked back to the painting on the easel—"this act of creating something unique is as close as I can come to understanding my own uniqueness in God's sight." She frowned, wondering if Woodrow could possibly understand.

But his expression told her he did.

She brightened. "Now, enough of all that," she said, pulling her hand away from his. "I found out yesterday that my first meeting with the committee is tomorrow night. Tomorrow I would like to visit the shopkeepers in Everlasting, talk to the owners and managers, find out how they feel about EEI."

"You're taking this role seriously, aren't you?"

"Well, of course," she said. "It's a ruse to find out what EEI's up to. Besides, what better place could I be in to fight for the rights of all of us shopkeepers?"

Woodrow nodded. "It occurs to me, Pearl, that God put just the right combination of spunk and fun and leadership abilities in you." He smiled. "I think you're just scratching the surface of your abilities."

Pearl looked up at him in wonder. "You do?"

He nodded again. "I do."

She shook her head slowly, narrowing her eyes. "I didn't think I'd ever live to see the day that those words would fall from your lips, Woodrow Hornberger."

He grinned. "I'll make you a deal, Pearl." His tone was half teasing, half tender.

"What kind of deal is that?"

"You just got through saying I'd put you in a little box."

She nodded.

"Well, my dear, I do believe you've done the same with me."

"Now, how's that?"

"You haven't believed that I could see beyond that image you've projected so long—that colorful, delightful creature you've always been to me."

Pearl was so stunned she could have fallen over. "Colorful? Delightful? Me?"

He nodded. "Not only have you guessed how I have seen you—you've also seen me, I daresay, as stuffy and rigid."

Pearl felt her cheeks color a bit.

"Isn't that true?" he asked.

"Well, not quite," she said, wondering how much she should tell. Well, why not? She'd just told him more about herself than she'd ever told anyone. She laughed. "You'd be surprised how I see you."

"Tell me," he said, looking apprehensive.

"Just the other day—when you came to my door?"

He nodded.

"Well, I looked up at you, standing there, looking so handsome, and the three words that came to mind were debonair, graceful, and stately." She smiled into his surprised eyes. "Rigid and stuffy never entered my mind."

He looked enormously pleased. "Well."

"We keep getting off the subject," she said. They were still staring into each other's eyes.

"Ah, well, yes. That's true," Woodrow said, then cleared his throat. "Ah, back to tomorrow night's meeting. Do you suppose there would be any objection to my accompanying you?"

"There wouldn't be from me," said Pearl sweetly, wondering why her heart seemed to be dancing. "I think you would be a tremendous asset."

"Hmm. You're the creative one of the two of us, Pearl—how do you think we can convince them that I'm needed on the committee?"

"Why don't we form a new organization?"

"What do you have in mind?"

"Listen to this," she said excitedly, as the thought began to take on substance. "I've always thought that it was odd that Everlasting didn't have its own historical society."

"That's true," said Woodrow.

"Well, let's form one. All of the Birds-of-a-Feather members will, of course, join immediately. Maybe Annie and Greg can help us with a charter. Print it out on their computer. We'll head around town to see if we can get other shopkeepers, docents, and musicians—anyone who has anything to do with the state park—to join. You'll be president."

"And as president, I'll insist on being part of EEI's committee." He grinned appreciatively.

"But of course, my dear," she said, resisting the urge to pat

239

him on the cheek. "Um, let's see. A name." She narrowed her eyes in thought. "How about the Everlasting Circle of History? Or since EEI's so fond of acronyms, ECH."

"You've done it again, Pearl," he said, looking for all the world as if he might kiss her. But he touched her cheek gently instead. "How about if I go out and tell the others—they're setting up camp at the Westbrooks', by the way—and sit down with Annie to devise a charter?"

"Perfect," said Pearl.

"Then, my dear, how about joining me for dinner tonight?"

"I would enjoy that," Pearl said, her heart sinking. "But I have other plans. I'm sorry. Charley—"

Just then another shadow fell across the open doorway. "Did I hear my name?" said Charley Stiles. "Sounds like I arrived just in time to defend myself." He laughed at his own joke and stepped inside to shake hands with Woodrow. "Good to see you, Woody."

The three chatted a few minutes about the campsite at the pond and their upcoming activities. Charley said that Theda, Flora, and Gabe had already signed up for the docent-orientation class that was to start on Saturday and run on consecutive Saturdays for six weeks. They'd all been pleased to find out that they could work part-time in the museum, dressed in period costumes, starting immediately. Wyatt and Charley had auditioned as street musicians and would begin playing the following morning, Wyatt on the harmonica and Charley on the banjo.

Woodrow was cordial as they talked, but there was definitely an air of disappointment about him, Pearl thought sadly. And she knew it had to do with Charley.

The three were interrupted by the sound of tires on gravel as another car slowed, then halted in front of the store.

"Your first customer!" Charley said triumphantly as he

stepped to the window and peered out.

"I don't think so," said Pearl, noting the official-looking black Mercedes. A chauffeur stepped out gracefully, opened the rear passenger door, then stood back as his passenger emerged.

"It's Senator Thorpe," said Woodrow.

CHAPTER
Seven

Woodrow watched in awe as Pearl Flynn charmed Senator Thorpe. She took matters into her hands immediately upon his arrival, made introductions, then gave him a tour of her studio, stopping to discuss each painting and its attributes, as if she'd been training all her life to play this role. Only it wasn't a role. Her unique and colorful artistry filled her heart so that her joy spilled out naturally.

Woodrow's admiration grew as he watched her giving Thorpe rapt attention. Her hands seemed almost fluid as she gestured toward her paintings, and her animated face took on a glow of satisfaction and self-confidence as she spoke. Woodrow wondered if she had changed that much…or if he was just now seeing through to her soul?

"I'd like to purchase one of your paintings," said Thorpe after the tour was complete. He smiled at her. "Which would you recommend for my Sacramento office?"

"Well, my goodness, Senator," said Pearl. "I thought you'd come here to talk about EEI—not to look at my work. Not that I'm displeased…"

He laughed. "Actually, I came out of curiosity, but now I find I'm so taken with your paintings that I don't want to leave without one."

"In that case, I would recommend *Main Street*." She strolled to the wall where the painting hung, and Charley and Woodrow exchanged glances. It appeared Pearl was about to make her first sale. "It will remind you of this charming town after it has become that model you said would be used throughout the country."

Woodrow exchanged another glance with Charley, who raised a brow. She was obviously baiting the senator. Woodrow held his breath, waiting to see what would happen next.

"Ah yes, Pearl. You're right, of course." Thorpe seemed extremely pleased that she'd remembered his words.

"Why, Senator," she said with a wink, then lowered her voice slightly, but Woodrow and Charley could still hear her words. "We all know that profit is profit. Progress is progress. If EEI's running of Everlasting is as successful as it appears, there will be profits to be had, am I right?"

A cold expression appeared in Thorpe's eyes, then quickly disappeared.

"I said at the meeting that I wanted to be in on those profits," she continued calmly. "There's nothing illegal about that, is there?"

"Of course not," he said brusquely.

"Perhaps EEI's been worried about the wrong thing. They've been concerned about all of us making a fuss about the amusement park, when what we really want is to share in the success of the model."

Senator Thorpe looked uncomfortable. "I believe these issues are best left to discussion at the committee meeting tomorrow night."

"That's something else I wanted to talk to you about," Pearl said sweetly, giving him another of her charming smiles.

"What's that?" Now Thorpe looked as if he couldn't wait to get out of the studio.

Pearl took him by the arm and led him back to where Woodrow was standing by the counter. "I suppose during your trips here you've heard of the Everlasting Circle of History."

"Ah, no."

"Well, it's a very strong group, and getting stronger all the time," she said seriously. "And Woodrow, besides being the lifeblood of the organization, is also its president. As an official part of the committee, I would like to invite him to join us tomorrow night."

Woodrow simply nodded and smiled at the senator, who was looking as if he knew he'd met his match in one Pearl Flynn. Woodrow supposed Thorpe had thought he would sweep in and charm Pearl into becoming his ally. Buying her painting was perhaps a calculated effort to buy her silence—or at least her gratitude.

"It would be an honor, Woodrow, to have you join us. But you must understand that it will be as a silent member only—no voting privileges. We had agreed to a limit of seven members. When I asked Pearl to join us the other night, she made up that final seat on the committee." He laughed lightly. "But don't feel badly—I'm not a voting member either."

Thorpe turned back to *Main Street,* strolling over to stand beneath it. "I do believe you're right, dear," he said to Pearl. "I'll take it."

She told him the price, and even though the amount was enormous for an unknown artist, Thorpe didn't even blink. "Yes," he said, pulling out his checkbook. "This will be perfect."

Pearl was so delighted she could only nod as he handed her the check.

"What scenes do you plan to paint next?" he asked her as Charley wrapped the painting in brown paper.

Pearl nodded to the unfinished canvas. "As soon as I complete this work, I'll continue with others of Everlasting. A friend just told me about an ancestor's gold mine. I might try to find it. I think it would make a wonderful subject."

Woodrow, still leaning casually against the counter, noticed that Thorpe's expression suddenly changed.

"Gold mine, eh?" he said, taking one end of the wrapped painting to help Charley carry it to the car. "Very interesting. I'd like to hear more about that on our next visit."

Woodrow suddenly felt a chill travel up his spine. There was something in Thorpe's expression that hadn't been there before. It was as if he were looking at Pearl in a different light, and it wasn't one of admiration.

She felt it too, because as soon as Senator Thorpe's driver had placed the package in the trunk, helped the senator into the car, and driven away, Pearl turned to Woodrow, her eyes questioning.

"What happened?" she asked. "I thought everything was fine until just before he left."

"Something changed in his attitude. I think he was disgruntled because he came here to sweep you off your feet." He chuckled. "And you obviously weren't about to be swept anywhere. You turned around whatever agenda he had and used it for your advantage."

Looking pleased at his words, Pearl picked up the senator's check again and studied it.

"Your first sale," said Woodrow. "How does it feel?"

She smiled into his eyes, and his heart skipped a beat.

"The best part about it," she said, "is that now we can afford to hire a lawyer."

"A lawyer?" Charley asked. "What for?"

Pearl laughed. "I thought that part would be obvious. We need to have someone go over every legality involved in the pending sale. There may be a loophole. Or a clue as to what's really at stake here."

"My brother-in-law's an attorney," said Charley. "He handles real estate. He's in Sacramento. I can give him a call."

"Good idea," said Pearl, and Woodrow nodded in agreement.

"Contact him as soon as you can. If we can get the paperwork we need from the EEI meeting tomorrow night, then he can get started on his search."

Woodrow narrowed his eyes in thought. "You've got something else in mind for Birds of a Feather, don't you? I mean, something besides our snooping around here in Everlasting."

"I've had a feeling from the beginning that Nuggetworld isn't the real issue."

"Nuggetworld?" Charley asked, puzzled.

"Goldyland, Digginsville, Bear Flags over Everlasting— whatever EEI decides to call it," Pearl said. "I think all that's a smoke screen they've thrown out to get us off track. I think this little committee is a ruse to give us the idea that they're letting us in on their secrets."

"Why do you think that?" Charley asked.

"Any corporation worth its salt wouldn't let the likes of me jump right into the saltshaker."

"Don't put yourself down, Pearl," Woodrow said gently.

She surprised him by chuckling. "I was about to say—or the likes of you, Mr. ECH president!" Then she paused a moment and frowned. "I wonder if EEI's the source of the theme park and organized-crime rumors. Maybe just to send us off on some wild-goose chase." She raised a brow. "Not a bad thing for Birds of a Feather."

But Woodrow didn't laugh. "Even if organized crime has nothing to do with it, I'm still of the opinion that these people are dangerous. Did you catch the look in Thorpe's eyes as he left?"

She nodded. "But he's a well-known state senator. He may be lining his pockets with EEI political-influence money, but he's too public a figure to go beyond that, don't you think?" She looked uncertain.

Woodrow couldn't resist reaching out to touch her shoulder—right there in front of Charley Stiles. "We can't be too careful." By now the afternoon sun was casting long shadows along the street outside. Soon it would be closing time, and she would head to the B & B—alone. "Pearl, I worry about you staying here in town without the rest of us."

"I'll be with Charley this evening," she reminded him, and he let his arm drop from her shoulder.

Woodrow checked his watch, not wanting to be around when the two left together. "I'd better be going myself," he said casually. "As president of ECH, I'm a busy man."

"Give my best to Annie and Greg," Pearl said, following him through the door and onto the rustic porch of Uniquely Pearl.

He gave her a quick wave as he got into the Land Rover. For a moment she stood on the porch, her colorful, long, sweeping dress looking as artistic as any of her paintings. He waved again as he rounded the corner, and when he looked into the rearview mirror, Pearl surprised him by blowing him a kiss.

The following night's EEI meeting was held in the City Hotel dining room. All the participants were seated at one long table. Since the senator was absent, an EEI spokesperson led the proceedings.

Pearl introduced Woodrow to the others in the group, and he was greeted cordially. A few asked questions about Everlasting Circle of History, but none of the six representatives seemed particularly curious or surprised they hadn't heard of ECH. As Pearl had pointed out the day before, it seemed almost too easy to weasel their way into the inner workings of this committee.

The meeting droned on through the evening. Each of the

committee members gave a report on topics such as environmental impact, parking issues, and publicity. Finally, Pearl was asked to give a report on behalf of the Everlasting shopkeepers.

"An issue has been raised," she began, "that needs to be handled before it gets blown way out of proportion." She had their attention immediately, just as she'd planned. Smiling sweetly, she continued. "You see, the rumors about the theme park simply will not die." She feigned a sigh. "I do believe that the only way to dispel them is to circulate a copy of the escrow papers for the sale of Everlasting. I know that some accounts of the contents were published in the *Gazette*, but the shopkeepers would like a full disclosure. They'd like to see what all was included in the offer."

Joe Horn, one of the EEI reps, a slim man with steel-colored hair, leaned forward across the table. He sat at the end opposite Woodrow and Pearl and seemed to be EEI's choice for leader of the group in the absence of Senator Thorpe.

"That document is confidential," he said calmly. "You can understand why it's not in the best interests of either the state of California or EEI to make that kind of information public."

"You are aware of the rumors?" Pearl persisted.

"Oh yes," said Horn, and the others around the table nodded their heads.

"I think the only way to put to rest all the innuendo is by providing full disclosure," said Pearl. "As I mentioned the other night, there are many who would like to be in on the profits if there is a business venture included in the sale." She frowned, as if considering a new thought. "They're clamoring for the chance, but also worried about things such as, well, for instance, zoning laws."

Woodrow stifled a smile. Pearl was doing it again: throwing out curveballs wild enough to make even the most sophisticated hitters dizzy. She gave them figures and statistics and quotes, wandering everywhere except across home plate until everyone around the table was yawning. Finally, she said, "Now, gentlemen, can anyone tell me if Everlasting is zoned for something as enormous as a theme park—a place that thousands might visit each day?"

The men exchanged glances, then Joe Horn shrugged. "I don't know what this has to do with the sale of the land. We've made our intentions very clear. We are not going to change Everlasting. There would be no reason for zoning to be an issue."

Pearl smiled and nodded happily. "If that's the case," she said, pausing as if a brilliant thought had suddenly occurred, "I've got an even better idea. Since you are adamant about Everlasting continuing as is, why not open the offer for investment to the community? Run the corporation just as some of the more innovative airlines run their companies. Community-owned, but EEI remains in control of the whole operation." She beamed. "What a perfect solution! If there are indeed profits to be made—we all win."

Woodrow watched as the EEI committee members fumbled with their responses, looking at each other, then back to Pearl.

She leaned forward. "The other night Senator Thorpe said that Everlasting would become more efficient and profitable under EEI, that it would serve as a model for other such historic parks around the nation. What better way to show your appreciation for the people who work here? I recommend that you pass on some of those savings, gentlemen. Let everyone get involved. I'll get started immediately with getting the word out."

Again there was hemming and hawing and clearing of throats. "Well, I do see your point, Ms. Flynn," said Joe Horn. "I'll certainly bring it up to the EEI CEO and board of directors. I would recommend that you, ah, not get the community all riled up over this. The profits are going to be negligible. This is, after all, a state historic park; we are doing this ultimately for the people."

"Well," Pearl said, "there *is* something else I might mention." Collective sighs rose from around the table. "I do believe if the shopkeepers and others in Everlasting could see all the documents related to this sale, they might not be so inclined to pursue the investment angle."

Again, Woodrow stifled a smile. Pearl was about to blackmail EEI.

"And why is that, Ms. Flynn?" asked Joe Horn.

"If the profits are truly negligible as you say, well, there really wouldn't be any point, right?" She gave him another of her sweet smiles.

"Yes, well, that's true," said Joe Horn. This time he glared at her. "We'll take the matter into consideration. We'll get back to you, and the, ah, other shopkeepers in Everlasting."

"Thank you," said Pearl. "When?"

His eyes pierced hers. "I said we'd get back to you. The timing is really up to us."

For a moment there was no other sound in the room. Woodrow realized with a stab of fear that Pearl had just made another enemy.

CHAPTER

T he weeks raced by for the Birds-of-a-Feather gang, and autumn began to creep closer to winter.

Pearl moved down Main Street on her usual morning stroll, talking to shopkeepers and owners, musicians, and vendors. She called out hellos, and once in a while, stopped to chat. The shops were now decorated for Christmas, and the result was charming. Twinkling white lights, Christmas trees, pine boughs, and cedar garlands had suddenly turned the town into a Norman Rockwell painting.

Escrow was still in process, due to close a few days after Christmas—only two weeks away. EEI was making a concerted effort to stall providing their promised deeds, disclosures, and escrow papers; they were also becoming more closemouthed than ever. The meetings had become cursory at best. Even the community of Everlasting had become complacent, willing to accept that EEI had the best of intentions for keeping the historic town exactly as it was now.

It was a Saturday, so all the Birds members, in gold rush costume, were working in their volunteer positions. Pearl turned into the mercantile to talk with Theda, Flora, and Gabe. She smiled a greeting to the three, who were milling about with some of the other docents waiting to give tours to park visitors.

Theda, dressed in cranberry red velvet and carrying a fur muff, waved a hello and strolled over to Pearl, her long skirt swishing around her ankles. Flora followed behind her sister, dressed in forest green satin that was trimmed with black lace.

Even Gabe was decked out for the season, his costume that of a dandy gambler. He looked up and nodded, then went back to his discussion with some of the park visitors about Everlasting's history.

Theda drew closer and whispered, "Have you heard that Senator Thorpe will be here today?"

"No, not a word," Pearl said, frowning. "When was it announced?"

"Someone from Sacramento called the museum. He's going to hold a press conference at the gazebo at noon."

"I wonder what he's got up his sleeve?" Flora said.

Pearl let out a sigh. She was beginning to lose her patience with EEI, their stonewalling, and especially their obvious ally, Thorpe. "Maybe we should spread the word—raise a bit of a ruckus in front of the press."

Theda grinned. "Exactly what do you have in mind?"

"I don't know yet."

The other two chuckled. "*Yet* is the operative word," Theda said. "I'm confident you'll think of something before noon."

Gabe stepped over to join them. "Think of something for what occasion?" he asked.

They told him of the senator's impending visit, and he looked worried. "I don't think we should take this lightly." He glanced around to see who might be listening. "I've heard only this morning that escrow might close early. I wonder if that's why Thorpe is coming today—to make some sort of announcement."

Pearl's heart sank. The three talked for a few more minutes; then she headed out onto Main Street again. Charley was just taking his banjo from its case, and Wyatt was standing, one foot propped on a log bench, warming up his harmonica. They both looked up and smiled as she approached.

"How's Everlasting's most famous artist?" Charley said with a grin.

"Not very well right now," she said. She told them about the press conference.

"My brother-in-law was planning to stop by this evening with his findings," said Charley. "I called him after classes yesterday, and he said that he'd finally made some progress getting through the web of red tape surrounding this deal. He sounded pretty excited."

"I wonder if he could make it here sooner?" Wyatt asked. "Maybe we're the ones who need to call the press conference."

Pearl nodded in agreement. "I've got his phone number at the shop. I'll call and see what we can set up."

But Charley looked doubtful. "His appointments are booked weeks, sometimes months, in advance. And, of course, that's not considering his hours in court." He noticed Pearl's crestfallen look and touched her arm. "Maybe he can give you something to go on by phone, then deliver whatever else he's got tonight in person."

She nodded, feeling more hopeful. "Where are we supposed to meet tonight?"

"I suggested Annie and Greg's. They've agreed—especially since most of us are already out there. Woodrow mentioned that it's probably not a good idea for all the Birds to be seen together in town."

"That's fine. Meantime, I'll give your brother-in-law a call and see what he's uncovered. Then I'll see everyone tonight. I plan to keep the shop open late since it's a Saturday so close to Christmas. Don't worry if I'm a bit late."

Main Street was now filled with visitors milling about, and Pearl said her good-byes to Wyatt and Charley, then stepped back to listen to them play. Even in the midst of her worry, she couldn't help smiling. The two men, dressed like mule skinners, played a lively "Oh, Susannah." People gathered nearer to listen, tapping their feet and humming along.

After a few minutes, she gave Wyatt and Charley a small wave and went on her way. Next she stopped by the *Everlasting Gazette* office to look for Woodrow. He'd taken a volunteer position, playing the role of editor in the *Gazette's* museum and explaining the 150-year-old history of the building and its artifacts to visitors.

Bess, the *Gazette's* current editor and museum curator, looked up as Pearl entered. "Well, hello, Pearl," she said pleasantly.

"Is Woodrow here?" Pearl asked.

"Downstairs in the museum, dear. He's preparing for our big morning."

Pearl was surprised. Woodrow hadn't said anything about a special group coming in. "Reporters?"

"Yes, dear. How did you know? From some of the biggest newspapers in the region. They're getting together in Sonora for their annual conference. They're usually in bigger cities. First time they've picked a little community."

Pearl nodded. The senator was obviously using their conference for his own press purposes.

"I'll run down and see Woodrow. I promise I won't keep him but a minute."

"He probably needs a break. He's been here helping everyone prepare since dawn."

Pearl headed down the stairs and spotted Woodrow by one of the ancient printing presses. He looked up and smiled a greeting. He looked more handsome than ever in his nineteenth-century editor's costume.

"Can I steal you away for a minute?" she asked. "Bess said you need a break."

"Ah, that I do," he agreed, taking off his green visor. "Let's go next door for some coffee. We can take it out on the terrace."

"Perfect," said Pearl.

A few minutes later, coffees in hand, they rounded the corner of the old Falcon Hotel and walked through the iron gate to a brick terrace behind the century-and-a-half-old building. A fountain bubbled a welcome, and some nearly spent winter roses circled the terrace, their light perfume carrying on the morning breeze. It was the kind of place Fred Astaire might have danced with Ginger Rogers, Pearl thought with a sigh as she and Woodrow strolled to a cast-iron love seat and sat down.

Pearl immediately told Woodrow about the press conference Senator Thorpe had called, and he nodded solemnly. "EEI's time line's been stepped up whether or not we're prepared," he said.

"I'll call the attorney, but we may be too late to stop the sale—if that's what Thorpe's about to announce."

"Do you have any idea what the attorney's found?"

"No, but I'll let you know as soon as I find out."

"I'm not going to be of much help today—of all days," Woodrow said. "I'm giving a talk to the newspapermen. I really can't get away."

Pearl suddenly smiled and arched a brow. "Newspapermen?"

Woodrow caught her look, threw back his head, and laughed. "No wonder I love you so! I know what you're thinking...that while I've got the media as a captive audience, I can give them some real infor—"

"What did you say?"

"About the captive audience, you mean?" he teased.

"No," she said. "Before that."

"About knowing what you're thinking?"

"Ah, no. Before that."

Suddenly, he caught her hand and lifted it to his lips. "Oh, you mean the part about loving you?"

She nodded, almost too stunned to speak. No man had ever before uttered those words to her. "Love?" she whispered, just to make sure she hadn't heard him wrong.

He smiled gently. "Haven't you guessed by now, Pearl?" For once she was speechless and waited for him to go on. "For weeks now, I've known. I've wanted to say something. I was waiting until we had some time alone, maybe in a special place." He laughed self-consciously, looking down at his worn costume, the ruffled armband on his sleeve. "I really didn't expect that time to be now. It's just that I've thought so often about the wonder of loving, it just, well, spilled out."

"You love me?" were the only words that Pearl could manage. "Me?"

"I know it's a shock, Pearl. And I couldn't hope that you'd care for me as much as I do you. I'll understand if you never want to see me again—I mean, in a romantic way. I promise, I won't ever speak of love again if you say so." His eyes searched her face.

"Me?" Pearl said again. "You love me?"

He chuckled softly. "Yes, Pearl. You."

"Oh, Woodrow," she said, breathlessly. "I—I don't know what to say." Her heart pounded so hard she thought he might hear it.

"You don't need to say anything, Pearl. Just know that you've been in my heart for a very long time."

She nodded wordlessly and drew in a very deep breath. "Woodrow, there's so much I want to tell you. I—"

Pearl stopped midsentence as the clamor of footsteps and a voice calling her name drifted from the street side of the terrace. She and Woodrow exchanged puzzled glances, then turned to see who was coming.

"It's Charley Stiles," muttered Woodrow. "I'd know his voice anywhere."

Charley, red-faced, carrying his banjo, galloped around the corner and into sight. "I just heard from my brother-in-law!" he panted. "On the cell phone. He's going to call you at Uniquely Pearl in just a few minutes. I told him you'd be there; then someone said they'd just stopped by and you weren't there, so I came hunting. I hope I didn't interrupt anything."

Woodrow let out a very deep, very long, very noisy sigh.

Pearl stood, gave Woodrow a tender glance, then headed back through the gate with Charley. He returned to his corner, banjo in hand, and she walked to her shop.

She unlocked the door and let herself in, trying to concentrate on the phone call she was about to receive—instead of the heart-thumping words Woodrow had just spoken.

Absently, she looked around her shop, noting the empty spaces on the walls. She'd sold four paintings, five counting the one that Senator Thorpe had bought. She had finished the painting of Annie and Greg's property, which she'd titled *The Pond*. It was framed and hanging in the place where *Main Street* used to be.

But try as she might, her mind wasn't on her paintings. It was on Woodrow and those three beautiful words he'd said to her.

Finally the telephone rang. Once…twice…three times by the time she'd raced across her studio to reach it. She slid onto the stool behind her counter and reached for the receiver.

A female voice asked her to hold for the attorney. A moment later, he came on the line. "Ben Johnson here."

"Ah yes, hello, Mr. Johnson."

"Ms. Flynn, I'm glad I reached you, though I plan to be out there tonight to give you all the details in person."

Pearl explained about the news conference, and when she'd

257

finished, Johnson said, "You can bring up this issue at the conference, but I've got the proof in hand. Without it, what you say is so much innuendo. EEI and Thorpe know that; they could easily turn the tables and make you look very foolish."

"What is it you've found?" Pearl could feel her heart pounding.

"I've uncovered some doctoring of the plot maps drawn for the purpose of the sale."

"What do you mean?"

"These are legal documents describing the exact property lines. Works the same whether you're buying a single dwelling or a shopping mall. Or a city, as in the case of Everlasting. The state has owned a certain acreage for a number of years, but a few weeks before EEI made their offer for Everlasting, the plot map was redrawn. There was no purchase recorded of additional land to bring about this change, but apparently someone went through old records to check on claims that miners had simply walked away from."

"Are you thinking what I'm thinking?" Pearl breathed into the phone.

"If it has to do with mineral rights, then we're on the same wavelength," Johnson said.

"I agree with you about needing proof," Pearl said. "But can you give me the location of the area that's been added?"

"Sure thing." She could hear him riffling through some papers. "Here it is." He gave her a detailed description of where to find the plot.

"Pearl," Johnson warned before he hung up, "don't go out there alone—if that's what you've got in mind. Escrow is due to close any day, and I wouldn't be surprised if EEI's got equipment in place and ready to roll."

"I'll be careful," she promised. "And I'll see you tonight."

Pearl quickly turned around the Closed sign to face the

street, locked the door, then strode back through town to the B & B. It didn't take her long to pull on a pair of blue jeans, some sneakers, and a heavy wool sweater. Minutes later, she was in the Camaro, heading to the main highway leading out of town. In her pocket was the map of Rainbow's End that Annie had given her weeks ago.

She only wished that Woodrow could be with her, or that she could have at least told him the news of her discovery. But he was probably in the middle of his talk to the newspapermen right now.

For the next hour, she wound through the Sierra Nevada foothills. The day had dawned bright and clear, but there were now clouds forming over the mountains, darkening every minute. California's winters typically didn't begin until January, so she wasn't worried about snow. But she could tell that the temperature had dropped.

She pressed on the accelerator in her hurry to reach a ridge of volcanic rock overlooking the valley. The ridge was mentioned on both the plot map that Johnson described and on the map that Annie had given her. She rounded several hairpin turns, then came to a turnoff. The road was narrow and covered only with gravel, but she knew by its location that it was the one she was looking for.

The road climbed upward now, and the gravel disappeared. Pearl thought suddenly of Woodrow's Land Rover. It was much more suited for this terrain than her Camaro.

The car bumped and thumped along the rutted road. A sheer drop-off was on one side and a thick forest on the other. Pearl whispered a prayer and kept driving, though now the car was barely creeping along.

One more rise, she thought, peering ahead. Then she should reach the ridge. She saw an outcropping of black volcanic rock just beyond the next curve and pointed the Camaro toward it.

A large rock suddenly appeared in the road in front of her, and with sickening realization, Pearl heard rather than felt the underside of the car hit the obstacle solidly. The Camaro halted. The dust that had been trailing behind her billowed and rose into the cloudy skies. She coughed as it covered the car.

Woodrow wrapped up his talk on the *Everlasting Gazette* by relating some of its colorful history. He told his audience of the fiery romance between Marcus Jade, who at that time was the editor-owner of the *Grizzlyclaw Gazette* in San Francisco, and the lovely Sheridan O'Brian, who'd come to Everlasting Diggins to find her missing twin brother.

After he and Sheridan fell in love, married, and decided to stay in Everlasting, Jade took over the *Herald Star,* renaming it the *Everlasting Gazette,* a name that had stuck through the following century.

Woodrow finished his talk with a focus on Jade himself. Ink was in the young man's blood. But so was the search for justice and truth. More than once, Jade laid his life on the line as he pursued every avenue to see that the people of his community knew the truth behind crooked politicians or others who sought to deceive. By the time Marcus Jade died in the 1930s, he'd received some of the highest honors that could be bestowed on investigative newspapermen of that era.

"In short," Woodrow concluded, "though the *Everlasting Gazette* may seem like small potatoes to those of you from the *Sacramento Bee* or the *Los Angeles Times,* it produced some of the most honest, forthright, and courageous reporters in the history of the gold rush and the decades that followed. Marcus Jade left us a legacy of integrity in reporting that we can't ignore."

Woodrow took a deep breath. The reporters were still

watching him attentively. "Now in that same vein, there is something else you must know. What I'm about to tell you cannot be proven, but perhaps you can help us prove our suspicions, using those same investigative skills that Marcus Jade was known for."

For another several minutes Woodrow proceeded to tell the men and women everything he knew to be true, and what he and others suspected, about the pending sale of Everlasting to EEI. The reporters took notes, writing almost furiously.

Finally he asked for questions. Hands shot up and voices called out. Woodrow took one at a time, answering each as best he knew how.

"We can't print any of this without proof," said a young red-headed reporter from the *Bee*.

"No one knows that better than I," said Woodrow. "If you print even our suspicions at this point, we could be held for libel."

"Do you think the press conference is to make some grand announcement about the sale?" asked another reporter.

"I would bet on it," said Woodrow. "I think, however, that if you bring up some of these allegations, perhaps the senator will become flustered. Maybe give something away."

"And you definitely think EEI's not going to turn Everlasting into a theme park?"

"Again, I can't say for sure. But it does seem to be a smoke screen for something else. The trouble is, that something else hasn't yet been discovered."

"Can we stay in touch with you?" asked a tall, thin woman sitting near the front. "Especially following the announcement—whatever it is—at the press conference today."

"Of course," said Woodrow. "And there's someone I'd like you to meet. She's actually been the driving force behind our efforts. Her name is Pearl Flynn. Perhaps you can interview her following the press conference."

A few more questions were asked; then finally Woodrow said, "There's a group of people here in Everlasting who have been working quietly behind the scenes for the past several weeks. As I said, Pearl Flynn is the driving force. But the others have been working equally hard to see that justice is done. You might want to interview them to get their perspectives." He gave their names and where they could be found.

Finally, his talk was over, and the reporters, after asking a few more questions, filed from the museum to head over to the gazebo. Woodrow exited right behind them and hurried over to Uniquely Pearl.

When he arrived at the front door and saw the Closed sign, he became alarmed. Pearl had left him to receive a phone call from the attorney. She must have left afterward. He headed immediately to the B & B, hoping to catch her there. Bea, the proprietor, said she'd seen Pearl leave in a rush a few hours before. But Pearl had only given her a wave as she drove off. And no, she hadn't any idea where Pearl was headed.

He hurried back into downtown. By now a large crowd was gathering around the gazebo, which had been decorated with small white lights and garlands of holly and cedar, and just as Woodrow was threading his way through the crowd, Senator Thorpe's black Mercedes drove into the gravel parking lot adjacent to the park.

There was a smattering of applause as the senator stepped before a lectern that had been set up for him. He smiled at the crowd, cleared his throat, and said, "Ladies and gentlemen, the announcement I'm about to make is one of vital importance...."

~ ~ ~ ~ ~

Pearl opened the car door, coughing in the still-rising dust. With a sigh, she stooped and looked under the car. Her worst fears were realized. The oil pan, or whatever it was called, was cracked. She could see a dark liquid dripping onto the rock, then trailing down into the soft, dusty soil.

No one knew her whereabouts, she suddenly thought, her shoulders slumping. She had left no messages for Woodrow, Charley, or any of the other Birds-of-a-Feather gang. It might be days before anyone discovered where she'd gone.

She looked around. Clouds were gathering, and a brisk wind had kicked up. She wrapped her arms across herself and shivered, looking around and trying to decide what to do next.

She'd come out here to find a gold mine, and she was close to the outcropping of black rock that both maps had described. So really, she thought with another deep sigh, she should continue on her quest by foot. Certainly no other alternative came to mind.

Trying to look on the bright side, she would merely go it alone and pray that someone would call Ben Johnson and find out about the information he'd given her.

They'd find out, of course, if he weren't tied up with clients. Or in court. Or at lunch. Or… She didn't let herself finish the bleak thought that he might be unreachable for the rest of the day.

She trudged up the incline, trying to keep her fears at bay.

Dear Lord, I know you're with me, she prayed as she walked. *No one else knows where I am. But you do! Give me strength to endure what's ahead. And courage, too, Lord, for I'm beginning to get a little worried.*

She looked up at the darkening clouds. If she was worried now, she could only imagine how she'd be come nightfall.

She pushed away the thought and instead pictured placing her hand in her heavenly Father's. She murmured the words of Isaiah 41:13: "For I am the LORD, your God, who takes hold of your right hand and says to you, Do not fear; I will help you."

After a few more minutes, she reached the top of the ridge. The outcropping of volcanic rock was right where it had been described.

She turned back to the south and could now see Everlasting. She smiled. It might be too far to walk, but it was comforting that the little village looked so solid and friendly in the distance. She glanced at her watch and, noting that it was just after noon, wondered what lies Senator Thorpe was about to tell.

She turned, letting her gaze sweep the surrounding area. Though she was standing on a jutting ridge, above her the mountains continued to rise, and to the north, a deep canyon swept downward. She pulled out the plot description the attorney had given her and the map of Rainbow's End and turned them this way, then that, trying to match them to her location. She scratched her head, turning in a complete circle, unable to make any sense of either.

Finally, she concentrated on the Shamus O'Brian map, narrowing her eyes as she scanned the horizon searching for landmarks. Slightly beyond the outcropping of black rock, he'd drawn a cut in the terrain with sheer granite sides. Rainbow's End, according to his record, was centered just below a stand of oaks near the base of the cut where a small stream flowed.

The canyon, or small valley, appeared larger somehow than what was drawn. This might be the same place, Pearl thought, if through the decades, floods and fires had eroded the original cut in the terrain; if new foliage had grown up enough to cover the cliffs and the stream at their base. Of course, those were pretty big ifs.

A glint of metal caught her attention near the bottom of the canyon. Pearl stepped to a higher part of the ridge and looked again. It appeared to be the roof of a crude shed, barely visible through the heavy foliage.

She looked at the O'Brian map again. No sign of any dwelling. But of course, she thought, what would be remaining after 150 years, anyway? But at least it was some sign of civilization, so Pearl studied the canyon, surveying the best route for making her way downward.

Small rocks and gravel slid down the path as she hiked into the canyon. Overhead the sky was darker still, and now the wind moaned through the trees. Pearl whispered another prayer and continued on her trek.

A pile of granite blocked her trail about halfway down. She reached for a small twisted pine growing between the rocks and grabbed onto it for support as she crawled to the highest point on the boulders.

Half kneeling, she halted suddenly, stunned at what she saw. About a hundred yards from her, just feet from the shed she'd seen earlier, was a pickup truck. Another was parked directly behind it, beside a dirt road that ribboned through the narrow canyon to the north. The road followed a small stream that she could hear bubbling along its rocky bed and rushing down small falls. The perfect conditions for a gold mine, she thought, remembering Shamus O'Brian's map. This had to be Rainbow's End.

Several men in hard hats stood talking near the corrugated metal shed. One was unrolling a large, rectangular sheet of paper, and the others were standing nearby. Their backs were to Pearl.

She calculated the distance with her eyes, wondering if she could sprint from the boulders to the far side of the little building, hide, and listen to their conversation. It was worth the risk, she decided. Slowly, she slid off the back of the boulders, hitting the ground below with a soft thud. She inched around the rocks, then peered out to see if the men had heard anything.

They were still absorbed in what Pearl thought was probably a geological study of some sort. She held her breath and tiptoed into a small stand of dogwood and pine.

The men's backs were still turned toward her, so she crept forward slowly, one step at a time. She had almost reached the edge of the copse of trees when a gray squirrel, looking down from a sugar pine, barked a warning, then barked again. And again.

Pearl froze in place, willing the little animal to shush. But the barking continued, and now a stellar jay had joined the ruckus, squawking without pause. He was joined by others.

First one, then all of the men turned around. As they started toward her, their looks were angry and menacing.

With a sinking feeling, Pearl realized she'd seen every one of them before.

Woodrow milled through the crowd at the gazebo, looking for Pearl. Theda, Flora, and Gabe had all told him that Pearl had definitely said she would be there. Charley seemed particularly worried and hovered near Woodrow while Senator Thorpe droned on about the wonderful improvements that would be coming to Everlasting because of EEI's control.

"Do you have any idea what your brother-in-law told Pearl?" Woodrow whispered to Charley.

Charley shook his head. "No."

"Do you still have your cell phone with you?"

"It's back in the car."

"How about giving your brother-in-law a call? Maybe he

can help us figure out where Pearl's gone. I can't help but worry," said Woodrow. "She was so sure about being here. Something must have come up."

Charley nodded. "You stay here—see what Thorpe's pulling this time. I'll go call and check back with you in a few minutes."

"Right," said Woodrow.

Thorpe had finally indicated he was about to spill his big news when Charley returned. He looked triumphant and worried at the same time.

"The key to this whole thing's been right under our noses!" he whispered loudly. "And from what we can figure, Pearl's gone to check it out."

From the podium, Thorpe's voice rose. "And now, ladies and gentlemen, you who love Everlasting and want to see it thrive—"

"What key?" Woodrow whispered to Charley, though he was still looking at Thorpe.

"He said that EEI's added parcels of land to the original acreage. And that's not all."

Thorpe's voice lifted as he continued. "Those of you who aren't ready to accept the status quo for either Everlasting's historical significance or for its bright and wonderful future—"

"What else?" Woodrow whispered loudly.

"Mineral rights! They've gone after mineral rights for the new parcels. I've got the plot descriptions," Charley whispered back. "From the same plot map my brother-in-law gave Pearl." He handed a sheet from his notepad to Woodrow.

Woodrow's mouth dropped open as Thorpe finally got to his point.

"Because, dear friends," Senator Thorpe cried, "the future is now! As of midnight tonight, Everlasting will officially and legally belong to EEI—Everlasting Enterprises Incorporated."

"It's gold they're after!" shouted Woodrow. "And they've found it. They've found gold!"

The melee that followed was akin to what had followed the shout of "Eureka!" during the original gold rush, Woodrow thought. Hollering and shoving and calling out questions, the reporters jostled Woodrow to the front of the crowd and handed him a microphone.

Out of the corner of his eye, Woodrow saw Senator Thorpe slink off to the safety of his chauffeured Mercedes. There would be time enough to deal with him later. Pearl was what was important now.

"It's not too late to stop the sale!" Woodrow shouted to the crowd. "But it's going to take all of us working together."

"There's a gold mine or maybe two out in these hills. EEI— or its parent company—is probably setting up to mine a newly discovered vein as we speak. And I say we stop them now."

"Catch 'em red-handed!" someone called out. "Let's go!"

There were howls of anger at EEI and shouts of willingness to help.

"Listen carefully, now," Woodrow said when he again had their attention. "This is a plot description telling exactly where this vein is located. Some of you are more familiar with the area than we are. I say let's head out together and put a stop to this deception once and for all." He read the description carefully and watched as some of the old-timers scratched their heads, then nodded.

"One more thing," he said. "Someone very courageous already headed out to search for these scoundrels. And we need to get to her as quickly as we can. Her life may be in danger."

Murmurs of worry rose from the crowd. "Who is it?" someone shouted.

"It's Pearl Flynn," he said quietly, then paused, thinking of how she had looked that morning, sitting next to him, her eyes aglow with affection. "A very special woman."

"Oh," came the almost collective whisper. "Uniquely Pearl—the artist."

"Let's be on our way!" shouted one of the reporters. The others began grabbing up their camera equipment.

"Hear, hear!" shouted a woman from the back row. "Everyone with four-wheel drives meet at Highway 41 just north of town!" The newspaper reporters took off en masse.

"Eureka!" yelled someone else as the rest of the crowd scrambled all directions. "Let's be off to find our Uniquely Pearl!"

CHAPTER
Ten

Pearl was ushered unceremoniously toward the small metal shed by Joe Horn, the men's leader. The others were also members of the EEI committee. Surprisingly, they hadn't even stopped to consider that she might not know why they were visiting the old gold mine, geological maps in hand.

"You're going to be very sorry you took it upon yourself to follow us out here," said Joe Horn just before he opened the shed door. The open padlock clanged against the metal siding. "You and your so-called Birds-of-a-Feather group should've learned a long time ago to keep your beaks out of places they don't belong."

"I was just scouting out a place to paint," Pearl protested, stalling while she thought how to get herself out of the dilemma. "Birds of a Feather doesn't have anything to do with where I choose for the settings of my paintings. This place is a natural for my work."

"You all think you're so clever," said one of the other men. "Pretending to be part of the town so you can save the day." His laugh was more of a scoff. "We've known what you and your group were up to from the day you rode into town in your white hats."

Narrowing her eyes, Pearl looked hard at the three men who were residents of Everlasting. They had originally been chosen to represent the community. Some representation, she thought. "So you knew about the mine all along?" All three shrugged and didn't answer. "Shame on you. I suppose you've simply stolen it from the rightful heirs with no regard for them. This is not fancy real estate finagling, gentlemen. This is theft, and you're no better than common criminals."

"That's enough," Joe Horn said with a laugh, giving her a shove toward the shed door. "We don't need a lecture. Besides, you're too late to do anything about it. It's a done deal as of midnight tonight, and no one's going to be around to dispute it. Least of all you, Ms. Flynn."

The padlock clicked into the slot outside the door. Pearl drew in a deep, frightened breath as her eyes tried to adjust to the darkness. There didn't seem to be any windows, and the only light was what filtered in through the joints between the sheets of metal siding.

She tried not to think about any little critters that might be in the shed with her. Rattlesnakes were probably hibernating by now, but there were always wood rats, deer mice, or even raccoons to worry about. Any or all of them might have made this old place their home.

Shivering, she stood as close to the center of the shed as possible so she wouldn't brush up against the spiderwebs or dust that lined the walls. This building was old enough to have years and perhaps decades of dirt and grime and rat droppings. She shuddered again, almost afraid to breathe.

The men didn't seem to care that she could clearly hear their every word. They spoke openly about their plans—the bulldozers that would arrive by dawn the next day, the workers and equipment on their way from San Francisco, the brokers in New York who were already awaiting the "product." Pearl quickly realized that they didn't plan to let her live to tell others what she'd heard.

By now her eyes had adjusted to the shed's dark, dusty interior. She moved around, examining the piles of old mining equipment. They were mostly scraps of old wood and rusted iron implements, picks and shovels and shallow pans.

Suddenly, she spotted a couple of six-foot boards of an old Long Tom at the back of the small room and knelt to rub her hand over the rough wood. These devices had been used for only a few decades beyond the gold rush, and she touched it almost reverently. Despite her fears, Pearl's curiosity got the best of her, and she moved from one piece of equipment to another. She even forgot her concerns about spiders and mice and lifted some of the lighter pieces of equipment to discover what was underneath.

Her eyes had adjusted better now to the darkness, and she noticed something the shape of a window frame at the rear of the old shed. It was so dark she thought it must have been boarded over, but she gingerly stepped over the debris until she was close enough to inspect it.

It was covered with layers of dust and dirt and spiderwebs. Wrinkling her nose in disgust, she reached one finger up to swipe through the grime. She felt the cold, solid surface of glass beneath her touch.

Looking around, she saw an odd cradlelike piece of equipment, briefly wondered what part of the mining process it had been used for, and pulled it to the window and turned it upright. Then she carefully stepped to its top and began to scrub at the window with her sleeve. Gradually the small room became filled with light. Not the bright light of a sunny day, but light nonetheless.

Smiling, she stepped down from the makeshift stool and brushed off her sweater. Now she could at least assess what equipment was in the little treasure trove, especially those pieces that would help in her escape.

But as she stepped back, her gaze fell again on the piece of mining equipment that so resembled a cradle. Curious, she knelt beside it, then laid it back down in its rightful position.

She realized it *was* a cradle. Made for a baby, not for gold mining. It was filled with webs and dust, and she gently turned it over to empty it and wipe it out. She ran her fingers over its still-smooth wood, in awe at such a find.

Her fingers felt a series of indentations on the underside of the cradle, as if something had been carved there. She turned it over, then toward the light from the window. Precisely spaced, the words were clearly legible: *To my darling sister Sheridan for your coming blessed bundle. May the wee babe never forget its Irish blood.*

Pearl was stunned. What a discovery! It was more precious than any vein of gold. This must be close to Shamus O'Brian's Rainbow's End—if not the very spot. She looked around at the equipment again. Could all this have been his? Perhaps he'd passed it on to members of his family. Only they never came back to claim his equipment—or the mine.

The men outside were speaking in more animated tones now, too low for her to make out, but definitely the sounds of arguing. Her knees trembled as she wondered if the dispute might be over how and when to take her life.

She needed a plan and looked frantically around, her gaze finally resting on the window. She grinned as a strategy formed.

She moved the Long Tom, the cradle, and other equipment into place. Then she worked out the timing of her plan. Finally, she stood on the upended cradle and again reached the window.

She lifted a heavy pick and shattered the glass, poking out the shards so that the entire window was nearly clear. She quickly tossed out a couple of pieces of equipment. They landed with loud thumps and rolled down the hillside.

For a moment there was a stunned silence among the men outside. It was immediately followed by the sounds of fast-moving footsteps and frantic voices.

Pearl scrambled under the Long Tom, letting it down to the floor so that it covered her completely. She held her breath as she heard the padlock click open.

Just as she expected, the men rushed in. "She's gotten away!" shouted Joe Horn. "Quick! Head around back. Find out where she's gone."

"Follow me!" someone else shouted.

"Hurry! I think she's gone toward the creek," yelled another.

Pearl waited until she heard their footsteps moving toward the streambed. Then she lifted the Long Tom and very quietly crawled out and tiptoed to the door. She carefully peered out. The area immediately in front of the shed was clear. At least for now.

She ran toward the cover of oaks and pines beyond the shed. When she reached the trees, she felt her heart pounding in her chest, and she stopped, gasping for breath.

There was an unnatural silence, almost as if the men had been caught up in some net. No voices carried toward her. No chattering of jays or squirrels. She shot up a quick prayer, hoping they were still heading in the opposite direction.

Finally, Pearl's heart calmed, and as the silence continued to reign, a grin of triumph crept across her face. She headed up the hillside.

She had just reached the outcropping of boulders when she heard the ruckus of cars and people heading along the dirt road leading into the canyon. She climbed to the topmost point and peered down, expecting to see the equipment the men had been talking about earlier.

To her amazement, she saw a caravan of cars and four-wheel drives heading up the road, clouds of dust billowing behind. There were dozens of cars, and as they halted, at least a hundred people spilled out of them.

But one of the last cars to arrive caught her attention. A

worn-looking Land Rover pulled off the side of the road, passing all the other parked vehicles until it reached the front and pulled to a stop beside the shed.

Pearl didn't wait to watch Woodrow step out.

She scrambled from her granite perch and ran down the hillside. As she made her way through the milling crowd of reporters, photographers, shopkeepers, street musicians, and even the Birds-of-a-Feather gang, people fell silent and stepped back to let her through.

She heard calls of "It's Pearl Flynn!" and "It's Uniquely Pearl!" as she passed.

"She's safe," someone nearby whispered. "Praise God, Pearl's safe!"

Finally she saw Woodrow. He was watching her, his face filled with relief and love. He held out his arms, and with a small cry, Pearl ran to him.

The crowd sent up a cheer, and she smiled up into his face. "I didn't get to tell you what was in my heart this morning," she said.

He merely arched a brow in that debonair, graceful, and stately way she adored.

"It's you, my dear, dear man. You are in my heart," she said softly. "How I love you!"

The crowd cheered again as Woodrow bent his head and kissed her.

Epilogue

Valentine's Day

In the old-fashioned balcony room of the City Hotel, Pearl stood in front of the oval, full-length mirror. Sighing, she watched her reflection as a very pregnant Annie Westbrook, the matron of honor, lifted Pearl's tulle veil off its hanger and carried it over.

"You look beautiful, Pearl," Annie whispered, her eyes misty.

Pearl smiled at Annie in the mirror. Her wedding dress was traditional only in its ivory color. Its handkerchief-lace hem and sleeves spoke of a style that was uniquely Pearl. More gypsy than Victorian, certainly more artistic than what one might consider elegant. She'd designed it herself.

Below the balcony, the musicians were already playing: Charley on the banjo, Wyatt on the harmonica. Two friends they'd made while working as docents had joined the duo with violin and flute.

"Okay, hold still now," Annie said as she placed the veil on Pearl's head. Pearl had also designed the headpiece, with its miniature sunflowers and mix of orange and yellow tiger lilies. "Take a look at you!" Annie stepped back. "Oh, my. You're a vision, Pearl."

Pearl turned and smiled. She did feel beautiful, perhaps for the first time in her life. To think of it…a bride at her age! She wanted to lift her arms and dance a jig.

"Did you know that my great-great-grandmother prepared

herself for her marriage to Marcus Jade in this very room?"

"No, I didn't," Pearl said, shaking her head thoughtfully. She was reminded of her wondrous find in the shed. "Did Greg finish his work on the cradle?"

"He did, and I can't wait for you to see it. He only sanded it lightly—just enough to remove the years of dust and dirt. Then he put on a coat of oil. It's oak, hand carved." She smiled, patting her stomach. "It'll be perfect for the baby."

Pearl nodded.

Annie caught Pearl's hand and squeezed it. "Greg and I are so glad you and Woodrow are going to live near us, Pearl. You're really part of our family."

Pearl swallowed hard and nodded. "I've never had a family before." She sighed. "So many years I lived alone, content, but not realizing what I was missing. Now here I am, a bride so in love I think I've suddenly set foot in heaven. And now that we're building a place so close to you and Greg and the babies, well—" she gave Annie a hug—"well, my dear Annie, I never knew God's blessings could fill me with such joy."

"What you've done for Everlasting, Pearl, can never be repaid. We're not the only ones who love you."

"What Everlasting's done for me is greater," she said softly, with no need to explain. Annie knew what Uniquely Pearl, her paintings, and the townspeople all meant to her. Oh yes. She'd been blessed beyond all measure.

A few minutes later, Annie helped Pearl down the stairs, through the parlor, and out onto the rock path leading to the gazebo. Every inch of it was covered with tiny lights, cutout valentines, and flowers of every color and description, compliments of the Birds-of-a-Feather gang, who must have cleaned out the supplies of every florist in a twenty-five-mile radius.

The gazebo and the lawn around it were filled to overflowing with friends from Everlasting and San Francisco. The instruments played softly as the minister walked to the center of the small bandstand; Woodrow took his place beside him, and Greg, his best man, stood beside Woodrow, grinning at Annie and Pearl.

Mary Beth and Shamus, skipping and jumping, started down the center path, dropping flower petals from baskets as they walked. Then it was Annie's turn.

The music of banjo, violin, and flute rose as Annie moved forward. On the road beside the gazebo, a team of six gray horses whinnied and shook their manes in front of an old stagecoach. The stagecoach had been decorated with flowers and valentine hearts, and old shoes and tin cans were tied behind. On the rear hung a sign: Just Married!

Annie reached the gazebo and turned to watch as Pearl stepped to the aisle and paused.

All music stopped except for a single flute that began to play some lively Irish music in honor of Shamus O'Brian and his Rainbow's End, just turned over to the people of Everlasting.

A hush of expectancy fell over the guests, and as one, they stood and turned toward the bride.

Pearl began to move down the aisle, a bit faster than most brides might have, she knew. But this was a joyous occasion and, by jing, she was going to look like she was having fun.

As she moved closer, Woodrow's eyes met hers. Pearl's heart danced, and she fought to keep her feet from following suit. Now that would be a trip down the aisle folks would remember, she thought, her gaze locked on Woodrow's face.

It would also be uniquely Pearl.

So she hiked her skirts just a tad above the ankle, danced a few quick steps of an Irish jig, then grinning at her groom, let herself be gathered into his arms.

~~~~~

My romantic hubby believes in showing love every day of the year. Why do the expected, he says, when the unexpected is so much more fun? I never know when his fancy may strike. On the most ordinary of days, I've opened the door to a delivery of an enormous bouquet of tiger lilies…or lilacs…or multicolored roses. Or I've found a little stuffed bear on my pillow, holding a red heart that says "I love you," or a silly greeting card on my desk, cheering me on as I write. His love transforms the most ordinary of days into days of celebration. He's taught me that we don't need to wait for those special days on the calendar to say "I love you." Little acts of love sprinkled throughout the year are life-changing and world-brightening.

Strawberry Delight

Preheat oven to 350 degrees. Mix together the following ingredients with a pastry cutter or fork until crumbly:
> 1/2 cup butter, softened
> 1 cup flour
> 1/2 cup brown sugar
> 1/2 cup chopped almonds, pecans, or walnuts

Spread in a shallow baking dish or cookie sheet. Bake until golden brown (about 15 minutes), stirring two or three times.

Beat one cup of whipping cream and set aside.
Place the following ingredients in a large mixing bowl:
> 1 cup sugar
> 1 tablespoon lemon juice
> 1 teaspoon vanilla

1/4 teaspoon lemon extract
2 egg whites
1 package frozen strawberries, unthawed

Beat for 2 minutes. Fold in whipped cream.

Sprinkle half of the butter-crumb crust onto bottom of 9 x 13 dish. Pour strawberry cream filling on top of crust. Top with remaining crust. Freeze until firm.

Diane Noble has published five novels and two novellas with Palisades under the pen name Amanda MacLean. Her first novel with Multnomah under her own name is *Tangled Vines,* releasing in February 1998. She and her husband, Tom, live in Southern California.

Write to:
Karen Ball
Barbara Jean Hicks
Diane Noble
c/o Palisades
Multnomah Publishers, Inc.
P.O. Box 1720
Sisters, Oregon 97759

PALISADES...PURE ROMANCE

⁓ PALISADES ⁓

Reunion, Karen Ball
Refuge, Lisa Tawn Bergren
Torchlight, Lisa Tawn Bergren
Treasure, Lisa Tawn Bergren
Chosen, Lisa Tawn Bergren
Firestorm, Lisa Tawn Bergren
Surrender, Lynn Bulock
Wise Man's House, Melody Carlson
Heartland Skies, Melody Carlson (March 1998)
Cherish, Constance Colson
Chase the Dream, Constance Colson
Angel Valley, Peggy Darty
Sundance, Peggy Darty
Moonglow, Peggy Darty
Promises, Peggy Darty
Memories, Peggy Darty (May 1998)
Remembering the Roses, Marion Duckworth (June 1998)
Love Song, Sharon Gillenwater
Antiques, Sharon Gillenwater
Texas Tender, Sharon Gillenwater
Secrets, Robin Jones Gunn
Whispers, Robin Jones Gunn
Echoes, Robin Jones Gunn
Sunsets, Robin Jones Gunn
Clouds, Robin Jones Gunn
Waterfalls, Robin Jones Gunn (February 1998)
Coming Home, Barbara Jean Hicks
Snow Swan, Barbara Jean Hicks
China Doll, Barbara Jean Hicks (June 1998)
Angel in the Senate, Kristen Johnson Ingram (March 1998)
Irish Eyes, Annie Jones

Father by Faith, Annie Jones
Irish Rogue, Annie Jones
Glory, Marilyn Kok
Sierra, Shari MacDonald
Forget-Me-Not, Shari MacDonald
Diamonds, Shari MacDonald
Stardust, Shari MacDonald
Westward, Amanda MacLean
Stonehaven, Amanda MacLean
Everlasting, Amanda MacLean
Kingdom Come, Amanda MacLean
Betrayed, Lorena McCourtney
Escape, Lorena McCourtney
Dear Silver, Lorena McCourtney
Forgotten, Lorena McCourtney (February 1998)
Enough! Gayle Roper
The Key, Gayle Roper (April 1998)
Voyage, Elaine Schulte

⁓ ANTHOLOGIES ⁓

A Christmas Joy, Darty, Gillenwater, MacLean
Mistletoe, Ball, Hicks, McCourtney
A Mother's Love, Bergren, Colson, MacLean
Silver Bells, Bergren, Krause, MacDonald
Heart's Delight, Ball, Hicks, Noble
Fools for Love, Ball, Brooks, Jones (March 1998)

THE PALISADES LINE

Look for these new releases at your local bookstore. If the title you seek is not in stock, the store may order you a copy using the ISBN listed.

Heartland Skies, Melody Carlson (March 1998)
ISBN 1-57673-264-9
Jayne Morgan moves to the small town of Paradise with the prospect of marriage, a new job, and plenty of horses to ride. But when her fiancé dumps her, she's left with loose ends. Then she wins a horse in a raffle, and the handsome rancher who boards her horse makes things look decidedly better.

Memories, Peggy Darty (May 1998)
ISBN 1-57673-171-5
In this sequel to *Promises*, Elizabeth Calloway is left with amnesia after witnessing a hit-and-run accident. Her husband, Michael, takes her on a vacation to Cancún so that she can relax and recover her memory. What they don't realize is that the killer is following them, hoping to wipe out Elizabeth's memory permanently....

Remembering the Roses, Marion Duckworth (June 1998)
ISBN 1-57673-236-3
Sammie Sternberg is trying to escape her memories of the man who betrayed her, and she ends up in a small town on the Olympic Peninsula in Washington. There she opens her dream business—an antique shop in an old Victorian—and meets a reclusive watercolor artist who helps to heal her broken heart.

Waterfalls, Robin Jones Gunn (February 1998)
ISBN 1-57673-221-5
In a visit to Glenbrooke, Oregon, Meredith Graham meets movie star Jacob Wilde and is sure he's the one. But when Meri puts her

foot in her mouth, things fall apart. Is isn't until the two of them get thrown together working on a book-and-movie project that Jacob realizes his true feelings, and this time he's the one who's starstruck.

China Doll, Barbara Jean Hicks (June 1998)
ISBN 1-57673-262-2
Bronson Bailey is having a mid-life crisis: after years of globetrotting in his journalism career, he's feeling restless. Georgine Nichols has also reached a turning point: after years of longing for a child, she's decided to adopt. The problem is, now she's fallen in love with Bronson, and he doesn't want a child.

Angel in the Senate, Kristen Johnson Ingram (April 1998)
ISBN 1-57673-263-0
Newly elected senator Megan Likely heads to Washington with high hopes for making a difference in government. But accusations of election fraud, two shocking murders, and threats on her life make the Senate take a backseat. She needs to find answers, but she's not sure who she can trust anymore.

Irish Rogue, Annie Jones
ISBN 1-57673-189-8
Michael Shaughnessy has paid the price for stealing a pot of gold, and now he's ready to make amends to the people he's hurt. Fiona O'Dea is number one on his list. The problem is, Fiona doesn't want to let Michael near enough to hurt her again. But before she knows it, he's taken his Irish charm and worked his way back into her life…and her heart.

Forgotten, Lorena McCourtney (February 1998)
ISBN 1-57673-222-3
A woman wakes up in an Oregon hospital with no memory of who she is. When she's identified as Kat Cavanaugh, she returns

to her home in California. As Kat struggles to recover her memory, she meets a fiancé she doesn't trust and an attractive neighbor who can't believe how she's changed. She begins to wonder if she's really Kat Cavanaugh, but if she isn't, what happened to the real Kat?

The Key, Gayle Roper (April 1998)
ISBN 1-57673-223-1
On Kristie Matthews's first day living on an Amish farm, she gets bitten by a dog and is rushed to the emergency room by a handsome stranger. In the ER, an elderly man in the throes of a heart attack hands her a key and tells her to keep it safe. Suddenly odd accidents begin to happen to her, but no one's giving her any answers.

∼ ANTHOLOGIES ∼

Fools for Love, Ball, Brooks, Jones (March 1998)
ISBN 1-57673-235-5
By Karen Ball: Kitty starts pet-sitting, but when her clients turn out to be more than she can handle, she enlists help from a handsome handyman.
By Jennifer Brooks: Caleb Murphy tries to acquire a book collection from a widow, but she has one condition: he must marry her granddaughter first.
By Annie Jones: A college professor who has been burned by love vows not to be fooled twice, until her ex-fiancé shows up and ruins her plans!

Heart's Delight, Ball, Hicks, Noble
ISBN 1-57673-220-7
By Karen Ball: Corie receives a Valentine's Day date from her sisters and thinks she's finally found the one...until she learns she went out with the wrong man.

By Barbara Jean Hicks: Carina and Reid are determined to break up their parents' romance, but when it looks like things are working, they have a change of heart.

By Diane Noble: Two elderly bird-watchers set aside their differences to try to save a park from disaster but learn they've bitten off more than they can chew.

BE SURE TO LOOK FOR ANY OF THE 1997 TITLES
YOU MAY HAVE MISSED:

Surrender, Lynn Bulock (ISBN 1-57673-104-9)
Single mom Cassie Neel accepts a blind date from her children for her birthday.

Wise Man's House, Melody Carlson (ISBN 1-57673-070-0)
A young widow buys her childhood dream house, and a mysterious stranger moves into her caretaker's cottage.

Moonglow, Peggy Darty (ISBN 1-57673-112-X)
Tracy Kosell comes back to Moonglow, Georgia, and investigates a case with a former schoolmate, who's now a detective.

Promises, Peggy Darty (ISBN 1-57673-149-9)
A Christian psychologist asks her detective husband to help her find a dangerous woman.

Texas Tender, Sharon Gillenwater (ISBN 1-57673-111-1)
Shelby Nolan inherits a watermelon farm and asks the sheriff for help when two elderly men begin digging holes in her fields.

Clouds, Robin Jones Gunn (ISBN 1-57673-113-8)
Flight attendant Shelly Graham runs into her old boyfriend, Jonathan Renfield, and learns he's engaged.

Sunsets, **Robin Jones Gunn** (ISBN 1-57673-103-0)
Alissa Benson has a run-in at work with Brad Phillips, and is
more than a little upset when she finds out he's her neighbor!

Snow Swan, **Barbara Jean Hicks** (ISBN 1-57673-107-3)
Toni, an unwed mother and a recovering alcoholic, falls in love
for the first time. But if Clark finds out the truth about her past,
will he still love her?

Irish Eyes, **Annie Jones** (ISBN 1-57673-108-1)
Julia Reed gets drawn into a crime involving a pot of gold and
has her life turned upside down by Interpol agent Cameron
O'Dea.

Father by Faith, **Annie Jones** (ISBN 1-57673-117-0)
Nina Jackson buys a dude ranch and hires cowboy Clint Cooper
as her foreman, but her son, Alex, thinks Clint is his new daddy!

Stardust, **Shari MacDonald** (ISBN 1-57673-109-X)
Gillian Spencer gets her dream assignment but is shocked to
learn she must work with Maxwell Bishop, who once broke her
heart.

Kingdom Come, **Amanda MacLean** (ISBN 1-57673-120-0)
Ivy Rose Clayborne, M.D., pairs up with the grandson of the coal
baron to fight the mining company that is ravaging her town.

Dear Silver, **Lorena McCourtney** (ISBN 1-57673-110-3)
When Silver Sinclair receives a letter from Chris Bentley ending
their relationship, she's shocked, since she's never met the man!

Enough! **Gayle Roper** (ISBN 1-57673-185-5)
When Molly Gregory gets fed up with her three teenaged children, she announces that she's going on strike.

A Mother's Love, **Bergren, Colson, MacLean**
(ISBN 1-57673-106-5)
Three heartwarming stories share the joy of a mother's love.

Silver Bells, **Bergren, Krause, MacDonald**
(ISBN 1-57673-119-7)
Three novellas focus on romance during Christmastime.